Making Connections: Language and Learning in the Classroom

Susan Hynds
Syracuse University

Making Connections: Language and Learning in the Classroom

Susan Hynds
Syracuse University

Christopher-Gordon Publishers, Inc.
Norwood, Massachusetts

Copyright © 1994 by Christopher-Gordon Publishers, Inc.

All rights reserved. Except for review purposes, no part of this material protected by this copyright notice may be reproduced or utilized in any form or by any means, electronic or mechanical, including photocopying, recording, or any information and retrieval system, without the express written permission of the publisher or copyright owner.

Christopher-Gordon Publishers, Inc.
480 Washington Street
Norwood, MA 02062

Printed in the United States of America

10 9 8 7 6 5 4 3 2 1   99 98 97 96 95 94

ISBN: 0-926842-28-5

To my grandmother, Marie Just

For bedtime stories

and the gift of laughter

Table of Contents

Chapter One: The Language Event
and the Learning Climate 1

Chapter Two: Language Purposes 23

Chapter Three: Stances Toward Learning 47

Chapter Four: Outcomes of
Language and Learning 71

Chapter Five: Case Study — Lauren:
A Personal Metamorphosis 95

Chapter Six: Choice in the Learning Climate 117

Chapter Seven: Independence and
Collaboration in the Learning Climate 145

Chapter Eight: Commitment: Exploration
and Permanence in the Language Act 173

Chapter Nine: Case Study — Rebecca:
A Leap of Faith 199

Chapter Ten: Evaluation 225

Detailed Table of Contents

Chapter One: The Language Event and the Learning Climate 1

    The Learning Climate 2
    The Language Event 2
    The Natural Process of Language Learning 3
    Extending This Process into the Classroom 3
    Designing the Learning Climate 4
        Reflections: Something You've Learned 4
    Designing Successful Learning Experiences 12
        Classroom Closeup: Peanut Papers 14
    Techniques and Forms for Language and Learning 16
    The Fallacy of Form Without Function 19
    Teacher Goals and Student Perceptions 19
        Explorations 20
        References 22

Chapter Two: Language Purposes 23

    Why We Use Language 24
        Reflections: The WHY of Language 24
    School Purposes and the Tyranny of Form 26
    Language for School Purposes:
        The Competency Exam 27
    Language for Human Purposes:
        Personal, Social, Artistic 29
        Classroom Closeup: Myself as a Reader and Writer 30
            Reflections: The Teaching Tale 33
        Classroom Closeup: A Tale of Two Teachers —
            The Journal Journey 35
            Getting Started 37
            Reaching Beyond the Classroom 38

    A Choice of Purposes 40
    Classroom Connections 41
  Bringing the Classroom to Life 43
    Explorations 45
  References 46

Chapter Three: Stances Toward Learning 47
  The Limits of Hierarchical Thinking 48
  Stage Models and Curriculum 49
  Learning Stances 50
    Replicating 51
    Connecting 52
    Extending 52
    Classroom Closeup: Reading the Response 52
    Reflections: An Apple for the Teacher 56
    Classroom Closeup: Genetics and the Environment 60
        Personal Connections: The Double-entry Journal 61
        Connecting and Extending:
            Parallel Reading and Writing 61
        Extending the Issues: Future Implications 63
        Extending The Form: Fiction Writing 64
        Extending Beyond the Classroom: Culminating Project 65
  Classroom Connections 66
  Drawing Connections 67
    Explorations 69
  References 70

Chapter Four: Outcomes of Language and Learning 71
  Outcome: Language Directed to Whom? 71
  Outcomes for Reading and Writing 72
  Outcomes for Listening and Talking 74
    Reflections: Learning Outcomes 75
    Further Reflection: Shifting Outcomes 76
        Heidi: Language for Self 78
        Catherine: Language for Intimate Others 80
        Kathi: Language for Distant Others 82

  Inviting Language 84
   Classroom Closeup: Seth's Story 84
    A First Step 85
    At School 86
    Reaching Out Through Language 87
    The First Breakthrough:
     Writing Toward Meaning 87
    More Meaningful Outcomes 88
    Moving Outward 89
   Classroom Connections 90
  Explorations 93
  References 94

Chapter Five: Case Study — Lauren:
A Personal Metamorphosis 95
 Lauren's Journal 97
 Looking Backward 112
  Explorations 114

Chapter Six: Choice in the Learning Climate 117
 Choice and the Learning Climate 118
 Reflections: Choice 120
 Creating a Climate for Choice 122
 Choice, Ownership, and Motivation 123
  Further Reflection: Pen Pals 124
 Closing Down and Opening Up 126
 Modeling Choice 126
  Classroom Closeup: Language for Learning
   in Mathematics 128
   Writing to Learn: The Math Notebook 130
   Writing to Explain: Instructions 132
   Writing Imaginatively: Story Problems 135
   Mathematics Beyond the Classroom 136
  Classroom Connections 139
 Frightening Freedom 140
  Explorations 142

References 143

**Chapter Seven: Independence and Collaboration
in the Learning Climate** 145
   Independence, Collaboration, and
      Learning Outcomes 148
   Sharing and Demonstrating 150
      *Classroom Closeup: Collaborative Reading
         and Response* 151
      Reflections: Collaborative Authorship 154
   Independence and Collaboration 157
      Classroom Closeup: Collaborative Writing 158
         The Collaboration Begins 160
         The Dream Team: Shared Responsibilities 161
         The Terrorists: Crawling Toward Collaboration 162
         "Our Classroom" 163
         From Collaboration to Community 165
   Independence through Collaboration 166
      Classroom Connections 167
   A Piece of the Whole 169
      Explorations 170
   References 171

**Chapter Eight: Commitment: Exploration and
Permanence in the Language Act** 173
   The Research Paper Nightmare 174
      Reflections: Reading Between the Guidelines 174
   Permanence and Exploration in the Research Process 176
   What's Wrong With This Picture? 177
   Exploring the Issue of Commitment in Language 178
   REsearching Research 180
      Further Reflection: Searching and REsearching 180
      Classroom Closeup: Project "Our Town" 184
         From Researching to REsearching 186
         Negotiating and Collaborating 186
         From Exploration to Permanence 187

    Randy and Mike: Collaborating and Cooperating 189
    "Process Grade" 192
   Classroom Connections 193
 From the Hypothetical to the Real 194
   Explorations 196
   References 197

Chapter Nine: Case Study — Rebecca: A Leap of Faith 199
 Rebecca's Journal: The Rollercoaster Ride 199
   Explorations 221

Chapter Ten: Evaluation 225
 Response 226
 Evaluation 226
 Grading 229
 Response Roles 230
   Reflections: Response Roles 230
     Role Switching 232
   Evaluation Problem Number One: Evaluating
     Student Growth 234
     Hanna: From Reluctance to Risk-Taking 235
     Moving Toward Independence 236
     Growth Spurts 239
   Evaluation Problem Number Two: Evaluating
     Groups of Students 242
     Discovering Competencies in Students' Texts 242
   Evaluation Problem Number Three: Assessing
     Student Attitudes and Beliefs 244
     Corey: "An Author When I Grow Up,
      That's Maybe" 244
   Designing a Grading System 248
   Classroom Connections 248
 Final Reflections 252
   Explorations 254
 References 254

Preface

Most people think that teaching is throwing information at students and hoping they'll remember it. But people on the receiving end have to catch it and do something with it, or no learning takes place. True learning is rather an act that requires us to call upon our past experience and present powers, and to rise and meet new information and ideas — transforming them into something useful, taking away their sanctity, their pure authenticity, and transfusing them into our earth-bound self so they develop a new authenticity and sanctity. It's a kind of alchemy, or fusion. In a true knowing place, teachers and students are surprising both each other and themselves. (Macrorie, 1984, p. 234.)

A dear friend once said that a good book doesn't just invite readers to read; it invites them to **participate**. I think that's also true of good teaching. That's what this book is about — helping teachers and students to create "knowing places" where everyone can make connections between their past experience and their present powers and where they can develop those powers through the language acts of reading, writing, speaking, and listening. It's about putting language to work in any classroom and helping students to use language not only to demonstrate knowledge but create and refine it as well. Finally, it's about creating a learning climate where students and teachers are always "surprising both each other and themselves."

I believe that teaching is transforming, but I don't believe that it's alchemy or magic in the medieval sense of changing base metals to gold or searching for the elusive elixir of life. Nor do I believe that teaching can be reduced to a strict formula or set of modern scientific principles. That's why this is not a cookbook or a workbook or a set of fixed prescriptions. It's more like an invitation for teachers to reconsider how they are teaching and to harness the power of language to promote learning all across the curriculum, from literature class to science, mathematics, or social studies.

As I began to write this book, I thought long and hard about how to present what I had to say. I wanted a way to write about teaching that wasn't preachy or didn't set me up as some kind of unshakable authority. I thought about how much I've learned from the hundreds of teachers I've met in workshops and classes over the past several years. I wanted to recreate the sense of community that emerges whenever teachers take time out of their busy, complicated schedules and spend a few days rediscovering the power of written and spoken language in their own lives.

But how do you develop a sense of community in the pages of a book, And how do you invite readers to rediscover and reflect upon their own learning processes when you can't be in the same room with them? In a sense, this book was written by other teachers. Some of them were my own teachers many years ago; others were my colleagues during the nine years I spent as a teacher of English and speech in high schools and middle schools; most of those who are quoted in the pages of this book are teachers I've worked with in workshops and classes during my time as a teacher educator in a university setting.

Rather than cluttering the pages with generic activities and assignments, I decided to present examples of real teachers and real students using language to learn in real classrooms. I wanted to share not only their stories of success but their disappointments as well. For that reason, their names and occasionally some small details of their experience have been changed to preserve their anonymity and that of their students. Each of their situations is, of course, unique. My hope is that their stories will speak to you no matter what your circumstances. Carl Rogers once described this paradox: "What is most personal is most general" (1986, p. 110)." I chose these particular stories because they have resonated with me in some way and taught me something about the art of teaching. I hope that they will do the same for you.

In this book, you will read about teachers and students from across the grade levels and across the content areas. When I first started to write this book, I was warned that it's not very wise to try to span the grade levels from kindergarten to high school. I'm grateful that my publisher didn't hold me to that maxim. My classroom teaching experiences have been on the secondary and middle school level, but I've also gained such a wealth of knowledge in working with elementary and early childhood teachers. I personally have never had much direct experience with students who have disabilities, but, fortunately, the special education teachers I've worked with have opened so many new worlds to me and have expanded my understanding of the ways in which all children are exceptional, all have special needs, and all deserve teachers who are willing to adapt instruction to those needs. The special kind of magic that develops when teachers from all content areas and grade levels get together in a workshop setting cannot be reconstructed in the pages of a book, but I can invite you to join a community of sorts — a community of other teachers, telling stories about what they do and why they do it. I hope that this kind of sharing will be more valuable to you than any maxims or precepts about teaching and learning that I might provide.

I must confess that I've got one other agenda in writing this book. I'd like to invite you to become more open to change in your current and future teaching. Someone once said that we do not learn from experiences that do not change us. That's true of our students, and it's also true of ourselves. Change doesn't come easily, even when we know it's ultimately good for us. As I began this book three years ago, I thought back to moments of change in my own teaching. I realized that for me, lasting change was always more incremental than cataclysmic. Over the years, I had created my own teaching style out of little snips of other teachers' ideas that seemed to work with my students, but I was never successful in bringing somebody else's idea wholesale into my classroom. I had to take what I needed and leave whatever didn't apply to my situation. I had to learn the art of reflecting and adapting.

Getting ideas was only part of the process. I also had to develop a theory. I've heard it said so many times that teachers are resistant to theory. How demeaning that is! In working with other teachers, I don't find them resistant to theory at all. In fact, I believe we're all looking for what I would call **practical theories** — ways of understanding our teaching that we personally create out of our own particular circumstances and adapt continually through the course of an entire teaching career.

That gets back to the part about books inviting readers to participate. There are several ways you can "participate" in this book. In each chapter, you'll notice some short learning experiences called **REFLECTIONS**, which invite you to write or sometimes talk with someone else about what you are learning in the course of your reading. After each of these reflections I've tried to include some examples of how other teachers reflected about the same ideas in their journals and logs. At the end of each chapter, there are some longer experiences called **EXPLORATIONS**, which take you a little further in reflecting upon various issues related to teaching. You can simply sit back and read this book if you like, considering how all of this applies to you and the students you teach, or you can try your hand at some of the more structured learning experiences I've provided for you, making your own personal connections and considering how each experience supported or impeded your learning.

As always, in the course of writing a book there are several people who deserve a sincere note of gratitude. Thank you to my parents, Chuck and Leone Hynds, for believing in me always; to Joyce Greenberg Lott, James Marshall, and Dorothy Watson, whose wise comments helped bring this manuscript to maturity; to Susan Scharoun; who kept me honest; and to Hiram Howard, who forced me to find my voice.

But most of all, a heartfelt thanks to all of the wonderful students and their teachers, whose words run through these pages: Kevin Ahern, Brigid Barry, Kristie L. Bliss, Deborah Brown, Frank Colabufo, Barbara Combs, Michele Dimon-Borowski, Marybeth Elliot, Linda Gangemi, Marilyn Gray, Christine H. Harding, Jackie Knowles, Mary McCrone, Laura Payne, Barbara Preston, Lynda Rill, Patti Scott, Nancy Sellmeyer, Ann Sherwood, Angela Sinopoli, Syndi Smith-Bierman, Theresa Stevens, Linda Stillman, Heather Thomas, and Linda McAvoy Turner.

References

Rogers, C.R. (1986). Some significant learnings. In J. Stewart (Ed.) *Bridges not walls: A book about interpersonal communication* (4th Ed., pp. 104-111). New York: Random House.

CHAPTER 1

The Language Event and the Learning Climate

I often feel sympathy with the job of a marriage counselor, only in my position I am called upon to fix not marriages that went wrong but writing assignments that went wrong. Sometimes, my classroom seems like a model writing community: Students are involved, interested, writing and improving. But at other times, it seems that no matter how much time I spend creating what I think will be challenging, interesting assignments that will motivate my students to attain even greater degrees of writing proficiency and enjoyment, something goes wrong. My class groans at the description of the assignment. They complain. They turn in incomplete work or don't turn in anything at all. Or perhaps they turn in papers, but to my utter puzzlement, they seem to have completely ignored the specific instructions I gave them for the task. Obviously, something clashed between by expectations for the assignment and the students' perceptions of the assignment. I ask myself, "Can this writing assignment be saved?"

— Beth

Beth is a high school English teacher in her fifth year. These comments in her teaching journal reflect how frustrating and difficult it is to design successful learning experiences for students. So many times there is an unexpected clash between our expectations and the ways that students perceive an assignment. Teaching, like writing, is a "composing process." It requires that we constantly reconsider and revise our ideas, searching always for that fragile balance between our goals and our students' expectations.

For my first five years as a high school teacher, I was too busy trying to get through the hectic school day to think very much about why my teaching ideas succeeded or failed. Like Beth, I found myself using ideas that worked and discarding those that didn't in a sort of haphazard fashion. I suppose eventually, by a trial-and-error process, I got to the point where I succeeded more often than I failed, but the failures, when they did happen, never seemed to get any less painful, unpleasant, or unexpected. Although I probably didn't realize it at the time, I didn't need a set of no-fail activities; I needed some way of looking at my teaching that would make me better at predicting and planning lessons that would suit my students' abilities and expectations.

The Learning Climate

Over time, I began to realize that whenever a lesson didn't go as planned, something I had done before or after the lesson, perhaps an offhanded comment that I'd made or the way I had arranged the room or my grading system — something in the classroom climate — had undercut my goals and caused my lesson to fail.

I discovered that one of the reasons it's impossible to create student-proof activities is that learning doesn't operate in a vacuum. The way in which we set up an assignment, what we say about it, and how we evaluate it — in other words, the learning climate we set up — profoundly influences what and how our students learn.

The Language Event

A few weeks ago, I was visiting a friend who teaches middle school, when I noticed a series of posters entitled "The Composing Process" above her bulletin board. I'd seen them before in other classrooms in the district. One poster says "Plan," the next says "Draft," the next "Revise," and so forth. When I asked my friend about it, she told me that all of the teachers in her district are required to display them in a prominent place in their room. We both had to laugh when I pointed out to her that, gradually, over the course of the year, her posters were becoming swallowed up by the reams of student texts that she was in the habit of stapling to the bulletin board.

The problem with these posters, as she and I realized, was that they seemed to assume, rather simplistically, that all writers move in a rigid sequential order through a process of prewriting, writing, and revising. In actuality, writers are often revising their ideas before those ideas reach the printed page, they are planning at the same time as they are drafting, and all writing is a sort of prewriting for other texts to come. Few learning processes are as simple as these districtwide posters or their accompanying scope and sequence charts seem to imply.

The movement from product to process in language learning has become a rather commonplace idea. It started a few decades ago, when we began to wonder about the actual learning processes that people engage in when they read, write, talk, and listen. Over time, we became more concerned with learners, their social and cognitive development, and less concerned with the correctness of their language. At the same time, we grew more aware of the social and cultural influences that surround learners as they engage in various language acts.

The Natural Process of Language Learning

It is rather widely accepted that language development arises out of a complex system of social interaction. As Vygotsky (1978) argues, young children are taught by adults to make their needs known, to demonstrate their abilities, to form social relationships through language. Through the important work of the whole language movement (see, for instance, K.S. Goodman, 1986; Y.M. Goodman, Hood, & K.S. Goodman, 1991), we've begun to accept that learners rarely learn to speak and write through mastering a set of isolated language skills. Instead, they learn a to use a variety of interrelated language processes naturally as they try to get their needs met or forge relationships with others. Ideally, in schools, this natural process of language learning continues as children learn to collaborate and communicate with teachers and classmates.

Extending This Process into the Classroom

This view of language learning has powerful implications for the classroom. It means accepting the notion that learning processes best develop as students learn to grapple with real intellectual problems, in the company of teachers and other students. Isolated exercises out of textbooks or worksheets rarely offer the kind of complex problems or the opportunity for social interaction that can be found in real life problems. Furthermore, isolated activities like spelling lists and grammar drills are usually associated with passing tests and pleasing teachers. Once these short-term goals are met, once the grades or praise are given, students often forget these isolated skills altogether. Just as there are no teacher- or student-proof language opportunities, there are no fixed sequences of skills that every learner must master at a certain age and no rigid steps that must be followed in every curriculum.

As a high school teacher, I quickly learned that all learners did not develop at the same pace and that those slick curriculum materials rarely worked the way the advertisements claimed. Yet, I wasn't sure how else to proceed. I wanted to develop a way to adapt my lessons to meet the unique needs of each student, at the same time as I was recognizing the needs of my classroom as a whole. I came to realize that this meant helping each student to build a repertoire of learning strategies that can be put into play in a variety of ways, depending upon the particular situation at hand.

Designing the Learning Climate

Over the years, I'd begun to look at my teaching in terms of what I will call some **dimensions** of language and learning. These dimensions are a sort of lens through which you might look at your teaching in a more systematic way. I'd like to begin by presenting all six dimensions in this introductory chapter and then discussing each in more detail in the chapters that follow.

My hope is that you will make the ideas in each chapter your own by taking the opportunity to reflect personally in the **Reflections** and **Explorations** sections and by reading and responding to the stories of other teachers. In the process, perhaps you'll discover that even the lessons you're most disappointed with can "be saved," in Beth's words. I'll begin by inviting you to do a bit of reflecting through writing.

Reflections: Something You Learned

For this first experience, I'm going to ask you to think of a time in your life when you learned something. It may have happened several years ago or just yesterday. You may have learned something profound like "the true meaning of life" or something practical like "how to make a strawberry pie."

After you've made your choice, simply freewrite without stopping for about ten minutes. As a way of keeping this experience purely free and exploratory, remember that you won't have to share the writing itself with anyone, although you may choose to share some of the thoughts you had as you wrote. The important thing is not the text that you create but the learning you engage in as you try to capture your thoughts in writing. If you get stuck, don't stop to monitor. Just write anything that comes to mind until you get started again.

As soon as you've finished, take a few more minutes to make a list of Essential Elements for Learning. As you make this list, try to think about the experience you just described. What elements had to be there for you to learn what you learned? Your list may include such things as "the freedom to fail" or "the guidance of a supportive adult." When you've spent a few minutes creating this list, you may want to discuss it or compare lists with someone else.

Here's one example. Amanda, an elementary reading teacher, participated in a summer workshop I had given on writing across the curriculum. She decided to write about the first time she learned to use a camera. As I read over her piece, I was immediately struck by the connections she was able to draw between her experiences as a photographer and her current experiences as a teacher as she helped students to "come up" out of the growth experiences in her classroom. As you read her text, you might want to try to think about whether there are any similarities between her piece and what you wrote:

When I first was handed a camera, I knew it was a special moment for me. Here was a way I could be an integral part of all things that were happening around me. I was painfully shy and not very healthy as a child. Photography became my escape. I could hide behind my camera. The excitement of the activities was now open to me even though I wasn't an active participant. I also found that I had a talent for "seeing things." It was my area of expertise. People sought me out because my pictures brought them pleasure. Being sick didn't matter when I was in my darkroom. No one was watching me. I could let up on my guard and delve totally into the process. I learned that I could teach myself. I would read and then experiment. Sometimes I would make a picture twenty times before I was satisfied. I also learned that even something so meaningful could become drudgery if forced upon you with no end. I discovered that it wasn't what I wanted to do for a career because that would ruin the magic for me. I also discovered that the only time I captured a comparable feeling of magic was working ... teaching... children. Watching a picture "come up" in the developer is rather akin to seeing a child develop in your classroom. The amount of tone and depth achieved depends a great deal on the care and skill and time you invest with the picture.

In thinking about Amanda's piece, consider what essential elements had to be in place for her to learn what she did. As an example, here is a list that was created by one group of teachers in the workshop Amanda attended (see Figure 1.1).

ESSENTIAL ELEMENTS FOR LEARNING

freedom to experiment	self-confidence (expertness)
respect/guidance of others	outside knowledge (reading)
freedom to struggle	privacy
supportive others	equipment/materials
praise	pride of achievement
admiring audience	pain (sometimes)
experimentation	prior knowledge (some)
time	freedom from evaluation
feedback	encouragement

Figure 1.1

All the items on this list may not be "essential" for every learning experience, but if you take this list as a starting place, you can begin to consider how many of these essential elements are readily available to students in your classroom. How much time, for instance, is available for students to work on and revise their work, how much opportunity is there for experimentation, how is failure treated, and how often can students work without the fear of immediate evaluation? As with most significant learnings, the best lessons about our teaching are usually right there in our own experiences as learners.

Reflections on Reflection

I'd like you to take a few moments and think not so much about the experience you described but about what it was like to write about a time when you learned something. In the next few pages, I'm going to lay out some of the basic assumptions of this book and ask you to consider your own writing and learning processes in light of these assumptions. I guess you could call the ideas in the next few pages my list of **Essential Elements**.

focused only on getting down the details of your experience. Gradually, as you began to make up your list of "Essential Elements for Learning," you might have assumed a connecting stance as you compared and contrasted your experience with what you believe about the learning process in general. Or you might have adopted an extending stance as you went beyond your original experience in speculating on some general beliefs you have about language and learning. Probably, you noticed that you shifted back and forth from among these stances at various points in your writing and thinking.

Although schools seem to focus on the development of language and the development of logical abilities, James Britton (1983) points out that learning has artistic as well as logical dimensions. According to Britton, logical learning involves accomplishing acts: communicating with others, demonstrating knowledge, changing yourself or the world in some particular way. Artistic learning, on the other hand, involves creating or appreciating an artifact — often a text of writing or speech. In artistic learning, we step back and contemplate ideas evoked from texts or create an artifact of our own.

As you wrote your piece, you might have focused more on the incident you were describing than you did on the words you were using to describe it. You may have been trying to capture what happened rather than worrying about how you wrote. But perhaps you did focus to a certain degree on the language itself. You may have planned to share your account with someone who mattered to you or have had an imaginary reader in mind as you played with choices of wording and phrasing, style, and tone. Probably, as you wrote, you shifted focus several times between these logical and artistic concerns.

Despite the value of artistic learning, logical learning predominates in schools. Learners are seldom given the opportunity to contemplate, appreciate, or engage in the artful creation of a text. Much school-sponsored writing is communicative writing, intended to show what one knows to a teacher-examiner (Britton, et al., 1975). Much school-sponsored reading is for the purpose of demonstrating knowledge about written texts on examinations or in formal papers rather than for the purpose of exploring the many personal and social meanings that potentially arise out of reading (Applebee, et al., 1982).

In creating opportunities for learning, we need to take advantage of both the logical and artistic potential of language. Beyond this, we must realize that learning seldom proceeds in a linear fashion through a set of levels or hierarchical skills.

Learners Move Constantly Between Self and World

Now stop for a moment and consider the **outcome** you imagined for your writing and what I might have done in the phrasing of the task to influence your perceptions of that intended outcome. If you believed that your writing would never be seen by anyone else, you probably directed your language only to **self**. If, on the other hand, you planned to share it with a good friend (**intimate other**) or if you believed that someone you didn't know very well, like a professor or a workshop leader, or some **distant other** would be reading it, your writing and thinking processes were probably more self-conscious. Chances are, you became more aware of the words you were using, the correctness of your language, or the tone of the text. Consider how the outcome of your writing shaped the experience for you and how it might have influenced your thinking processes.

I tried to frame this particular writing experience as a private, exploratory reminiscence rather than a planned, public performance. That's why I said: "As a way of keeping this experience purely free and exploratory, remember that you won't have to share the writing itself with anyone, although you may choose to share some of the thoughts you had as you wrote."

I've found that it's a good idea never to present a language activity without letting everyone know in advance whether and how it will be shared. Especially in the first few days of a workshop or class, I notice that group members become visibly nervous at the prospect of sharing their writing with strangers. Providing the option of not sharing the writing itself but simply sharing the ideas behind it is one way of minimizing these fears a bit. If I do want my students to produce some sharable pieces, I can let them know in advance and give them some choices about which pieces to share.

James Moffett (1968) argues that language users are moving constantly along two dimensions, from self to other, and from self to the world. Sometimes our language is focused totally on ourselves, as we read for pleasure, listen appreciatively, talk to ourselves, or write privately. At other times, our language may be focused on someone close to us or someone we've never met.

Although it may seem convenient to believe in a neat curriculum of developmental stages, the movement between self and world is not rigidly sequential or stagelike. Sometimes language users begin fairly close to self, and at other times they begin at a point beyond themselves. The movement between self and world is a perpetual balancing act; there is nothing linear or sequential about it. Very young children, perhaps because of their exposure to books and stories, often begin by writing fantasy, creating characters and situations distant from their actual life experience. Older students, on the other hand, must often be encouraged to move toward the concrete — staying close to phenomena, exploring what happens, before moving on to what might be.

It's a good idea to ask yourself whether your students' reading, writing, speaking, or listening will most likely be focused on themselves or on someone else, perhaps a distant or an intimate other. Then consider what you are doing in the way you set up a language activity to influence their perceptions of those outcomes and whether you might open up their choice of outcomes in any way.

Learning and Choice Are Intricately Related

In the writing task that I posed for you, I tried to set up some general parameters within which you could make some choices. In this particular case, I didn't want to offer absolutely free choice in topic. Because I wanted you to reflect on your own learning processes, I decided to focus the writing rather generally on "A Time When You Learned Something." Within this fairly general framework, I'd hoped the choices for your writing would seem rather open.

I suggested, for instance, that your learning experience "may have happened several years ago, or just yesterday," and that you could choose to write about "something profound like the true meaning of life or something practical like how to make a strawberry pie." I was trying to model some possibilities, in case you might feel stuck for something to write about, but I was also trying to give you enough space to find your own relationship with your topic.

Still, you may have brought some rather negative feelings and experiences to this writing task. Even within these rather broad parameters, you might have had difficulty finding a topic because you were focused on getting it right. Or you may have been resentful of me for framing the topic at all, especially if you are a more independent person who is used to setting your own agendas and finding your own topics.

The fact is that we can never know how all of our students perceive a learning experience. We are always in the business of making educated guesses about that. One thing is certain, though: Every choice that we make in designing our curriculum influences the choices that our students have. The important thing is to become more reflective about choice, closing down only what is necessary, and inviting choice-making whenever possible within the limits of what we are trying to teach.

Learning Moves Between Independence and Collaboration

There are times when we need the privacy to work out our own ideas away from the presence of others. At other times, collaboration with others allows us to enrich and extend our learnings. Since this is the first bit of reflection I've asked you to do, I wanted your writing to be entirely private at first. I didn't want you to worry about anyone else's reactions but to be free to come to your own independent conclusions. I had hoped that you would make some connections between your thoughts and someone else's later in the process, but I wanted to make sure you got a chance to capture your original ideas before sharing them with others.

Depending upon whether you were working with a partner, with a group, or by yourself, there might have been an opportunity to compare your own private learnings with someone else's at a later point. In this sharing process, you probably found that your learning became transformed in some way, as you responded to and reflected upon the ideas of others. The point is to consider when learners need to arrive at ideas independently or when they might benefit from collaboration with others. Better still, it's nice to allow the students themselves some choices about how collaboratively or independently they want to work.

Language Can be Exploratory or Permanent

In framing this particular writing experience, you'll notice that I made sure to say, "The important thing is not the text that you create but the learning you engage in as you try to capture your thoughts in writing." I also told you not to monitor your ideas but to "write anything that comes to mind until you get started again."

The concept of freewriting comes from the work of Peter Elbow (1973), and is a technique that allows the creative processes to proceed, unencumbered by conscious thoughts. By telling you to focus more on the ideas than on the written text itself, I was trying to set up a situation where ideas could be tentative and exploratory rather than permanent. Most likely, the more you were able to make yourself believe that this text would not be seen by others, the more exploratory you could afford to be in your writing.

Let's say, though, that at a much later point you find yourself using some of the ideas from your freewriting in a more polished text. Your language would move from this rather tentative, unguarded place into a more permanent form, and your thinking would change in the process. You might find that as you wrestle over decisions about how to put your ideas into words, you end up learning things that you never thought about before. It's a good idea to be conscious of when your students' language is likely to be tentative and exploratory or when it is likely to be more permanent. Each kind of experience is valuable; each produces a different kind of learning.

We Are Not Only Informed By Language, We Are Transformed By It

As James Britton (1983) has observed, learning is not a uni-directional process, moving from teacher to student, but an essentially social activity, where teachers and students learn "with each other and from each other" (p. 221). Beyond this interactive view, I believe that learning is a **transactive** process, where learners are transformed in fundamental ways by what they read and what they write, what they hear and what they say (You might want to read Louise Rosenblatt, 1990, for a good definition of "transaction.").

Real, substantive learning is not often found in a one-way transmission of information from teacher or text to student but is a process of mutual exploration and change. Learners not only demonstrate what they know through using language; they also discover and develop it, and they grow as language users with every meaningful learning experience.

As you wrote this text or developed your list of essential elements, or perhaps as you read what Amanda had written or shared ideas with friends, you may have found yourself thinking about something that had never occurred to you before. At that moment, you were fundamentally changed by the process of using language to learn. Language is a means of both understanding and changing ourselves and the world around us.

Designing Successful Learning Experiences

In figure 1.2 (on page 13), I've included a chart which you might use in understanding various aspects of your teaching in a more systematic way. Each time you think about some aspect of your teaching, you might begin by asking the questions posed here.

Often, it's hard to predict from a lesson plan what might go wrong in a particular classroom activity. Usually, though, when our ideas go wrong, it's because the learning climate doesn't support what we are trying to accomplish with the language experience. Unfortunately, the learning climate is often intangible. It doesn't show up in the lesson plan. Let's consider a brief example from one teacher's classroom.

DIMENSIONS OF LANGUAGE AND LEARNING

The Language Event

The Learner Dimension: Purpose
What is the learner's purpose in using language?

Personal   *Social*   *Artistic*

The Learning Dimension: Stance
What kind of learning does the language event support?

Replicating   *Connecting*   *Extending*

The Language Dimension: Outcome
To whom is the language directed?

Self   *Intimate Other*   *Distant Other*

The Learning Climate

The Learner Dimension: Choice
How much choice do learners have in the learning environment?

Open   *Closed*

The Learning Dimension: Collaboration
How independently or collaboratively do learners work?

Independence   *Collaboration*

The Language Dimension: Commitment
How exploratory or permanent are language acts?

Exploratory   *Permanent*

Figure 1.2

Classroom Closeup: Peanut Papers

Maria is a fourth grade teacher in her first year. She is disappointed and perplexed by an assignment that backfired:

I don't know what went wrong! I thought I had the most creative idea, and it just plain flopped! It was George Washington Carver's birthday this week, and our whole school was invited to be involved in a contest to see who could put together the best display out in the hall. So I brought in this really great thing for my kids to do—at least, I thought it was really great! I had cut these pieces of paper in the shape of peanuts. I handed them out to the kids and I said, "Write a story about George Washington Carver on these pieces of paper and hand them in at the end of class. Tomorrow I'll put them all up as part of our class's entry in the contest." Well, I wasn't prepared for their reaction. I mean, it really flopped big time! I had all kinds of moans and groans: "I don't know what to write about! Can I have another piece of paper? I wrecked mine." And those were the best comments! Most of the kids just sat there in a daze or fell asleep. I was shocked. I thought they'd really get into this, and it just plain bombed. It makes me really scared to get that creative again!

Maria's comments are familiar to every one of us who ever had a creative idea that went wrong. It's tempting to go back to something familiar — a tried-and-true assignment. In these situations, we often feel a little rudderless as we set about revising our original ideas.

As Maria looked closer at her assignment, however, she realized that the techniques she began with, the language she used to introduce the assignment to her students, and the assumptions she made about their motivations were powerful hidden predictors of her success or failure. Given time to reconsider what she did, Maria herself was able to reflect upon this:

I see now that I really didn't give the kids any choices. I just told them to write a story on George Washington Carver. I started out, then, by limiting the form and the topic of the assignment right from the beginning. I also didn't give them any choice about whether they wanted to enter this contest. I just assumed that they'd be excited by the idea of competing with the other classes for recognition. Some of these kids had come from very rigid classrooms, where they had never had any kind of open-ended or "process" writing experiences. They'd done a lot of worksheets and sentence exercises, but they'd never been asked to write many longer pieces. Here, only a few weeks into the year, I was asking them to go public without a safety net. I see now that forcing them to write a final draft onto those pieces of lined paper was a total mistake. They had to get it perfect the first time. There was no chance of getting help beforehand, drafting, or revising. Everything was permanent right from the start. If I had it to do over again, I'd set it up much differently. I'm glad that we, as teachers, can learn from our mistakes as we go!

ð

If we consider Maria's activity in light of those six **dimensions** in figure 1.2, we might begin by asking what purposes Maria's students saw in the activity, what kinds of learning stances the activity supported, and to whom their language was directed. It appears that Maria wanted her students to use language for **artistic and social** purposes (writing and sharing a story). She wanted them to use language in a way that they might **extend** their knowledge about George Washington Carver or perhaps help them to make **connections** between his life and some larger themes. Finally, she was asking them to direct their language to a group of **distant others** (the entire school). Not a bad set of goals!

As Maria observes, though, some aspects of the learning climate immediately undercut her objectives. First, the lack of **choice** was a problem. Maria realized that she was asking her students to be creative in a climate that encouraged conformity in topic, purpose, form, and audience. In addition, she was a relatively new teacher in the school, and the students were apprehensive about sharing their work with an unfamiliar teacher and classmates, not to mention the whole school. Maria had assumed that they would enjoy **collaborating** as a class to produce a winning display in the schoolwide contest. The fact that students were forced to go public too soon rather than to draft their writing privately made this particular assignment threatening. To make matters worse, many of the students had not been exposed to writing anything longer than a word or a sentence. She was asking them to take the risk of publication before they had been given time to experiment and explore what they wanted to say.

Finally, by closing down so many aspects of this writing assignment, she forced her students to write in a very **permanent** way. By failing to allow for revision, conferring, or feedback, and by demanding that stories be written in final draft form, she made sure that every aspect of the assignment demanded total commitment; nothing was tentative, exploratory, or disposable. Luckily, as Maria has noted, we all have chances to revise our teaching as we go.

The connections between the language event and the learning climate must never be underestimated. If we want our learning opportunities to succeed, we must begin by realizing that our teaching begins even before the bell rings. If we greet our students at the doorway, eager to chat with them about what they're thinking, writing, and reading about, we've set up an inviting climate for language. If we're open to negotiation in posing learning opportunities for them, if we offer options rather than fixed-course assignments, we set up an atmosphere of openness. If we give them chances to fail and opportunities to work toward success, we allow them to use language in exploratory rather than permanent ways.

Even the way we talk about the learning experiences we provide, the nonverbal behaviors surrounding our lessons, the ways in which we comment (or fail to comment) on student work shape the ultimate experiences with language and learning that they have. Our tone of voice, the way our room is arranged, what we say to students about the assignments we give — all ultimately influence their learning processes.

Techniques and Forms for Language and Learning

I often find it useful to work from a list of different techniques and language forms in designing opportunities for my students to learn through language. This list is a starting place for discovering all the possible ways to frame a particular learning task.

It's important to remember that most language techniques can take many different forms. For example, brainstorming is often treated as a prescribed form of writing or talk. This can be misleading. If my version of brainstorming always involves large group discussion and a teacher-made list, then students who are shy in a large group or those who need to write things down for themselves will not be able to take advantage of this learning tool.

It's useful, then, to consider brainstorming a technique that can take a variety of forms rather than a prescribed form itself. Oral brainstorming by a group of students, led by a teacher who writes words and phrases on a chart, is different from written brainstorming, in which one writer makes a private stream-of-consciousness list in a journal. Both are different from group brainstorming, which can occur without the help of a teacher and may not result in a written product.

Even today I find myself creating new versions of what I thought were prescribed language forms. It's important to question whether our forms of language are really more generic techniques that can take on a whole variety of language forms. This helps us to question constantly how fixed particular language activities really need to be.

Here is a preliminary list of techniques that you might consider in framing learning opportunities of your own. The list isn't meant to be exhaustive; it's intended as a starting point for you to begin thinking about the great variety of ways to foster language and learning experiences in your classroom. You'll probably want to add to it as new ideas come to you.

A PRELIMINARY LIST OF TECHNIQUES

BRAINSTORMING	DRAFTING	HYPOTHESIZING
FREEWRITING	RESPONDING	FICTIONALIZING
CLUSTERING	CORRESPONDING	IMAGINING
MAPPING	NARRATING	PROPOSING
DRAWING	REPORTING	ARGUING
CHARTING	PERSUADING	PROBLEM-POSING
DIAGRAMMING	DRAMATIZING	EDITORIALIZING
FREEWRITING	DISCUSSING	IMPROVISING
NOTING	SPEAKING	REVISING
TRANSCRIBING	INTERPRETING	CONFERRING
OUTLINING	PERFORMING	TAPING
SUMMARIZING	DEMONSTRATING	FREEREADING
	RECORDING	INTERVIEWING

Figure 1.3

I gave this preliminary list of techniques to a group of elementary and secondary teachers in a summer workshop, similar to the one that

Amanda was in. I asked the members of this group to help me to brainstorm a more specific list of **language forms** that could be used in creating different versions of these techniques (see figure 1.4). As you will notice, this group decided to cluster their list of language forms according to three categories: writing, talking/listening, and reading/response. Interestingly, though, they discovered that a form such as the **journal** might appear in more than one place on the list. Such lists, then, are never neat or definitive — they are only starting places from which to work.

LANGUAGE FORMS

WRITING:

LETTERS	RESUMES
ESSAYS	MEMOS
POEMS	APPLICATIONS
STORIES	COMMENTARIES
DIALOGUES	EDITORIALS
RESEARCH REPORTS	BOOK REPORTS
JOURNALS	SONGS
SKETCHES	CRITICAL REVIEWS
ANECDOTES	FIELD-NOTES
REQUESTS	PROPOSALS
CHARTS/GRAPHS	MONOGRAPHS
APPLICATIONS	PUZZLES
RESUMES	SCRIPTS
LISTS	NOTES
DRAWINGS	DIAGRAMS
CONCEPT MAPS	RESPONSE PAPERS
NOVELS	CARTOONS
PHOTO ESSAYS	DIRECTIONS
DIARIES	FICTIONAL NARRATIVES
STORY PROBLEMS	AUTOBIOGRAPHIES

TALKING/LISTENING

SMALL GROUP DISCUSSIONS	INTERVIEWS
DEBATES	MOCK LEGISLATURES
DRAMATIC IMPROVISATIONS	SPEECHES
DRAMATIC ENACTMENTS	ORAL INTERPRETATIONS
PANEL DISCUSSIONS	MONOLOGUES
CONVERSATIONS	CHORAL SPEAKING
PAIRED DISCUSSIONS	POSTER SESSIONS
COLLABORATIVE LEARNING GROUPS	ORAL DEMONSTRATIONS
JOKES	SKITS
STORYTELLING	TASK GROUPS
SCRIPTED DIALOGUES	ORAL REPORTS

READING/RESPONSE

SILENT READING	RESPONSE JOURNALS
RESPONSE LOGS	DRAMATIC SPIN-OFFS
RESPONSE GUIDES	SCENE IMPROVISATIONS
DIALOGUE JOURNALS	ORAL READING
CRITICISMS	READERS' THEATRE
BOOK REVIEWS	CHORAL READING
BOOK TALKS	ILLUSTRATIONS
CHARACTER SKETCHES	IMAGINARY DIALOGUES
REWRITES OR PARODIES	THINK-ALOUDS

Figure 1.4

The Fallacy of Form without Function

If you will notice, I did not present these techniques and forms until after I had introduced the idea of the intricate relationship between the language act and the learning climate. Many curriculum guides and "how-to" books offer similar lists of techniques for using language across the curriculum. However, form in the absence of function tells us little about the kinds of thinking in which our students engage. Depending upon the purposes for which they are used, letters-are-not-letters-are-not-letters, reports-are-not-reports-are-not-reports, and so on. Within any one language form, there is an endless array of possible learning stances, purposes, and outcomes, all of which influence the way we use language to learn. To organize our curriculum in such a way that letter writing or essay writing begins in a particular grade is pretty limiting. As you've probably realized, writing a letter to an author demands different kinds of thinking processes than writing a letter to a good friend or writing an unsent letter to yourself.

Since one discourse form can be used for so many different purposes and outcomes, building our entire curriculum upon a sequence of language forms doesn't get us very far. Forms and techniques of language must be chosen in light of our language goals (the stances, purposes, and outcomes we want to support) and our learning environment.

Teacher Goals and Student Perceptions

Just as we must realize that form alone tells us little about the kinds of thinking we are asking our students to adopt or the outcomes and purposes toward which they decide to direct their language, we must also understand that our intentions for the language user may bear little resemblance to how he or she perceives the language and learning experience we provide. We may, for instance, ask our students to write a letter to some elected official for the purpose of influencing public policy, only to find that they have written the letter to **us**, for the purpose of getting a grade. Or, we may ask them to write expressively for their own self-understanding in a journal and discover that they have written very perfunctorily to us, for the purpose of fulfilling our assignment.

There is one thing that I've discovered over and over again: When people use language for things that count and share that language with people who count (including themselves), motivation will follow. One of our most crucial goals should be finding a way to make our classrooms places that support this important work.

Finally, it isn't enough to simply hand out a list of learning options or to offer as many of the forms and techniques as we can in the course of a school year. Good teaching demands that we are always somewhere within easy reach of our students, setting the tone and creating the climate within which our students' good ideas can bloom into being. We simply cannot be somewhere else and expect our lessons to succeed. More than this, it's important to begin with our students, not with our list of techniques. In each individual student lies a clue about what kinds of experiences are best for the class as a whole.

Meg, for instance, is a middle school English teacher. In her teaching journal, she reflects on the importance of starting with the student as the first source of ideas for teaching:

> *The more I teach, the more I am convinced that teaching has much more to do with showing someone how to tap into their natural, inner resources as people — not just as students — and much more about unlocking all the information and talent that is already inside a person than trying to stuff it all into someone's head.... Every kid I teach is a writer and a reader. They are all in different places and have different futures. My expectation is that all of my kids leaving middle school will know themselves as readers and writers and will have a sense of how that aspect of who they are fits into their daily purpose-filled lives. If they learn how to spell more words correctly or if they can talk about symbols and themes in literature, if they can write well-constructed sentences and speak fluently — all the better. But if they go into high school with the belief that reading and writing have a purpose in their lives, and if they know how to use them to accomplish the myriad goals they set for themselves, then that is what will determine whether or not they have really learned and whether or not I have really taught.*

Explorations

The following learning experiences are intended to help you in exploring some of the ideas in this book. You may choose one or several. Feel free, also, to modify them or create your own, if you feel more comfortable doing so.

1. **Letter to the Author:** As you read through this chapter, you might want to imagine that you were going to write a letter to me, the author of this book, explaining any ideas that occurred to you as you read. You might want to keep a running a list of everything that strikes you in a particularly strong way. This may be something you have

questions about, that you disagree with, or that you find particularly appealing. When you've finished reading, go back over the list and circle items that you would like to comment upon. If you want to send your letter to me, the address of my publisher is in the first pages of the book.

2. **Friendly Correspondence.** Another possibility is for you to write a similar letter and send it to a friend or fellow teacher who might benefit from some of the ideas you've encountered. In your letter, you might want to tie these ideas into some experiences that the two of you have shared in your teaching.

3. **Unsent Letter.** If you'd rather not send your letter off, you might want to draft an unsent letter. Even though you don't actually intend to send it, you could use this writing opportunity to clarify some of the ideas you've encountered. Sharing this letter with a partner or a larger group might be a good way of clarifying and extending some of your thoughts.

4. **Group Exploration.** Find a group of four or five other people who have also read this chapter. For this project, you'll need some chart paper and some felt markers. Each of you should begin by freewriting individually for about five minutes, capturing your initial response to what you have read. When this time is up, circle one or two words or phrases that seem to lie at the heart of what you've written. Choose one person to write these words or phrases on the chart paper as each member calls them out. After this preliminary list is completed, group members can take turns talking about the word or phrase they suggested. Continue working in this way until your group feels that it has exhausted most of the possibilities.

5. **Charting Your Response:** After discussing the main concepts of this chapter, your group might want to make a drawing, a diagram, a chart, or some other visual illustration that represents your group's thinking in some way. You might share this map, drawing, or chart with a larger group when you're finished.

6. **Create Your Own Exploration:** Design your own opportunity to write or talk about anything that you feel will enhance your understanding of what you just read and experienced. Feel free to share both the learning opportunity and any texts you created with a partner or a group.

References

Applebee, A.N. (1982). *Writing in the secondary school: English and the content areas.* NCTE Research Report No. 21. Urbana, Illinois: NCTE.

Britton, J. (1983). Language and learning across the curriculum. In P. Stock (Ed.), *Fforum: Essays on theory and practice in the teaching of writing.* (pp. 221-227). Upper Montclair, New Jersey: Boynton/Cook.

Britton, J., Burgess, T. Martin, N., McLeod, A. & Rosen, H. (1975). *The development of writing abilities (11-18).* Schools Council Research Studies. London: MacMillan Education.

Elbow, P. (1973). *Writing Without Teachers.* New York: Oxford.

Goodman, K. (1986). *What's whole in whole language?* Portsmouth, NH: Heinemann.

Goodman, Y.M., Hood, W.J., & Goodman, K.S. (Eds.) (1991). *Organizing for Whole Language.* Portsmouth, NH: Heinemann.

Moffett, J. (1968). *Teaching the universe of discourse.* Boston: Houghton Mifflin.

Rosenblatt, L.M. (1990). Retrospect. In E.J. Farrell & J.R. Squire (Eds.) *Transactions with literature: A fifty-year perspective.* (pp. 97-107). Urbana, Illinois: NCTE.

Vygotsky, L. (1978). *Mind in society.* Cambridge, MA: Harvard University Press.

CHAPTER 2

Language Purposes

ప్ర

I really don't know the dates. They never appeared too have any importance. I can see pictures words and storeis but my mind is blocked by a stone slab; My memery is hazed by something that I can't understand. Looking back I see a train full of toys and was tring to get up a hill but if it did I don't know because I don't seem to remember. In sixth grade I started reading lots of books by myself. My faverite was called THE BOOK OF THREE. After that I started wizing threw books like Streams of Silver.... Now that I'm in seventh I don't like reading with the class at all. Instead my eyes wonder off to finish stories and read others. I do that so much that when we read some storeis I've already read them.

(Jake, seventh grade)

ప్ర

Reading Groups

I listen to the others read,
I listen to how they sound.
It's like they know how to read,
How to read since they were born.
And me sitting there by myself,
Feeling all alone.
One person away,
From my appointment with doom.

Then it was my turn to read,
With sweat dripping down my neck I started to read
After a while I started getting used to it.
That's what got me interested in reading!

(Melissa, seventh grade)

There is an old saying that our students will never remember what we taught them; they will only remember how we treated them. How many of our students like Jake and Melissa learned to read, write, talk, and listen in spite of, rather than because of, what we taught them? I have a hunch that when our students begin to divorce themselves from what they're learning, we've probably focused on school purposes and ignored the **human** purposes behind the language activities in our classrooms. The next few pages will focus on some of the reasons why people use language and some ways we can create learning experiences that harness these authentic human purposes.

Why We Use Language

We often hear about motivation, as though such a commodity could be produced or enticed from reluctant students by some external force. The problem with this notion is that motivation from the outside is rarely long-lasting or successful. We may temporarily engage in an activity because of some outside pressure, but at some time we must find our own personal purposes and intentions, or we will quickly lose our commitment. Motivation cannot be found in a grab bag of gimmicks or activities; it can only emerge in a climate where learners see the personal purposes behind their language acts.

Reflections: The WHY of Language

As a way of better understanding the notion of human purposes, I'm going to ask you to participate in a short writing-to-learn experience. After you've finished, you might want to share what you learn with another person or with a group.

Begin by taking out a sheet of paper and making a list on the left side of the paper of all of the different kinds of reading, writing, talking, or listening that you do right now in your life. Try not to monitor what you put on your list. Just freewrite for about five minutes.

When you've completed your list, go back and place a star beside each kind of writing, reading, talking, or listening activity that you engage in with the most investment. It's not important whether you enjoy doing it. It's only important to choose those activities you engage in most avidly.

*As soon as you've completed this process, ask yourself: What are the **human purposes** behind the language activities I selected? What do I get out of using language in these ways? What's my payoff, in human terms? In the right hand column, list these purposes beside each language activity on your list. This double-entry journal or dialectical notebook is a technique that was developed by Ann Berthoff (1981). It allows you to recall or replicate some aspect of your experience and then to move beyond these concrete terms to speculate about the "why" behind them.*

If you aren't working with a group, you might want to compare your list with the one in figure 2.1, which was formulated by a group of teachers.

Invested Language Activities	Human Purposes
class papers and reports	to succeed, get grades, to please someone
shopping lists	to remember
listening to music	to enjoy, savor
watching TV and movies	to enjoy, to escape
reading textbooks	to understand
reading novels	to escape, enjoy, be entertained
letters to friends	to give, share, clarify
applications	to get, to succeed
memos	to clarify, remind, organize
poems	to create, enjoy, share
notes on meetings	to remember
oral presentations	to clarify, explain
phone conversations	to share, to enjoy, to gossip
lesson plans	to remember, organize
journal writing	to understand, create, remember, learn
letters of complaint	to get, be understood, solve a problem

Figure 2.1

In comparing your list with this one, you might be surprised by a couple of things. The first is that many of the "invested" language activities in your everyday life may not be typically found in classrooms. It's astonishing how seldom students in schools are asked to make lists of things they really need; to send notes to friends; to engage in casual conversations; to read, listen, or experience anything for pure pleasure.

The second surprising thing is that you may have starred an item (for example, journal writing) as an "invested" language activity only to find that others see it as totally perfunctory. It's interesting, on those occasions, to probe for the reasons why the same activity can be compelling to some people and perfunctory to others. Usually, when we have negative perceptions of a task, we are using language to please others that we care little about rather than ourselves. One person may see journal writing as a way of creating a personal history, understanding life events, or letting off steam. Another may see it as an mandatory assignment, a chore, a meaningless task assigned by a teacher.

It's difficult to determine just how our students view the language experiences we provide for them. One thing is certain, however: If our students use language for school purposes rather than human purposes, the chances for long-term investment and real learning are greatly reduced. Sometimes, only those students who want to please teachers and succeed in school are likely to learn anything of lasting value.

You might want to keep your list handy and add to it from time-to-time. It's not a bad idea to be constantly on the lookout for ways to use some of these invested language activities in your own classroom. For now, let's consider another problem with most of those school purposes.

School Purposes and the Tyranny of Form

In making your list, you probably discovered that you read, write, talk, and listen in order to solve problems, make personal connections, explore the unknown, and remember and reflect upon important information. Unfortunately, in classrooms, language activities are often far removed from these human concerns. Here, students (as opposed to learners) use language in order to: inform, persuade, demonstrate, exemplify, describe, narrate, recall, and analyze. A good many things that happen in school involve the learning of language forms.

There is no inherent problem with experimenting with different language forms. We get a great a deal of pleasure out of telling stories, persuading others to our point of view, describing an incident to someone who wasn't there. The problem comes, though, when students engage in language activities for the sole purpose of convincing a teacher that they can successfully reproduce a language form. Students who never discover those human purposes for using language seldom see their learning experiences as authentic and invested.

Let's consider an example. Most large-scale writing competency examinations ask students to engage in some kind of argumentative writing. Unfortunately, the *real* reasons why people engage in argumentation are often lost in the process of writing for the competency examination. Ask yourself about the last time you used persuasive language. Were you writing to an elected official to change public policy, arguing with a loved one about some misunderstanding, trying to convince your partner to go on a long-deserved vacation?

In every case, it's a good bet that you used language to fulfill some basic human needs: to be understood, to change an unpleasant situation, to get your feelings out in the open and convince someone else of their worth. It's not very likely that you engaged in persuasive language to convince some unknown audience that you could construct five grammatically correct paragraphs and supply three valid reasons for solving a problem with which you have had no previous experience. Underneath the school purposes (learning a language form), we must find some real human purposes, or the language experience may be viewed as perfunctory and divorced from real learning.

Language for School Purposes: The Competency Exam

The following examples are paraphrased prompts from the 1988 NAEP (National Assessment of Educational Progress) examination in writing. They are examples of what the test makers call "Writing to Convince Others to Adopt Your Point of View" and "Writing to Refute an Opposing Point of View." As you read over the examples, you might want to put yourself into the role of a student who is encountering them for the first time. For what purpose would you be writing? And what aspects of these writing prompts might actually limit your success?

Spaceship: Decide whether creatures from another planet should be allowed to return home or be detained for scientific study, and convince others of this point of view. (Grade 4)

Dissecting Frogs: Write a letter to a science teacher discussing and supporting views on dissecting frogs in science class. (Grade 8)

Radio Station: Give reasons why the class should be allowed to visit a local radio show despite the manager's concerns. Grades 4 & 8)

Recreation Opportunities: Take a stand on whether a railroad track or a warehouse should be purchased. Defend your choice and refute the alternative using arguments based on possible recreational opportunities. (Grades 8 and 12) (Applebee, Langer, Jenkins, Mullis, & Foertsch, 1990, pp. 71-75)

One look at these writing prompts reveals some problems. It's hard to imagine, for instance, that the average middle school or high school student would be in charge of purchasing a warehouse or a railroad track (or even interested in purchasing one, for that matter). Consider how many eighth grade students would bother to write a letter to their science teacher explaining their views on frog dissection. Wouldn't they most likely deliver those views in person? Furthermore, how many will actually be dissecting frogs in eighth grade science class? Would the students or their teacher be in a position of convincing a reluctant radio station manager to allow a group of young people to tour the station? More important, will they be able to reconstruct a real radio station manager from the test-maker's hypothetical version? Considering the fact that their letters will be delivered to an anonymous evaluator and not a real radio station manager, it's not surprising that students frequently forget the most important aspects of the business letter, such as the return address and signature.

In deference to the test makers, there are real reasons for constructing items like these: They allow generalizability over time and across large groups of students. However, as Ernest Boyer has argued:

> Tests are a useful barometer of how well schools are doing; they do not come close enough to individual children or provide sufficient information to the teachers. And by reducing students to numbers, we may tell children they are failures before they've discovered what they might become (1986, p. 21).

Students who are instructed in writing for competency examinations should be dealt with fairly and honestly. They should be told up front that they are engaging in a very specific kind of language — a test. They will need to invent a context and an audience, to write within a specific time frame with little opportunity for revision, and to conform to a rigid form. Their actual audience (we and they know it) will be an anonymous rater who has been trained to look for competencies, not for originality or honesty. Their purpose in this exercise will be to demonstrate mastery of a form and to pass a test. Our candor might allow them to adopt a real intention (passing the test) and not ask them to pretend that they are actually writing to a crotchety radio station manager or an imaginary science teacher.

Aside from the competency examination question, we might consider if it's ever possible within the walls of school to create opportunities for our students to find personal investment and purpose in their reading, writing, speaking, and listening. If we consider the reasons for using language in the first place, we might find that their reasons are very much like those discussed at the beginning of this chapter.

Language for Human Purposes: Personal, Social, Artistic

Several years ago, James Britton (1975) examined texts produced by students from the ages of eleven to fifteen in the United Kingdom. He and his colleagues asked teachers to submit the writing that their students did in school and to describe briefly the context within which the writing was produced. In analyzing more than 2,000 texts, the team explored two questions: "Who is it for? and What is it for?" (1978, p. 15).

Britton's team came up with three *function categories* to describe the school texts they analyzed: "expressive," "transactive," and "poetic." The spectrum from expressive to poetic was classified by the researchers as language in the "participant" role, and the spectrum from expressive to transactive, as language in the "spectator" role.

According to Britton, language in the participant role is for the purpose of getting things done or taking part in events. Letters, public speeches, discussions, are examples of language in the participant mode. Language in the spectator role, on the other hand, is used for contemplation of "our own or other people's experiences, or ... the imagined events of dream or fiction" (1978, p. 17). In the spectator role, "the utterance itself moves into the focus of attention, becoming an end rather than a means to something outside itself" (1978, p. 19). Poetic writing, the reading and writing of imaginative fiction or literary essays, and listening for pure pleasure are examples of language in the spectator role. In Britton's model, expressive language is a "matrix from which, in favorable circumstances, both transactional and poetic writing are developed" (1978, p. 18). Thus, according to Britton, all language is used to some extent for personal expression.

Britton's model of language functions is a useful framework for classifying the texts of language that students produce. It is important to note, however, that Britton's system was not an analysis of students' stated purposes for using language. As teachers, we need to focus on our students and the many purposes for which they use language in their lives.

I'm going to propose three basic purposes for which learners use language — **personal, social, and artistic**. These purposes are closely related to Britton's function categories, but they focus on the language learner, rather than the language itself. Consider these brief definitions:

> **Personal.** When language is used for personal purposes, the focus is on the **self**. Learners use language to understand, to remember, to reproduce, to express, to explore personal connections, to appreciate something privately.
>
> **Social.** When language is used for social purposes, the focus is on the **other**. Learners use language to give, to get, to share, ingratiate, to understand and be understood by another.
>
> **Artistic.** When language is used for artistic purposes, the focus is on some kind of **text** or artifact of reading, writing, or speech. Learners use language to enjoy, contemplate, admire, immerse themselves in a creative act.

Classroom Closeup: "Myself as a Reader and Writer"

To better understand the purposes for which students say they use language, I'm going to focus on a group of students in an urban middle school. At the beginning of the term, Meg, their teacher, was curious to know more about their early experiences with reading and writing. During the first few weeks of their seventh grade year, she asked them to write a brief account, entitled "Myself as a Reader and Writer." Meg explained that their memories of learning to read and write would be useful to her in getting to know them better. As they were writing these pieces, she conducted routine conferences with them about their early and later experiences as readers and writers. In their accounts, you will discover many human purposes for which they use language.

For example, at an early age, Aaron learned to use language for social purposes, impressing the girls in his class:

> *The first experience I had as a writer was when I was in preschool. I used to write "Roses are Red Violets are Blue" poems to girls that I*

thought were cute. The teacher used to read the letters to the girls that I sent them to. If they liked it then they would let me share their lunch with them. Then I would kiss them on the cheek. Then I would steal all their fingerpaint and they got mad and they used to hit me.
—Aaron

Tameka also uses language for social purposes. Early on, she learned the value of reading and writing from her grandmother, who had been a journalist for a large city newspaper. Later, Tameka passed this appreciation on to her own father, as she learned to read along with him:

My first reading experience was with my grandmother. She wrote for the Chicago Tribune and she used to tell me about her childhood and the clothes she used to wear etc. that also inspired me at 4 years old. My second reading experience was when my daddy sat down and listened to me read to him and we started to read together. (see he never graduated from high school and it's not only helping me but him too.) Sometimes I would read and he would help me with the big words. If we both couldn't figure it out we would ask my mother and of course she would know. Well that was the second and best learning experience 10 years old. Those were the most inspiring experiences that I remember.
—Tameka

Karen uses language for more pragmatic personal reasons — to realize her career goals. Here, reading and writing serve a vital purpose in her success in school and in her future plans.

In ... seventh grade I still find myself doing alot of reading on aerospace technology. I want to be an astronaut and I realize that in the future alot of reading will be required of me. I would also like to see myself reading more fictional works. I think that it is more important if not equaly to do fictional reading as well as nonficitional reading, because through nonfictional reading you learn to communicate better. The papers that are writen for high school as well as collage benifit from the non-ficitonal writing styles these books contain.... When I go babysiting it's like a ritual for the kids to have a bed time story. I hope that my children will show as much inthusiam towards reading as the children I babysit.
—Karen

Matt writes for artistic, personal, and social purposes as he dreams of becoming rich and famous:

When I was in the fifth grade I began writing limmericks. That is a fun form of poetry. Poetry is something that interests me. Most of the time I write, I write raps or slow raps. Hoping to make some money oneday and be come famous.

—Matt

Claudia discovered writing for artistic purposes as she developed her exquisite handwriting:

I really started to like writing because my hand writing started to improve alot. I would just sit down and start to write because I thought I really was cooking. I use to love when the teacher gave us dittos to do, because I just wanted to look at the way I was writing my name. Fourth grade I really liked to write because mostly all of my teachers told me that I had beautiful writing.

—Claudia

Jake, on the other hand, learned that reading and writing in schools was a punishment, of little value to his teachers in its own right:

In fifth and sixth grades I started to do assignments that were more complicated than before. My teachers were really strict about reading and writing. Sometimes if we didn't pay attention we had to write out of an encyclopedia. Then after we got all done the teachers would rip all the papers up.

—Jake H.

Unfortunately, in Jake's case, his teachers never seemed to get beyond school purposes in the experiences they provided. By asking him to copy words out of an encyclopedia and by tearing up his papers, they sent him powerful messages about the purpose (or lack of purpose) behind the language acts in their classrooms.

It's important to become aware of how our students see the purposes behind the language opportunities we provide for them. Their comments tell us that, like us, they use language for a whole host of personal, social, and artistic purposes: to succeed in life, pass the time, capture or understand the events of their lives; to build relationships, impress others, share important ideas, or discover a heritage of values; to create a beautiful artifact of words or images and, in the process, forge a unique identity as artisan and creator.

Reflections: The Teaching Tale

Just as these middle school students discovered the value of telling the stories of their early experiences as readers and writers, we can discover many valuable things in the stories we tell about our experiences as teachers. For several years as a high school teacher, and later as I began to work with other teachers, I found myself growing increasingly disenchanted with the traditional lesson plan. Although I knew it was important to think about my goals, activities, and evaluation schemes in advance, the typical skeleton lesson plan was a drudgery to create and revealed little about what actually went on in my classroom. I can remember my first years of teaching, when I wrote lesson plans only on demand and often after I'd taught the lesson, to please some administrator or department chair.

These days, I've discovered a great deal of value in writing, telling, and sharing stories of practice. These **teaching tales** *can be written or talked about before or after we have designed and implemented a lesson. They can focus on our own teaching or someone else's. These rich narrative accounts help us to discover a great deal about the teaching and learning process.*

Interestingly, our first attempts at telling stories of teaching reveal much valuable information about what we emphasize or what we consider unimportant. When our teaching tales are a list of strung-together activities with little explanation about our goals, our students' needs at the moment, or our classroom climate, it's a hint that perhaps we focus on activities to the exclusion of more hidden aspects of our curriculum. When we fail to mention our students' responses to what we do, it's perhaps a hint that we are not focused on the impact and outcome of our teaching.

As a source of further understanding and reflection, you might want to create a teaching tale of your own. Usually the initial drafting process takes about thirty minutes or so. As you continue to read this book, you can refer back to your original teaching tale, adding information you've forgotten or reflecting in writing about issues and ideas from each chapter. If you are working with a group, you can periodically share drafts of this account with others as a way of understanding some of the concepts that you are reading about.

As you begin drafting your teaching tale, remember that the object is not to create a permanent and polished piece of writing but to capture an experience you had in your own or someone else's classroom as fully as you can. Here are some possible ways to proceed:

Recollections of teaching. Try to capture an experience you had as a teacher. This might have been a lesson that succeeded or one that failed or fell short of your expectations. Recall the incidents of this experience in as much detail as you can. Try to paint a picture in your mind of what happened. You might want to begin by making some sketchy notes, a map, or a list of main events.

Recollections of learning. If you have never taught before, you might want to recall a vivid or striking experience you had as a student in someone else's class. You may want to write some preliminary notes or freewrite for a while as you try to imagine everything you can about the situation. Try to picture what your teacher and other students looked like. What were your teacher's exact words? What were your exact words? What were you being asked to do that made this experience so vivid for you?

Once you have a first draft, your might want to read what you wrote aloud to a partner and ask him or her to report what he or she heard as well as what wasn't in the narrative. You can then switch roles and do the same for your partner. Remember to listen appreciatively, openly, not critically. Each of you might want to make a list of everything you heard in your partner's teaching tale. At the end of this process, you might try to write a revised draft, in which you add details that you might have missed the first time (for example, focusing in more depth on how students responded to particular aspects of the lesson). Such a process of revising and reconsidering not only reveals valuable clues about why things worked or didn't work but also helps you to focus beyond a listing of activities, to the purposes behind them and their impact upon other people in the situation.

Depending upon the time available, you might do a variety of things with these teaching tales. You may decide to take them through several

> *revisions, each time elaborating on some aspect you had forgotten. You may decide to write comments in the margins or create a double-entry journal, taping another sheet of paper onto the original, and speculating in writing about particular things worked or didn't work. If you wrote a story of failure, you might decide to rewrite it as a success story, describing the experience as it would have been in a best-case scenario.*

These narratives of practice have several advantages over those sketchy lesson plans, with their lists of objectives, materials, and activities. They help you to become aware of several aspects of a lesson, including the climate within which it was presented. The writing process itself also helps you to better discover and explore ideas about teaching. Best of all, these narratives, written down in free moments throughout the year, can become a rich anecdotal record of your teaching.

As an example, I'm going to present some excerpts from the teaching tales of a middle school and a high school English teacher. Sandra and Gail were participants in a summer workshop with me. The two teachers decided that Sandra would spend several days in Gail's classroom, taking observational notes on what went on, while Gail would keep a journal focused on the same events. At the end of three weeks, they agreed to put their ideas together and see what they could learn from the experience. Interestingly, their experience illustrated all the different human **purposes** for which Gail's students learned to read, write, speak, and listen in her classroom.

Classroom Closeup:
A Tale of Two Teachers: The "Journal Journey"

Gail is a middle school language arts teacher with several years of experience. Sandra is an English teacher who has recently returned to school to complete her master's degree in English education. When Gail announced one day that she was planning to implement a journal writing project for the first time in her seventh grade classroom, both women decided to work together, keeping a written record of the experience.

At the outset, Sandra agreed to visit Gail's classroom for two weeks, making observations and keeping a journal of her own thoughts and insights. Gail also agreed to keep a journal and to write her version of the experience afterward. Their final teaching tales would provide an opportunity for them to share their perceptions of the experience and, hopefully, to learn something from it. Although they eventually shared their texts, the two women agreed to give themselves a couple of weeks to write about the experience privately. In the meantime, Sandra and Gail were free to chat informally about various aspects of the class.

Sandra recalls:

> *With no classroom of my own and eager to be in one, I was delighted to observe another teacher. Gail was a veteran teacher with children the ages of mine; I had enjoyed getting to know her earlier in the term. She had been particularly supportive of me in my apprehensions about returning to school.*

Gail recalls:

> *Because I was directly involved in the journal activities with my students, I was pleased when Sandra, a member of my university group, asked to come in to observe the dynamics of the two weeks.... She would afford me an objective, insightful perspective on what had become a perplexing issue. Hopefully, she would save me from the streets!*

Gail was excited about embarking upon what she called her "journal journey." She described the project as an "odyssey during which the students could practice their writing and we could communicate with each other in writing." At the same time, Gail had misgivings about the role of journal writing in her own life. She mused:

> *I wish I could report that my personal [journal] entries were prolific and entertaining. Unfortunately, they were sparse. It was only because of Sandra's inquiries that I was motivated to write at all. So meager were the offerings that they seemed unimportant. I valued the time and energy I spent in response to students in their journals more.... Even though I was not personally drawn to the use of a journal, this did not seem to get in the way of doing some useful things with my students. Perhaps approaching the issue honestly is all I need[ed] to do [.]*

Gail's reluctance about using journals in her own life became a compelling issue for Sandra as she observed the classes. In recalling her first observation, Sandra wrote:

> *Never having seen [Gail] teach before, I wasn't fully aware of her state of mind until she told her students, "Would you please take out—your journals." Her voice dropped perceptibly at this word, revealing the dread she felt.*

Early on, Gail confided to Sandra that she had never used the two beautiful leather bound notebooks that friends had given her on the birth of her first child and her first trip to Europe. She admitted:

> *Although at times, I occasionally yearn to pore over every minute detail of my son's first few years or that thrilling year in Florence, the yearning does not create a sense of loss or guilt sufficient enough to motivate me to keep a journal today so I can record all of those rich tomorrows! Why not? ... What motivation creates a journal keeper, a selfless yet selfish scribe who traps her yarns to be spun in old age or by posterity? ... I enjoy talking, listening, and trying to get to the meat of an issue. I appreciate the eye contact, the facial contortions, the flinches or other body language which help me on my way, as connections are or are not being made.... My inability to give the journal a place in my life would be of no concern if I was not a language arts teacher.*

Getting Started

Despite some initial discomfort about her own relationship with journals, Gail was eager to give the project a try. On the first day of the "journal journey," Gail told her students that they would be producing entries of one page or more and that she would respond to one row of students per day. They would receive no grades other than a check mark. As soon as the first assignment had been given, Sandra recalled, "the students scattered to corners, nooks and crannies of the room. Only two or three remained at their seats." It was obvious that Gail had arranged the room for comfort. Students had brought in pillows, and Gail eventually brought in a rug from home.

Interestingly, on that first day, Gail circulated around the room but did not choose to write along with her students. Sandra observed: "[Gail] had chosen to discuss grades rather than write, testimony to her attitude about writing." During her observation, Sandra wrote to herself:

It's hard to watch [Gail] struggle. She says her hand hurts when she writes! We talked about earliest writing experiences and she suggested that they color our feelings far more than we realize. I jokingly suggested that maybe she didn't like writing in journals because she was afraid of what she might find out about herself. She said that might be true.

For the next several days, Gail's journal odyssey brought her and her students increasingly in touch with the power of writing to shape, transform, and illuminate the events of their lives. Gail began by assigning general topics each day that she hoped would relate to real classroom situations. In the first entry, for instance, she asked her students to reflect on their current grades and their goals for the next marking period. From that beginning, students wrote on topics such as whether their study of grammar was helpful to them or whether they would recommend *The Hobbit* to a friend.

Although her first requests for journal entries were somewhat controlled, Gail felt that the topics were authentic enough to generate engaged writing. This seemed to play itself out on several occasions. One student, Ned, used the journal to clear up some misunderstandings with Gail about his past grades and his future goals. Another student, Nikki, shared her journal entry about grades and goals with her father, who arranged a conference with Gail soon afterward.

In the very first days of the project, however, both Gail and Sandra became aware that many students were still not writing or saying much. To get them more engaged, Gail decided to ask each student to list three gripes. Alongside each gripe, they were to write the name of a person to whom they might write for a solution to the problem. After students starred the most important gripe, they began a letter to that person in their journal. Gail recalled in her own journal that "this was, to date, the most exciting project. Students' frustration with their gripes led to some good discussion." When one student expressed a fear about sharing her gripes with parents, the class launched into a discussion of constructive criticism and appropriate tone in writing.

Reaching Beyond the Classroom

About this time, a rather serendipitous event served as a turning point for the project. On the day that students were supposed to write letters about their personal gripes, Gail recalled that Tom "couldn't see any purpose in carrying on a discussion with the principal about a book he had torn. He figured it was a no-win situation." Ironically, in the middle of the discussion, the principal, Mr. M., walked in. After the laughter quieted down and Mr. M. learned about the situation, he encouraged Tom to write the letter. He told the class about another student who, just that week, had written him a letter and was able to change his original opinion on an issue. Sandra recalled that Mr. M. "drew stick figures on the board to illustrate the path the letter had taken, pointing out, finally, that the [complaining] student had been right." Peter prepared his letter and gave it to the principal.

When the students returned from lunch, Sandra remembered how excited they all were. Much to his amazement, Tom had received a letter back from the principal. Although Mr. M. remained unconvinced of Tom's point, both Gail and Sandra noted that the experience had been a good lesson in the power of the written word.

The journals continued to play significant roles in the students' lives as the days wore on. Tiombe, for instance, used her journal as a way of opening a conversation with her father about a personal problem. She reported that her father "had tears in his eyes" as they talked. Gail reflected: "If I had such an experience at age twelve, would I be a journal writer now?"

Near the beginning of the second week, Gail took advantage of a districtwide contest, called "WAD" (War Against Drugs). She asked students to "begin a piece in any genre about drug prevention among youth." After a brief discussion of genre, the students scattered and began to write. The project proved to be so compelling that they asked for more time and were eager to "share even the earliest attempts."

By the beginning of the second week, the students and Gail had discovered several purposes for their writing and sharing. They used the journals to express themselves, to preserve their memories, to clear their minds, and to communicate with important people like parents, teachers, and administrators. Gail reflected: "Although time consuming, the permanence of the journal compared to conversation seemed to lead my students and me to a better understanding of each other." In one case, for instance, Gail got into an disagreement with a student about something that had happened in class. By turning to her own journal, Gail was able to point out her exact words, as well as this particular student's response. Because she had a record of the event in her own journal, she succeeded in convincing the student of what had actually happened. "Perhaps," Gail concluded, "it was time for me to recognize the journal as worthy of more than a mere flirtation. After all, once again, it had saved me!"

Over the two-week period, Gail and her students were able to use their written and spoken language for many authentic purposes. They directed their words to each other, to parents, teachers, administrators, and, privately, to themselves. In responding to people close to them as well as more distant audiences, they discovered the power of their own language to shape and clarify their experiences.

Indeed, Gail had created a safe and inviting climate for her students to use written and spoken language. Although she had begun by asking for a minimum of one page, she eventually told students to draw a line in the journal if they ran out of valuable thoughts and write about anything they wished.

A Choice of Purposes

She provided even more choice as the days went by. One day, she suggested that students write about "anything in any form they wished." Perhaps not surprisingly, her students had some trouble with this. Sandra remarked: "Given that the group was so well adapted to structure and the regulations of teachers, it was not surprising that they had trouble with complete choice." Eventually though, Sandra concluded that "they loved the freedom of choice — it was getting started that was so difficult for them." By the end of the two weeks, they still wrote within the limits of a rather general topic, but the choice of how and in what form to write was left totally up to them.

Gail was able to build a sense of support and community by negotiating various aspects of her classroom activities with the students. For example, she asked her students to set their own individual goals and give suggestions about grades as part of the journal writing experience. At one point toward the end of the two weeks, she began by asking her students to work in groups of six to eight. As each student read his or her journal entry aloud, the other group members took notes on important issues. These issues were listed on large sheets of paper and later shared with the rest of the class. At the end of this project, Gail asked her students to list the other group members in their journal and award a grade for participation, followed by an explanation. Gail mused:

> *The students' perception of their performance as well as the performance of others within the group that I gleaned from reading the journals were enlightening. The only students within one group who didn't mention the spit wads were the ones who shot them!*

As students shared journal responses, they learned some important lessons about how they were perceived by others in the room. Although Gail admitted that asking students to suggest grades was "good news for some and bad news for others," the students learned that "certain behavior doesn't go unnoticed and can be detrimental to the group's progress, particularly a group which is interested in a good grade!"

In all, the journal project was a great way for these students to engage in exploratory writing that allowed them to reflect on events in and beyond their classroom walls. Writing about emotional issues before talking about them allowed each student to work out powerful feelings before sharing them with parents, administrators, teachers, and peers. As Gail later reflected:

> *Could it be that the journal is a way of giving life meaning, of keeping things alive? ... If I write to purge, a seemingly useful purpose, that which appears on the page lives and therefore has the potential to renew pain ... Perhaps herein lies the argument for the usefulness of some temporary writing and some permanent writing!*

By the end of the experience, Gail was convinced of the need to provide many more opportunities for her students to use journals. As for her own relationship with them, she reflected:

> *I have begun to identify moments in my life as potential journal moments and have actually written a couple of pages in one of those dusty old books since the project ended or, I should say, since we paused on our classroom journal journey. The flirtation has recurred. Whether it will result in a lasting relationship remains to be seen. . . . I'll continue to provide opportunities for my students to use journals in my classroom, and I'll keep that dusty old book near at hand, at home, in case I get the urge to use it as I did again yesterday. Perhaps this project is the spark which will rekindle the desire? Perhaps I just talk a good line. Only time will tell!*

Through writing about and analyzing her own teaching, Gail discovered a whole host of purposes for which her students might use a journal in their daily lives. Perhaps more important, she found several personal reasons for writing herself. As Sandra and Gail have discovered, using language to re-see and revise our teaching provides a powerful tool for learning about and continually refining our important work.

Classroom Connections

At this point, the whole business of discovering the purposes behind our students' reading, writing, talking, and listening may seem altogether too tricky and elusive. It's easy to see **our** intentions for the language experiences we provide, but discovering **their** perceptions and intentions is another matter. How do we begin to probe the underside of their language acts, to discover the "why" behind them? Here are some ways to begin.

Ask Them.

Start with the obvious. Jake, Melissa, Aaron, Tameka, and their classmates wrote the "Myself as a Reader and Writer" pieces in this chapter at their teacher's request. As they shared these memories over several days, they decided to extend these initial writings into a larger project, where they interviewed each other, shared what they found in the larger group, and conferred individually with their teacher about their early experiences with language. Many of them had never been asked by a teacher about their memories of reading and writing. Most were more than happy to respond. Their personal accounts were indeed helpful to Meg, who planned her next semester with their comments in mind. It's often a good idea to ask your students about their purposes for using language. They'll probably tell you!

Conduct Periodic "Mini Studies".

In personal conferences with your students, you may want to ask them periodically to identify which activities they engaged in with the most investment. You'll probably be surprised at the variety of their responses. If they are at a comfortable point and can be honest, you might be shocked at how **few** of their learning experiences were invested. This should not be discouraging to you. Not everything they do in or outside of school demands their undivided attention and enthusiasm. From this starting place, though, you can begin to get a sense of what kinds of activities seem most purposeful to your students and why. You might ask your students occasionally to write "process accounts" in their logs and journals, to give you an idea of what your assignments and activities were like for them.

Make the Implicit Explicit.

I'm always surprised at how often I fail to let my students know explicitly the purposes behind what I do. I seem to feel that they will grasp these purposes by some kind of ESP or mental osmosis. I am more embarrassed when I look back at my lessons and realize that I didn't have a real purpose behind some activity and just assumed that my students would find their own meaning in the experience.

Oftentimes, especially if I have been able to create a comfortable atmosphere for learning, my students are more than happy to do things just because I asked them to, but my students learn more when I can be clear about my purposes and when my students' purposes for using language coincide with mine. I need to be more explicit about my purposes, bringing them to the surface of everything I do. I cannot trust that everyone will see the significance of the learning experiences I provide.

Open the Options.

Go back over the list of invested language activities you made earlier. Ask yourself if there is any way of making these invested activities a part of your curriculum. Could students write notes to each other in science or math class? Could they keep a personal journal as part of a social studies unit on some historical period? Could groups of students and teachers keep shopping lists of possible mini research projects on their next trip to the library? Could students write notes to you in a suggestion box or notes to each other in response to class readings on a computer networking system? Could there be opportunities for students to simply read, watch, or listen, with no responsibility for response?

Now look at your list of human purposes for using language. Can you set up opportunities for students to use language, not just as a way of demonstrating knowledge but as a way of sharing, giving, creating, ingratiating, understanding, exploring, or simplifying their lives? The main point is to stop stopping at school purposes and to recognize the potential human purposes behind every language act in your classroom.

Bringing the Classroom to Life

Of course, in the real world students will have to pass competency examinations, learn to write research papers, and master the form of the business letter. To deny them access to knowledge about these forms is to limit them in future academic and career settings. However, if school purposes dominate our curriculum, we may lose the learners for whom school holds little fascination.

If our curriculum says that it is important for students to write narratives, we might dig underneath our assumptions and ask ourselves why. What is the use of stories? When do we tell them most avidly? What are the stories that populate our everyday lives? The answers are all right there in front of us. We tell jokes to ingratiate ourselves and enjoy the company of friends. We recount events for others to share our experiences or to get the opinion of an objective observer. We write fictional narratives as a way of exploring our identities as authors and delighting in the beauty of our own creation.

Sadly, some students are never able to find human purposes in the things they do for school. For them, language and learning are divorced from each other, and school is divorced from the realities of the world. Consider the case of Andrea, a seventh grade student. In her "Myself as a Reader and Writer" piece, she recalls:

> *My reading life started before school. At day carer. It was a big wieth hous on a died end street. The old lady who lives thare is named Ms. Carter we called her Moma Carter. She was like a grandmother to me the way a grandmother really should be. Nice and kind always there for you. My real grandmothers lives in New Orleans. She would read to us and write the names of thing on them. We would watch T.V. shows like Sesame Street, Mr. Rogers and Pinwheel. My worst reading experience was in second grade. Where I failed as you know. It's so far was the worst grade experience I've ever had. I remember is after I had made the decision to stay in second grade another year. I didn't under stand the problem. The teacher said "Don't wherry you'll get it next year. And that's my grade school experience. Thous were the most powerful reading experiences I ever had so be carreful of what you tell, teach and treat a student you could destroy or biuld there foucher in what ever thay may do.*
>
> —Andrea (seventh grade)

Andrea recalls her early experiences as positive and productive. She read, wrote, listened, and talked in a purposeful way, with the supportive guidance of a loved and trusted adult. She did not need to convince someone of what she knew. Her language counted in its own right. Often, reading, writing, and listening were forms of entertainment, which, not surprisingly, resulted in more learning.

We might imagine that Momma Carter praised and nurtured Andrea's early language attempts, modeling for her and the other children the enjoyment and power of their developing literacy. Unfortunately, we don't know what happened between Andrea's positive early experiences with language and her later school failures. We can only wonder how many students like Andrea will reach adulthood, never finding their own personal purposes for language. What happens to these students by the time they become adults? Some may never graduate from high school, others may fall victim to the materialism, crime, and carelessness that surround their daily lives.

For Andrea and her classmates, there are opportunities to find meaning and purpose in their school activities. Stories of failure need not populate the world of school. Hopefully, learners like Andrea, Melissa, and Jake can discover the powerful human purposes behind their language acts.

Explorations

1. **Literacy History:** It might be interesting to interview someone about his or her first experiences as a language learner. This person might be one of your students, a good friend, or a relative. Work from a list of questions (i.e., "When did you first learn to read? to write? to speak in public? How did/do you feel about reading and writing? What were your teachers like?). Feel free to add other questions not on your list as they occur to you. Take notes on the interview. At some later point, read over your notes carefully and see if you can determine the purposes for which this person uses language. Write about what you find in your journal.

2. **Exploring Old Territory:** It might be enlightening and fun to find an old lesson plan and rewrite it as a teaching tale. Enrich it. Expand it. Add details that seem important, such as the students' reactions, the appearance of the room, and so forth. Once you have created a draft you feel comfortable with, write an account of what you learned from the experience of revising or reseeing this lesson plan.

3. **Classroom Exploration:** If you are teaching, tape record one of your classes. If possible, transcribe the lesson so you can see the text of teacher and student talk. As you look over the transcript or listen to the tape, take notes on whenever you seem to be making students explicitly aware of the purposes behind their language acts. Note what proportion of activities are presented with no stated purpose. When purposes are stated, take notes on what kinds of purposes you tend to gravitate toward. When you are through with your mini-analysis, write about what you have learned in your journal. If you don't have a classroom of your own, you might want to tape someone else's classes and follow the same process.

4. **Tales about Tales:** Look back over the excerpts from the teaching tales of Maria, Sandra, and Gail, presented in this chapter. Choose one story that interests you and write an imaginary letter to the author, telling her what you learned in her account about language and learning. You may share your ideas later with a group or might keep them in your notebook or journal, adding to and revising them as you go.

5. **Create Your Own Exploration:** Invent your own language exploration, focused on what you have learned from this chapter. Use any of the forms and techniques available to you. You might want to share the writing and your exploration with a partner or a group.

References

Applebee, A.N., Langer, J.A., Jenkins, L.B., Mullis, I.V.S., & Foertsch, M.A. (1990). *Learning to write in our nation's schools: Instruction and achievement in 1988 at grades 4, 8 and 12.* Princeton, New Jersey: Educational Testing Service.

Berthoff, A. (1981). *Forming/thinking/writing: The composing imagination.* Montclair, NJ: Boynton/Cook.

Britton, J. (1978). The composing process and the functions of writing. In C.R. Cooper & L. Odell (Eds.), *Research on composing: Points of departure.* (pp. 13-28). Urbana, Illinois: NCTE.

Britton, J. Burgess, T., Martin, N., McLeod, A. & Rosen, H. (1975). *The development of writing abilities (11-18).* Schools Council Research Studies. London: MacMillan Education.

Boyer, E. (1986). *The Carnegie Foundation for the Advancement of Teaching: The 81st annual report*, pp. 15-22.

CHAPTER 3

Stances Toward Learning

In Susan's middle school science classroom, students routinely conduct and write about experiments, keep learning logs, work in task groups, and generate and explore their own questions about scientific problems. Still, she wonders about how to nurture their intellectual growth without pushing them too far:

There's the question of development. I mean, do we throw it at them faster, or do we give them some sort of core and then expand on it? I have problems with the part about "throwing it at them faster." Because then, when you're done, where are you? But that is the push in our schools. We have to get a two-year program into one. That's the "accelerated concept." So, in our school, they teach sixth and seventh grade social studies all in one year. And in my opinion, it creates monumental problems, because some kids just aren't ready for that. They might be really excited by it, really able, but they aren't able to fit all of that new knowledge in.

How many of us are familiar with Susan's concerns? We wonder what intellectual tasks are appropriate for our students at particular phases of their growth. There are all kinds of "scope and sequence" charts to tell us where are students should be at particular points in their development. But we wonder if these models are limiting students rather than encouraging them grow in their own special ways. Often, our notions of development become a sort of self-fulfilling prophecy, in which we lead students away from what they can see, feel, describe, or remember in favor of what they can analyze and make generalizations about. This view of learning often underestimates and marginalizes learners who are below developmental standards or ideals.

The Limits of Hierarchical Thinking

Many approaches to language are based upon the Piagetian (1959) concept that learners progress from fairly concrete and egocentric to more abstract decentered kinds of thinking and behavior. According to this model, learners move from the world of concrete experience to the world of symbols. In the classroom, opportunities for learners to comment and build upon what they can see, feel, hear, and directly experience are gradually replaced by the study of symbols, abstractions, words, and numbers.

Yet, Howard Gardner argues that if we are to describe the intricate process of human development, "it is necessary to include a far wider and more universal set of competencies than has ordinarily been considered" (1985, p. x). While acknowledging our indebtedness to Piaget, Gardner criticizes a "monolithic emphasis upon a certain form of thinking" that ignores the other kinds of competencies that can be developed; for example, "those of an artist, a lawyer, an athlete, or a political leader" (1985, p. 20). Unfortunately, schools reinforce this rather monolithic view of development. From the time most children enter school, the goal is to lead them gradually away from concrete, sensory, intuitive kinds of thinking toward more abstract thought, with very little consideration of the broad spectrum of competencies that need to be nurtured at every level of development.

Because they are thought to be intellectually impoverished, children in the primary grades are often allowed to engage in story writing, self-expressive talk, reading, and listening for pleasure. In a worst-case scenario, they learn isolated skills out of workbooks, but only rarely are they asked to analyze, speculate, or think critically during these formative years. At the same time, older children are weaned away from more concrete, expressive tasks because these are thought to interfere with the development of analytical thought. As a result, in many schools, research writing doesn't appear in the curriculum until the upper grades while the personal narrative begins to disappear after grade four. It should not be surprising, then, that a great many students have trouble thinking in more abstract ways when they reach the upper grades and are suddenly thrust into the unfamiliar process of creating the persuasive essay or speech, the research paper, the literary or scientific analysis.

Young children are actually far more competent than we had previously believed (Donaldson, 1978). As Gardner notes, many of the details of Piaget's model are "simply incorrect," neglecting the fact that "children can conserve number, classify consistently, and abandon egocentrism as early as the age of three — findings in no way predicted (or even allowed) by Piaget's theory" (1985, pp. 20-21).

James Moffett, who based much of his early work on the theories of Piaget, argues that "a lot of evidence implies that even very small children make rather high-level inferences, although it is doubtful that they "think out" such inferences as adults might" (1968, p. 23). Moffett believes that "The goal [of curriculum] is not so much to attain the higher levels as it is to practice abstracting all along the way. No greater value is ascribed to one level than to another. Both concreteness and abstraction are dangerous and valuable" (1968, p. 25)

Unfortunately, many developmental stage models have been used to paint a deficit view of learners at the lower levels of the spectrum. Tom Newkirk criticizes this "deficit-hunting" (1985, p. 594) and challenges the current notion "that one must pass through the lower levels in the act of producing higher level discourse — like having to pass through Atlanta, Georgia to get to Daytona Beach" (1985, p. 595).

Although children do demonstrate some rough developmental sequences, particularly in the early years, there is much variability in the ways that learners move through these global sequences. It is a mistake to believe that we must follow rigid sequences in our teaching. Newkirk calls for models of development more sensitive to the complexity and diversity of children's language and to the multiplicity of ways in which that language is learned:

> The beginning of writing development cannot be limited to a single source or matrix. Expository writing cannot be viewed as developing *out of* narrative writing for the simple reason that beginning writers attempt exposition as well. A more adequate model will show the ways in which development occurs in a variety of discourse forms (1985, p. 602)

But what has been the effect of hierarchical thinking on schools?

Stage Models and Curriculum

Unfortunately, hierarchical thinking often shows up in published curricula and textbooks in the form of rigid, lockstep procedures and tasks, beginning with concrete description and leading eventually to more abstract analysis. For example, the composition and language arts curriculum in the state where I live begins by acknowledging the complexities of children's language development and recognizing that "cognitive growth occurs over time, at often disparate rates, in some areas while other areas regress or stabilize, and is greatly affected by changing needs and interests of individuals" (New York State Education Department, 1985, p. 8).

However, despite the earlier cautions against rigid views of development, the later sections of this curriculum document reveal the predictable shift in emphasis from narration and expression in the early grades to persuasion and description in the latter grades. The goals for students K-3 include only the following: "to express self," "to narrate," "to explain." It is not until grades four to nine that "to describe" and "to persuade" appear in the curriculum. By the time students reach levels ten through twelve, emphases on expression and narration begin to wane, in favor of tasks that involve explanation, description, and persuasion.

This curriculum plan seems to rest on two faulty assumptions. One is that students' purposes for using language are somehow embodied in distinct forms (narrative, exposition, persuasion). In fact, this is seldom the case. Narratives often contain the seeds of argumentative language, expository and persuasive essays often contain narrative, and all kinds of language forms are often dependent upon rich description for their effectiveness. Centering a curriculum around form alone fails to address issues of student growth.

The other false assumption involves the curriculum sequence. It is regrettable that students in the primary grades are not asked to engage in descriptive or persuasive tasks which might prepare them for the more formal tasks they will encounter in the later grades. By the same token, it is regrettable that students in the upper grades are rarely asked to tell stories or to play with language in tentative, exploratory ways as a way of informing their more formal language tasks.

Unfortunately, this more expanded, inclusive view of development that Gardner, Newkirk, and others talk about is not easily translated into simple, teacher-proof guides for practice. Leading students in a neat sequence from literal to abstract may seem like a good idea — indeed, its very teachability makes it attractive to textbook writers and curriculum planners. Unfortunately, these tidy sequences do not capture the ways that learners actually learn and use language. We need models that recognize and embrace the messiness of learning and growth — models that nurture all learners, not just those at the higher levels of a neat developmental spectrum.

Learning Stances

I am going to draw some distinctions between **learning stances** and **thinking levels**, since talk about levels of thought is often imbued with notions that higher is better. As I am defining it, a **learning stance** suggests an attitude or position toward an event rather than a more or less advanced or "valid" **level** of thinking. The notion of learning stances is a way of avoiding the kind of rigid hierarchical thinking that often shows up in textbooks and curriculum guides.

yet to understand allows us to bring familiar ideas to unfamiliar tasks, making them more manageable. Connecting abstract concepts with our own personal experiences makes our learning more invested and more personally compelling. Connections with the ideas of other people in and outside of our classroom enrich our understanding of complex ideas.

Extending

We take an extending stance whenever we move beyond an event in order to hypothesize, speculate, elaborate, and expand upon it. In doing so, we bring our learning beyond what is at hand into the realm of the possible and plausible. Although extending is often thought of as a higher level skill, we often shuttle between replicating an experience and extending beyond it. Generalizations and abstractions that are never placed in a real world context can be as superficial as literal replications that are never pushed beyond the realm of concrete experience.

Learners move swiftly and almost imperceptibly in and out of these three basic stances. Let's say, for instance, that our overall stance is one of replicating. We are in the process of writing in our journals about an argument we had with someone, for the eventual purposes of understanding what happened. Within this replicating stance, we might shuttle back and forth between various kinds of thoughts and experiences, reflecting on how we were treated and speculating about what will happen in our next encounter with that person. However, in terms of our underlying intentions, for the moment, our basic stance is one of reproducing or **replicating** an event.

These learning stances are not mutually exclusive. Eventually, we may move from this **replicating** stance to a combination of **connecting and extending** as we switch to writing an unsent letter to our friend for the purpose of further clarifying our feelings about the incident. Each learning experience demands a constant shifting of stances — connecting, extending, replicating — in no particular order. Now let's consider how to recognize the kinds of learning stances our students may be adopting.

Classroom Closeup: Reading the Response

As a way of illustrating how to "read" students' language for evidence of their learning stances, I'd like to take you into a middle school classroom. Marcus, Angie, and Jennifer are students in a seventh grade English class who have been writing about their personal reading in response logs. Meg, their teacher, routinely calls her students up to her desk on conference days to chat with them about their independent reading. She also uses their journals as a tool for evaluating the kinds of learning stances they are adopting.

In these excerpts, notice how Marcus and Angie begin with an initial replicating stance but eventually move back and forth through a variety of other learning stances.

Marcus has just read a few chapters of *Fade* by Robert Cormier:

This book is about a boy that can disepear. It runs in his family, because there is a picture where his uncle disappeared right before the picture. I don't think in real life something like this could happen. Sure, I believe in ghosts and aliens, but a person disappearing? No, I don't think so. I have only read a few chapters so far. From what I read, I think he can only dissapear in danger. This is because when he was about to be killed, he disappeared but didn't know it. So far, he hasn't learned that he could disappear. Do you believe in aliens? I think there has to be, because there are so many other galaxies and planets. I don't think earth would be the only place with life.
—Marcus

Marcus begins by recapping the basic plot of Cormier's novel to set the stage briefly for his later comments to Sandy, his response partner, who has not read the book. He moves quickly from this replicating stance to an extending stance, sharing his hunches about space aliens and speculating about life on other planets.

Now consider Angie's response to *Fall into Darkness* by Christopher Pike:

I haven't read very much of the book but what I have read is semi-confusing. It starts out sort of abrupt by saying that Sharon McKay was accused of murdering her best friend, Ann Rice (This is in the prologue). The catch is that Sharon is innocent but no one believes her and there was no body found. Right now Sharon is on trial and she's so scared. In fact, I'm scared also. I guess this is a good way to start a story because it gets people interested. At least, I'm interested. I got to put myself in Sharon's place, & I think that's one of the best advantages in reading. If I were in Sharon's shoes, I would be having a breakdown and be very scared as well as sad, lonely, and defenseless. What I like about Christopher Pike is that he gives the story from all the different characters' point of view so it's more of a mystery than it is.

—Angie

Like Marcus, Angie begins from a replicating stance, but she quickly moves into an extending stance, describing the author's "semi-confusing" techniques, which she seems to understand a little better through recapping the story. She then switches from this extending stance to a connecting stance as she discusses the story's effect on her ("In fact, I'm scared also."). Her final comment about Christopher Pike's technique of presenting the story from multiple points of view indicates that she is putting herself in the shoes of the author for a moment ("...he gives the story from all the different characters' point of view so it's more of a mystery than it is."). Thus, Angie moves back and forth from an initial replicating stance to a process of making personal connections with the story's protagonist and with the author.

Unlike Marcus and Angie, **Jennifer** seems to stay within a replicating stance in her response to Robert Newton Peck's *A Day No Pigs Would Die*:

The story I read was about a boy who had a father that slottered pigs for a living. And one day the boy got a pig as a presant from one of the neighbors and he named it pinky, well, it got older and one day the boy went to a fair with a neighbor to show Pinky and the oxen for prizes. Well the oxen and Pinky won. Later on in the book the family was running out of food so they had to slotter Pinky. Then early in may his father died in the barn. They had a funeral and the book ended.

—Jennifer

From her rather replicative comments, we might get the impression that Jennifer views this writing task as a sort of book report, in which she must convince her reader (or teacher) that she has actually done her reading. Unlike Marcus or Angie, Jennifer seldom ventures into the realm of connecting or extending.

It is important, though, not to invalidate Jennifer's response just because she stays within a replicating stance. For some reason, in this early phase of her response, Jennifer feels more comfortable with replication than with any of the other learning stances. She may be simply coming to terms with what she is reading by casting it in her own words. Perhaps also, considering the way in which journals often masquerade as book reports in some teachers' classrooms, staying within a replicating stance may be a sign of social competence rather than a deficit.

As teachers, our task is to begin with Jennifer's preferred stance and build upon it, not to lead her immediately out of it into the realm of connecting and extending. Eventually, Meg will invite Jennifer into other learning stances, but first she understands the need to build a safe environment where risks are encouraged. Meg's students assume a replicating stance often in their journals. They share the plot of what they read because their response partners and their teacher might not have read the same thing. Or, they read books and stories aloud as a way of simply enjoying and savoring the experience of reading together. Meg realizes that through replicating the events of the text, they are able to capture their initial tentative responses and, in some cases, eventually extend their understandings. In her words:

> *Even if this "book report thing" is all a kid ever does, you can use it to set up patterns later on. The tricky part is seeing not so much the isolated event — what they're writing down in the journal at that moment — but making connections with it later and beginning to use their replications to see patterns. You can say "this type of plot line seems to be running through the books that you like. You seem to prefer books that have this kind of plot line." What gets written down in journals is a raw material that you can use for all kinds of purposes later on.*

Far from being a "lower level" skill, replicative language allows learners to make connections with others, to remember and reproduce information, to savor a moment, or to understand more clearly the events of their lives. In capturing the exact dimensions of something, learners can come to understand, to appreciate, and to see it in greater detail and complexity. Often, our surface replications are just the tip of a much bigger and more abstract thinking process. One of our fundamental tasks as teachers is to support and nurture our students as they try out a variety of learning stances.

Just as it's important to provide opportunities for replication, it is equally important to point out potential areas where students might make connections between texts and between their ideas and those of others in the classroom. Finally, it's important to create a climate where risk-taking and speculation is valued — a place where students can extend beyond the information given and create their own understandings.

Reflections: An Apple For the Teacher

As a way of understanding the concept of learning stances more fully, I'd like to invite you to participate in a little experiment. This is an idea that you might use with your own students, especially if you're trying to teach them about the power of observation in a class like creative writing, science, or art. If you decide to participate in this activity, you will notice that you will move at various points from among replicating, connecting, and extending stances.

Usually it's fun to do this experiment in task groups of four or five, but you can do it by yourself if you like. First, you'll need some simple objects: a notebook, a pencil, an apple, a ruler, and a knife. If you are working with a group, each of you will need your own pencil and notebook, but you can share the apple, ruler, and knife. You will also want to pull your chairs in a circle around a table so that everyone can work together.

Replicating. *For this first phase, concentrate on describing the outer appearance of your apple, focusing only on what can be observed. No matter how tempted you might be to jump to more abstract thinking, try to be naive about what you are seeing; accept nothing at face value. Avoid generalizations like "fruit" or "Golden Delicious." Instead, try to stick to concrete descriptions. For instance, if you notice that your apple is speckled, you might try to discover whether the speckles are evenly or unevenly distributed, where they are closer together and where they are farther apart.*

You will be recording your observations in a double-entry journal. Each person should draw a vertical line down the center of a sheet of notebook paper. On the left hand side, write the word "observations." The right-hand column will be labeled "hunches, hypotheses, and questions." For the first part of the experiment, you will stick to a strict replicating stance, noting only those features that are directly observable in the left-hand column. The object is to note as many observable details as possible so you can make comparisons with other group members or generate hunches and hypotheses later on. You may decide to work independently for a few minutes before sharing responses or work collaboratively from the start.

> *After you have worked for several minutes, it's time to cut the apple open. As you work, you might want to develop some kind of plan. You might begin by cutting one part of the apple horizontally. After you've noted your observations about this cross section, you might want to cut the remaining part vertically, describing various features as you go. Be creative, and don't feel restricted to words. You might want to draw some simple diagrams if they are helpful to you in describing your findings.*
>
> ***Connecting and Extending.*** *After you feel that you have exhausted your list of observations, take several minutes to list hunches, hypotheses, questions, or speculations on the right side of the journal, alongside particular observations that suggested them. At this point, you will move out of the replicating stance and into connecting and extending stances.*
>
> *After you feel that you've gone through most of the possibilities, you might want to share your questions and hunches with others in the larger group. If you are working in a classroom or workshop setting, someone might want to keep a master list on the board or a flip chart. For every observation suggested by a group, you can see if other groups (with different apples) observed the same thing. This process might give you an idea of which findings are generalizable rather than random or idiosyncratic.*

Here's an example of one person's thinking process. Heidi is a high school reading teacher who also works as a curriculum supervisor for her district. Her double-entry journal is shown in figure 3.1. As soon as she and her group generated an exhaustive list of descriptive features in the left-hand column of the journal, they set to work generating a list of hunches, questions, and hypotheses from their initial observations.

Heidi — Double-entry Journal

Observations

- Stem
- not round
- 5 bumps on bottom
- speckled with white
- Red
- Light red streak
- Brown & light green fuzzy stuff where the blossom was on the bottom

- Fruity smell
- Small dents and bruises
- stem is thicker at both ends, thinner in the middle
- Darker red at top
- 2 1/4" at top, 1 3/4" at bottom
- 2 3/4" high on one side, 3 1/4" on another
- Height varies
- Stem is approximately 3/4 in. long
- Rounded at top
- Bigger at top than bottom
- Tapered
- Smooth
- Elliptical
- Brown Stem
- Silent
- Bumpy
- Convex/Concave
- Blemished
- Hard/soft
- Waxy surface
- Opaque
- Stands up on either end
- Fits in hand
- color is uneven
- speckles closer

hypotheses, hunches, questions

- What's the life cycle?
- How does the shape change as it grows? Does it grow down — gravity pull
- Is Red Delicious a cross or pure breed? What crosses are made from it (Mackintosh? Empire?)
- Research Question: What is this * called and what is its purpose?

- Are they sprayed? Alar? Are they dyed? Waxed?

- How do you identify a Red Delicious apple?
- Is the sunniest area darker?
- Is it like when you blow up a balloon? Does it start w/ all its speckles and grow into it?

Figure 3.1

In discussing which items to include, Heidi and her group explored many hunches. For instance, they noticed that the apple was not round and that the end opposite the stem was noticeably smaller in circumference. This generated a discussion of whether the apple grew downward (pulled by gravity) or whether the stem end was bigger due to the greater availability of nutrients in the stem end. As the group noticed that the color was uneven and the speckles were unevenly distributed, they speculated about whether the sunniest area was darker or whether the speckles grew apart as the fruit expanded with age. After their discussion, they generated the following list of researchable topics for future projects (see figure 3.2).

Hunches, Hypotheses, Researchable Ideas

- What is the star shape called?
- Is the top darker because the sun hits it more?
- Are there seeds inside? Do they correspond to the 5 bumps on the bottom?
- Does every apple have the same number of seeds?
- Are these apples dyed or waxed?
- Is the star shape on the bottom of every apple?
- Is one end always larger than the other (at every phase of the life cycle)?
- Do the seeds begin to form on the top or the bottom?
- Does seed formation relate to (symmetry) # of dots and points
- What makes apples juicy or dry?
- Are apples from the top of the tree better than from the bottom?
- What determines the weight of the apple?
- How do apples "know" when to fall off the tree?
- Why do apples turn brown when cut open?
- What are the speckles on the skin of the apple? Do all varieties of apples have them?
- What is the life cycle of an apple?
- Why is an apple called a "fruit" and not a vegetable?
- Are the dots the filaments that carry nourishment to the seeds?

Figure 3.2

At the end of the whole process, Heidi took a few minutes to write about what she'd learned. She speculated about how "modern" growing techniques, and a "mass production" mentality may have altered this simple fruit:

Apple Writing
I wonder how this apple is different from/similar to the fruit they called an apple a thousand years ago. This smooth, nearly unblem-

ished beauty, larger than my fist with its sweet dense fruit. Has years of breeding made the color darker, the size larger, the shape more uniform (did any apple always have those five bumps and gently tapered shape?) And what has been lost? Did the crisp snap of a first bite get lost in an attempt to improve its good looks and sweet taste? Is it my imagination or are Red Delicious apples getting more and more rectangular — the easier to pack? Is the fact that there's no worms or insect holes to cut out worth the toxic sprays I have to eat with my apple? There's a message here about "new and improved" — about what we value and what we leave behind. About choosing appearances over insides.

In this phase of her learning process, Heidi used many of the details she gathered earlier in her observations: the apple's tapered shape, the five bumps, its size and color. Eventually, she went beyond these initial descriptions to speculate about the social consequences of modern production techniques. Thus, from her initial replications, Heidi and her colleagues were able to come to a new and more personally meaningful understanding of this rather ordinary object.

In the next section, you will see how one science teacher invites learners in her classroom to adopt a variety of learning stances in understanding more about the world in which they live.

Classroom Closeup: Genetics and the Environment

In her experience as a sixth grade science teacher, Susan has become convinced that a subject like science can be enhanced by language activities that go beyond the traditional written examination and memorization of textbook material. Her philosophy of language is consistent with her philosophy of scientific inquiry. She reflects:

There is a constant modification of preexisting theories in sciences, so students' writing needs to be in constant revision as they evaluate their own thoughts. This kind of constant reevaluation of ideas often leads to what I call the "aha" of science, that unique insight into the very nature of the scientific how and why.

In her teaching, Susan often begins by asking students to go back and read the works of famous scientists. Beginning from this rather replicative stance, they begin to connect with and extend beyond the ideas they are reading about. In teaching a unit on genetics, for instance, Susan encourages her students to arrive at their own "aha" experiences by connecting the ideas of famous scientists with their own lives:

> Reading the ideas of scientists such as Albert Einstein, James Watson, Francis Crick, and Rachel Carson allows students the insight that these people have made via writing.... [S]tudents can see that a great deal of scientific inquiry happens by chance thoughts that these larger-than-life figures have and by the tentative uncertainty of their discoveries. In reading Watson's "Finding the Secret Life" from The Double Helix, students will get a sense of the non-rational intuitive nature of scientific explorations. Such phrases as "tried to puzzle the mystery," "the answer suddenly hit me" leap off the pages to show that writing allows the writer to make the transition from the observed to the unknown on paper as well as in the laboratory.

Personal Connections: The Double-entry Journal

After students have read about the scientific discoveries of the past, Susan asks them to make some personal connections. In double-entry journals, her students begin by listing some of their own physical characteristics. Alongside each trait, they make a note of wherever they observed the same or similar traits in their parents. As Susan and her students share these initial lists, they discuss how similarities in physical characteristics occur within families and begin to arrive at some basic principles of genetics.

Connecting and Extending: Parallel Reading and Writing

Next, Susan's students play a game she calls "Gene Detectives." She hands out a chart of the pea plant traits that Gregor Mendel used in his genetic experiments. Students are then asked to speculate on a series of questions in their journals. For instance, she asks:

> When two tall pea plants are crossed (one fertilizes the other) their offspring includes both tall and short offspring. When some of the short offspring are then crossed, only short offspring result. How can this be?

Here, there are certain genetic principles that Susan wants students to understand. To encourage exploratory thinking, she stresses the fact that several responses to the same question might be equally valid. Soon her students begin to move from a replicating stance into making personal connections and extending beyond the basic ideas they have been given.

Each day, as the students respond to her questions and record their hunches in journals, Susan asks them to read excerpts of Gregor Mendel's own writing. This kind of parallel reading allows them to develop a deeper understanding about how scientists must often pursue their insights and hunches without knowing what the end result will be. The process of connecting their own discoveries with those of Mendel makes their learning more permanent and personally invested.

In the very earliest phases of the unit, Susan keeps a pretty close hold on the general topic of students' writing and discussion while encouraging them to explore their own unique connections. As a way of encouraging exploration, speculation, and a variety of responses, Susan provides opportunities for students to record and grapple with their ideas in very tentative ways, through such techniques as concept mapping and clustering. Their thinking during this exploratory phase moves in and out of all three learning stances.

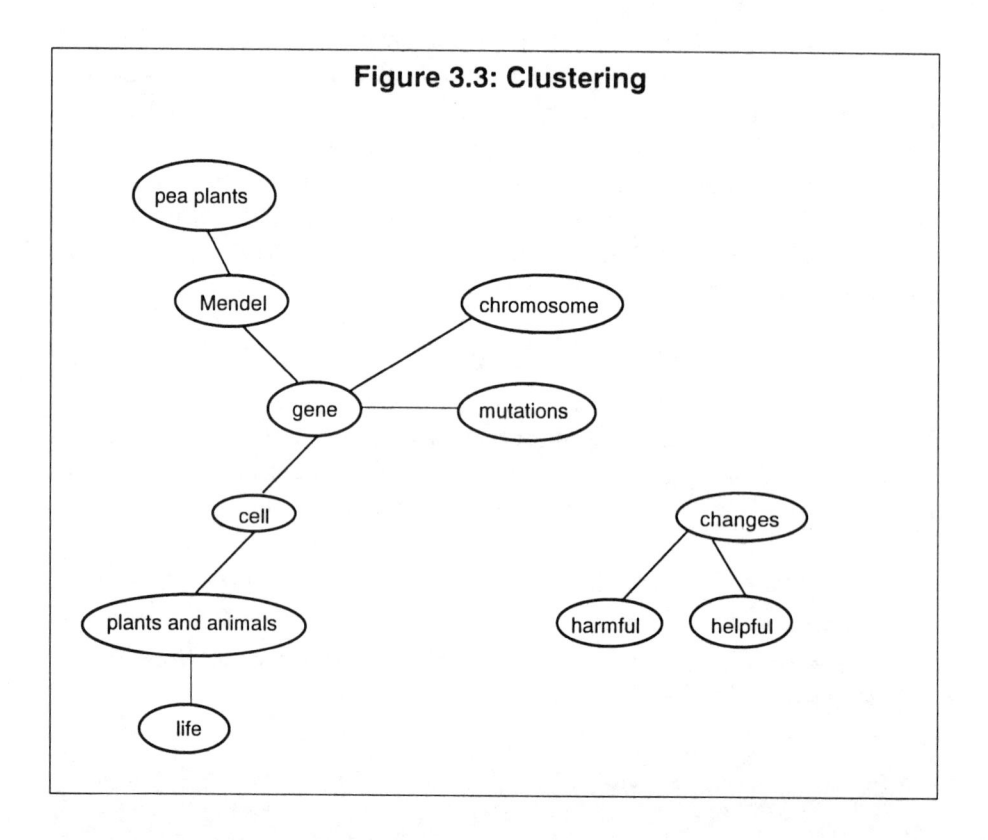

Figure 3.3: Clustering

In responding to the discussion of Mendel's work, one student produces the following cluster in his journal (see figure 3.3)

Clustering ideas like this is a way of helping students to replicate their first tentative thoughts and associations before asking them to go public. This replicating process is important since students are often too quick to give up on their own ideas in the midst of a class discussion. Once students have been allowed to capture their first ideas, they are then free to compare ideas from their concept maps and clusters with each other.

In Susan's view, the tentative process of clustering and concept mapping helps students to draw connections between abstract ideas and their own real world. In her words, such a thinking process "addresses the students' age-old question: 'When will I ever be able to use this stuff.'"

Extending the Issues: Future Implications

Eventually, as Susan's students come to understand the nature of genes, she leads them to consider the technological and ethical implications of genetic research and genetic engineering. In the early phases of the unit students seem to believe, rather unreflectively, that it would be wonderful to create organisms of super-human size and strength. They ignore the potential negative repercussions of genetic engineering. As a way of shaking up some of their misconceptions, Susan uses science fiction stories and movies. In her words:

> *Frankenstein started as a wonderful application of robotics that turned into a horror in "reality." Genetically engineering cells to enhance characteristics also sounds attractive as a possible way of creating "super" organisms, large fruit, more resistant plants, or more productive organisms. But a scientifically literate society needs to appreciate other potentially harmful side effects, resistant disease-causing organisms, effects these genetic mutants might have on other organisms, and other unforeseen circumstances.*

To help her students to better understand the delicate relationship among all organisms, Susan brings in a science fiction movie in which a colony of ants have been genetically engineered to tower in size over humans. After students have some time to enjoy the movie, Susan gradually leads them toward a discussion of what she calls the "web of life," or the "delicate interaction between organisms." "Historically," Susan argues, science has provided us with tools such as pesticides that are worshipped as miracle cures for what ails. DDT is a prime example of a substance that was used before the potential effects were carefully studied and the consequences considered.

For example, after explaining something about the gene for height, Susan asks her students to work in groups, brainstorming and later freewriting individually about the potential consequences of the initial changes in the gene. Here the students use each other as "sounding boards," coming up with a number of "good and bad case scenarios."

Extending the Form: Fiction Writing

Interestingly, Susan points out that sometimes the students who seem to have the least amount of scientific aptitude come up with the most creative ideas when allowed some choice about how to cast them into writing or speech. At one point she offers the option for her students to write science fiction stories about the potential hazards of genetic engineering. One student in particular surprised her:

> Buddy is a severely physically handicapped child that has been conditioned to try to finish all assignments as soon as humanly possible. I often am frustrated in my attempts to elicit any extra iota of effort from him. I imagine that if he could swat me away like a fly he would. After giving students independent writing time, I asked if anyone would like to share their ideas. Buddy's hand went right up, a miracle in itself. I maintained my composure, though, and asked him if he'd like to share his "story" with us. He read us a story that immediately conjured up in my mind George Orwell's Animal Farm (I later shared this notion with Buddy). He talked about thoughts animals would have if they were given the capability to communicate with people. At first, they said nice things (we provided them with homes and food) but later in his story he changed his mind. The animals became indignant about how badly humans treat them, hunting them and changing their land. This idea generated in my class a debate over the morality of man's manipulation of the natural world. It also provided a starting point for other students' writing.

Students like Buddy constantly remind us that nearly all learners can go beyond the information at hand if given the proper forum for expressing their ideas.

Extending Beyond the Classroom: Culminating Project

At some point, the topic switches to issues of environmental advertising. Susan brings in a copy of a brochure from MacDonald's restaurant, describing the company's environmental policies. After discussing the information in the brochure and weighing the pros and cons, Susan's students proceed to collect their own examples of ecological advertising from magazines and newspapers. In addition to looking critically at these advertisements, Susan and her students discuss which magazines and newspapers carry the majority of the environmental advertisements and what their motivation might be for doing so.

With this fairly structured series of activities behind them, Susan's students are now ready to work in groups, creating their own culminating projects. At this point, Susan feels fairly free to open up the choice of topic and form altogether. Some students elect to write their own science fiction stories while others write scripts to be audiotaped as radio plays or videotaped as movies.

Thus, Susan begins by asking her students to read and understand the written words of famous scientists as a way of modeling for them a new way to explore and create tentative ideas of their own. This process enables them to draw new connections and extend beyond the basic information in their textbooks in ways that simply presenting facts does not. In our current science teaching, Susan reflects:

> *The classroom becomes an arena for only presenting facts; we assume that students will make the connections on their own. Perhaps we are turning people away from science because often in the classroom science becomes compartmentalized and oriented towards too few "right" answers. We tend to shun controversial ideas or questioning of what we believe to be accepted scientific concepts. Facts are presented in rapid-fire succession with little time spent digesting these facts.... We have not given students the incentives to make the connections between these facts and their lives. Unless we draw students into the scientific process, we will be living in a world destroyed by a population of people who never considered the end-result of the knowledge we have gained.*

As you can see, there is no set sequence that everyone must follow in learning about the world. Learners move constantly back and forth between replicating, connecting, and extending stances in coming to understand the events around them. Through this process, they enrich, extend, amplify, and come to terms with their experiences in new and exciting ways.

Classroom Connections

It may seem, at this point, that any interference in students' natural learning stances may short-circuit their understandings and dismantle their thinking processes. While there are, perhaps, more grains of truth in this notion than we'd like to believe, there are ways to think about learning stances without limiting or pigeonholing student learners. Here are a few.

Reading Student Responses.

Take a look at your students' writing folders, learning logs, class notebooks, papers. Listen to their talk in class discussions until you have a feel for what kinds of learning stances they adopt most often. Do certain students appear to prefer one stance over another? Do some seem unable to switch learning stances when particular situations demand that they do?

Once you have decided what particular students' favorite learning stances seem to be, back off for a minute and consider carefully whether it's really necessary to tinker with their natural learning processes. Consider the possible logic behind students' learning stances. Are they incapable of doing so, or simply unaware of the possibilities for shuttling back and forth from one stance to another? Have they been rewarded in other teachers' classrooms for rather limited kinds of learning and responding?

Students who appear to write summaries or book reports when they are asked to adopt an extending stance may do so out of habit rather than inadequacy. They may have spent many years in classrooms where teachers demand rote paraphrase of predigested information. They may be fearful of going out on a limb because they learned in other teachers' classrooms to stay very close to what's safe and familiar. They may not, in short, be aware that other options for learning exist. Other students may be stuck within an extending stance, hanging on to unreflective generalizations rather than switching into connecting and replicating stances necessary for challenging, questioning, and enriching their hypotheses.

Opening the Options.

Once you have explored some of these questions about your students' preferred learning stances, sit down with them and explain that there are many ways to learn and many choices about what learning stances to adopt at particular moments in the process. Demonstrate these possible learning stances in your comments and questions to them. Show them when they appear to switch from one learning stance to another in their written work. Go through their journals, logs, and other texts, bringing these connections and insights about their learning stances to the surface. Then ask them about why they responded as they did. You might be surprised at their responses.

Checking on Yourself.

Take out your daily planner or lesson book. Look at the sequence and form of your lessons. Ask yourself about your intentions in each phase of your lessons. Are you conscious of the learning stances you expect your students to adopt, or are these stances unimportant to you? When particular learning stances are important, or when there are options, do you make these expectations and options clear? Do you provide a classroom climate where replicating is as legitimate as connecting or extending?

Look at the overall balance of learning stances in each lesson or across several lessons or units. Do you appear to gravitate more toward one learning stance than others? How do your preferences play themselves out in the daily events of your classroom? For example, when ideas are remote from students' experience, they may need to be shown how to make personal connections and associations. When they seem to be lost in concrete details, they may need to be shown how to extend, speculate, and take intellectual risks.

When you're done looking at your intentions, look at examples of your students' language again. Do their learning stances match your intentions? Are there ways of making these intentions clearer? Do you sometimes set up a hidden curriculum where you appear to invite extending responses but ultimately reward replication of your thoughts and opinions? There are, as you see, no "dos" and "don'ts" in the learning stances that your classroom can nurture and support, except perhaps for this one: **Do** try to make your classroom a place where **all** learners are able to come to language and thinking in ways that are most appropriate for them.

Drawing Connections

Ken was an art major as an undergraduate. After pursuing a career as an artist, he began a brand new career as an English teacher. In his journal, he recalls a favorite teacher in art school who taught him how to shift among a variety of learning stances, challenging the obvious, uprooting the familiar, and drawing connections between the unknown and the understood:

John Berman taught us how to do the "Alley Cat" in class one day. He put on some jazz and began dancing around the room. He was a small, grey-bearded man with a pot belly and little wire-rimmed glasses. He smiled a lot and laughed at himself quite often. We laughed too. One time, he asked us to make white using only blue and yellow. He asked us to make happy lines, sad lines, sexy lines, fast lines, and slow lines. He asked us to make "rubbings" of everything from subway walls to tombstones. He asked us to copy masterpieces using only cut-out bits of paper from magazines. By this time we had stopped laughing. We were convinced he was nuts. John Berman taught light, color and design.... We never knew what he was talking about or teaching. Much of what he taught was in the realm of hard science; the "Doppler Effect" and such. As art students, many of these lectures were completely foreign to us. After spending the better part of two semesters with him we began to see the light. We couldn't describe exactly what we had learned but we felt the change and saw it in our work. Looking back, it seems like much of what he was doing was teaching us how to make connections with seemingly unrelated information. At least that's what I think; it's still not entirely clear. It does seem to me, though, that as I grow a little older and experience a few more things, that things that happened years ago come back to me in different ways when I struggle to understand things that happen now. I see it in my writing all the time. Perhaps at nineteen years old my memory bank didn't have enough stored in it to make connections. My mind simply reacted to what was put in front of it. Reflection doesn't seem to be a strong characteristic of most teenagers. At thirty-two, though, things come into my mind all the time that never had any significance before and seem very important now. I think John Berman would like that.

Ken is right. Often our most significant learnings come to us long after we have left the classroom. Connections, put into play many years earlier, suddenly surface, coalesce, and bloom into new learnings. Replications and recollections of former events connect with current experiences and gather new significance.

There is no predictable timetable for these flashes of insight and understanding. Because learning is often delayed and hard to measure by multiple choice tests, it becomes tempting to focus on what is teachable and testable, rather than what might someday result in significant learning. Sadly, it is often much easier for students to mimic a teacher's understandings than to create their own, especially when the payoff of risk-taking usually doesn't outweigh the penalty of straying from the safety of correct answers.

The notion of development as a long-term, often messy process is just as risky and frightening for us. If there are no right answers at the back of the book and no neat developmental sequences to follow, then how do we grade and respond to student learning, how do we plan our curriculum in responsible ways, what do we say to parents and administrators when they ask about our students' growth?

The answer is simple and, therefore, very complex. We begin with our students, learning from them about the learning stances they must adopt to create their own understandings. From this tenuous and inchoate beginning we discover, with them, the individual paths they must take in exploring the uncharted territory of these connections and explorations.

Explorations

1. **Journal Exploration:** Read the text of Ken's journal entry. In your learning log or on a separate piece of paper note wherever Ken seems to shift from among the stances of replicating, connecting, and extending in his writing. If possible, compare your hunches and guesses with a partner or a small group of people. Take this chance to explore points of agreement and points of controversy in how each of you seems to "read" the underlying stances that Ken has adopted in his piece. The point here is not to decide who is "right" but to begin to come to some agreements about how evidence of particular learning stances might be visible in your students' writing.

2. **Stance Switching:** As a way of discovering your own learning processes, you might want to find something you have written recently and decide whether you have written it from a replicating, connecting, or extending stance, or some combination of these. Now, "re-vise" (as in "re-see") the piece by rewriting it from a different stance. For instance, if you wrote a reminiscence, you might want to transform it into a fantasy piece, an essay about a related topic, or a fictional account of the same event. When you are done, write a short account in which you describe how writing the piece from a different learning stance changed your thinking about the topic or event.

3. **Educational Artifact:** If you have taught or are teaching, find one of your lesson plan books and treat it as an artifact that someone might have unearthed in an archeological find. From this rather distanced perspective, look at one lesson or a series of lessons. For each lesson or phase of the lesson ask yourself, "What learning stance/s did I expect my students to adopt?" Take some notes on your findings. As soon as your have completed your writing, go back and see if you appeared to favor one learning stance (replicating, connecting) over the others, and why. Then ask yourself how your students might have viewed the learning experiences you provided. Did you get the sense that they might have adopted learning stances that were different from those you intended? After you have pondered these questions, write about what you found in any way that feels comfortable.
4. **Create Your Own Exploration**

References

Donaldson, M. (1978). *Children's minds*. London: Fontana.

Gardner, H. (1985). *Frames of mind: The theory of multiple intelligences*. New York: Basic Books.

Moffett, J. (1968). *Teaching the universe of discourse*. Boston: Houghton Mifflin.

Newkirk, T. (1985). The hedgehog or the fox: The dilemma of writing development. *Language Arts, (62),* 593-603.

New York State Education Department. (1985). *Composition in the English language arts curriculum K-12*. Albany, New York: New York State Education Department.

Piaget, J. (1959). *Language and thought of the child*. Trans. M. Gabain. London: Routledge and Kegan Paul.

CHAPTER 4

Outcomes of Language and Learning

Today I sat on my back deck in a lawn chair, "watching" the wind as it sent patches of sun and shade over the grass. And I realized something about learning — you never see it, really. You only see the effects of it; you notice it in the movements of your shifting beliefs. Learning lives somewhere in the negative spaces that surround your changing behaviors and actions; it's always elusive and "visible" only in its effects. Maybe that's why some kids leave my classroom showing no outward signs of growth. Then one day, maybe five years later, they come back and thank me for something I've taught them. It's so funny how those things happen. And the sad part is, that kind of learning never shows up on a test.

—Rachel

Rachel is a twelfth grade science teacher. Her observations remind us of the frustration and exhilaration we all feel as we search for visible signs of our students' growth. It seems that our students' learning always eludes us just as we try to measure or capture it. Their learning is shaped, defined, and directed by the many outcomes and audiences for which it might be intended. Even though those outcomes may not even be visible, they influence the learning process in significant ways.

Outcome: Language Directed to Whom?

It's remarkable just how much classroom language is directed to no one in particular and received only by a teacher. How sad this fact becomes as we consider that kids of all ages are natural sharers and performers. Donald Graves proclaims:

Children want to write. They want to write the first day they attend school. This is no accident. Before they went to school they marked up walls, pavements, newspapers with crayons, chalk, pens or pencils ... anything that makes a mark. The child's marks say "I am." (1983, p. 3)

Just as they want to write, they want to talk and be heard, to read and share their reading with others. And yet how much writing, reading, listening, and talking do kids do to prove to someone in authority that they have done their homework? How much of their language is for unreal or imagined audiences who never respond? On the other hand, just as they are often limited in terms of the audiences they address, they also have limited opportunities for privacy in the typical classroom. How often are they allowed to engage in language experiences that are for themselves alone — private, personally meaningful, and unaccounted for?

Part of the problem has to do with the unique constraints of this place called school. It's hard to bring the world into the classroom — to find real audiences for students' writing and talk beyond the teacher. School is an incredibly public affair. It's difficult to give students the chance to use language privately and without the threat of evaluation. There is so little time. It may seem a waste to do anything that doesn't ultimately count toward a grade.

I use the word "outcome" rather than the more familiar word "audience" because, unlike writing and talking, reading and listening aren't directed toward audiences. However, they are directed toward certain outcomes. As you will see in the next few pages, these outcomes shape our students' language as well as their thinking.

Outcomes for Reading and Writing

One day I was talking with some eighth grade students in a middle school English classroom about their reading. I was amused and a little distressed by Tomell's comments. Although most of us probably think of literature as something to be savored and enjoyed, Tomell had obviously learned somewhere along the line that literature is something to be quickly gleaned for its main points. He seemed to bring the same strategies to bear on his reading of literature that he used in reading textbooks. He remarked rather casually:

[M]y mom like taught me how to speed read so I can really read quickly. I can get the whole book, and it's great to be able to do that, to read a book like that when you've got to write a book report and, my dad reads too a lot, 'cuz he's an economist and so he has to read a lot of journals and stuff, so he can really read fast too.... [I]f you

speed read, you pick up the main topic of each paragraph and sometimes, that's the only important point in the whole paragraph. [Authors] draw everything out — they say the most important thing and then they describe it, and some of the describing parts are real boring.

To those of us who read and teach literature for its aesthetic possibilities, Tomell's view of reading may come as a shock and a disappointment. Somewhere along the line, he learned to approach literary reading in the same way as informational reading — as a technical skill to be mastered, not a uniquely individual, private, aesthetic experience.

Clearly, as Louise Rosenblatt (1978, 1985) has pointed out, different kinds of reading are appropriate for different kinds of texts. Literature lends itself to aesthetic reading, while textbooks, reports, and other informational documents usually lend themselves to reading for information. Unfortunately, perhaps because it's easier to test comprehension than aesthetic involvement, most classroom reading seems to be for the purpose of memorizing and carrying away knowledge rather than for the purpose of becoming personally involved in the reading experience. As a result, in school, outcomes for reading are often collapsed into one kind: reading for evaluation or examination. Study guides and introductory pre-reading experiences, however well intentioned, often set up messages that the reading of literature should be no different than the reading of textbooks.

Just as literary texts are often read in informational ways, textbooks are often treated as repositories of undisputed knowledge rather than invitations to consider and challenge an author's ideas. They are often skimmed and studied in classrooms for the information they "contain." On the contrary, learners should be constantly urged to create new meanings from books by working collaboratively (in small groups and pairs) or by working alone (in journals, logs, and other kinds of private language experiences).

Of course, writing has a broad spectrum of outcomes, too. In the real world, we direct our written language to people we hardly know (in business, political offices), to people we know well (friends, relatives, significant others), and to ourselves (in journals, diaries, shopping lists or notes scribbled in the privacy of our home or office). Most of us have been told by teachers to "consider our audience" when we write. In this sense, the writing classroom is one place where outcome or audience is conspicuously considered.

All of this talk about "audience awareness" can be pretty confusing though. Remember the first time you were asked to consider your audience when you wrote? You might remember feeling somewhat at a loss. There were few audiences for your writing beyond the teacher. Even when you were asked to write for more distant audiences, you probably knew that your teacher would still be the final reader, the arbiter of correctness, good taste, and style.

The blame doesn't lie solely with teachers. It's so hard in classrooms to set up situations where students use language for real world outcomes. We may ask our students to direct their language to others beyond ourselves, but more often than not, time and expediency force us to act as intermediate audiences, making guesses about how future employers, governmental officials, and other teachers will receive their words. This is unfortunate because when students actually do engage in authentic conversations with others, they begin to develop audience awareness in a personal and lasting way. As they see their words make, or fail to make, impressions on real listeners and readers, they learn valuable lessons about language and about learning. The difficult part is in creating a climate where those conversations among readers and writers can take place.

Outcomes for Listening and Talking

Consider the possible outcomes for listening. Often we simply immerse ourselves in a pleasurable listening experience, privately gathering images and ideas, judging, criticizing, or evaluating. But classrooms are usually more public than this. In schools, students usually listen for the purpose of taking in information from an authority. It's no secret that, on the whole, teachers do far more talking than students (Marshall, 1989). Much of our teacher talk is in the form of procedural directives, such as "turn to page 422," or questions we already know the answer to, such as "Does anybody know the capital of New York?" (Mehan, 1979).

We can be aware of how often we take center stage in classroom conversations, but awareness doesn't always solve the problem. I've known the truism about teachers talking more than students for quite some time now. Yet, try as I might, I still catch myself talking more than my students and leading them to my own preset conclusions. Most of the time, all I can do is to remove myself physically from the center of the arena, to set up a learning opportunity that forces students to listen and talk to each other, to explore their own questions as these arise.

Somewhat paradoxically, then, there are few opportunities for learners in schools to talk, listen, read, and write for self alone. On the other hand, there are also few opportunities for them to direct their language to audiences other than teacher. As the outcomes of their language change, students' learning also changes.

Reflections: Learning Outcomes

I'd like to ask you to think for a moment about the different outcomes toward which you direct your language in your everyday life. In chapter two, I asked you to make a list of the kinds of reading, writing, speaking and listening activities you engage in during the course of your life. Now, I'd like you to go over that list one more time. On a separate sheet of paper, or beside each item on your list, try to note all the different outcomes toward which each language activity might be directed.

For example, "notes" may be one item on your list. Think of the many possible outcomes toward which you direct the notes you write. These outcomes may include: "self" (reminder notes), "children" (directions and requests), "friends" (invitations) or "colleagues" (memos). When you're done, you might want to compare your list with this one, created by a group of teachers (see Figure 4.1):

LANGUAGE OUTCOMES

Language Activities	Outcomes
class papers and reports	professors
shopping lists	self, family
listening to music	self, family, friends
watching TV and movies	self, family, friends
reading textbooks	self, professor, other students
reading novels	self, professor, other students
friendly letters	friends, acquaintances, colleagues
applications	future employers
memos	colleagues, supervisors
poems	self, good friends
notes on meetings	self
oral presentations	friends, strangers
phone conversations	friends, family members, colleagues, employers, strangers
lesson plans	self, supervisor, professors
journal writing	self
letters of complaint	businesspeople, editor of newspaper, politicians

Figure 4.1

Notice that the language outcomes on this list seem to fall into three categories: Language for self, language for intimate other, and language for distant other. Here's a brief description of each.

- **Language for Self**. This is language that is totally private. Because no one will ever share our ideas, we can afford to play with intellectual possibilities without thinking about an observer or evaluator.
- **Language for Intimate Others**. This is language that is directed to people close to us. We read, write, speak, and listen for, and in the company of friends, trusted colleagues, relatives, spouses, and children, to name a few.
- **Language for Distant Others**. This is language that is directed toward those we may have never met. These people may be heroes, adversaries, elected officials, or nameless people in remote buildings.

Try to classify each item on your list into one of these three categories. Consider how that particular outcome influenced the kind of thinking you engaged in as you read, wrote, spoke, or listened. Experiment a bit. If writing business letters to strangers is on your list, consider how your writing and thinking might be different if you directed the same letter to someone you knew well or privately to yourself.

Finally, consider why some language acts are more invested than others. For instance, it might seem on the surface that writing or talking to an intimate other is easier than writing to a stranger, but this isn't always the case. In fact, it's sometimes easier to direct our language to strangers than it is to people who are important to us. If writing a letter of apology to a loved one is harder than requesting some information from an agency, consider why that is. What makes the two outcomes so essentially different? Write for a few minutes about what you learned.

Further Reflection: Shifting Outcomes

Now, let's move a bit beyond this simple exercise to experience firsthand how the outcomes of your language influence your thinking processes. This particular writing experience will take a bit of imagination on your part.

> *Writing for self.*
>
> Begin by sketching out some notes about a topic you might like to write about. This writing will be something you won't have to share with anyone, but I'd like you to choose a topic that isn't so personal that you might have difficulty sharing your ideas about it at some point. Because no one else will see what you wrote for this first bit of writing, you can feel free to write in any way that suits you. Take about ten minutes to explore freely on paper whatever you might like to write about.
>
> When you're done, take another few minutes to write a "process account," in which you describe what this writing experience was like for you. Did parts of the experience seem uncomfortable? Why? Were there some aspects of the writing that you enjoyed? Why? Where did you get stuck, and where did ideas seem to flow?
>
> *Writing for An Intimate Other.*
>
> As soon as you have finished this exploratory writing, I'd like you to keep the same topic, but this time try to direct your thoughts to someone you know very well. To make the situation more real, you might actually plan to send off what you wrote to this person. Write for about ten minutes before coming to a stopping place. If you aren't finished, you can write "to be continued" at bottom of your piece. When you're done, take a few more minutes and write a process account describing this particular writing experience.
>
> *Writing to A Distant Other.*
>
> Now, direct your writing to a more distant audience. You may have to vary the topic slightly to do this, but try to stick as closely to your original topic as you can. Possible audiences may include the editor of a newspaper, a professor, an author, someone in the business and professional world, or the readers of a popular magazine. When you've written for about ten minutes, write a process account of what it was like to write this piece.

In looking back over your writing, you probably discovered that the issue of language outcomes isn't very straightforward. Although writing to ourselves may seem very easy, there are times when it doesn't seem nearly as satisfying as directing our language to and getting response from others. It's usually easy write or talk to good friends because we can worry more about what we say than how we say it. But there are times when intimate audiences are more threatening than distant audiences, especially when we believe that there will be important consequences to what we write or say. Or what about those times when it's easier talk to some stranger on a bus or in an airport because, quite frankly, we aren't concerned about the consequences of communicating to someone we may never see again?

You might be surprised to find that the writing situation that was easiest for you might have been the hardest for someone else. Some people find it easiest to communicate and correspond with others; to them, writing for self seems pointless and dull. Other people are shy or reluctant to write to more distant audiences and would prefer to write privately.

Let's consider the case of three teachers. Heidi, Catherine, and Kathi had participated in a two week-workshop with me a couple of years ago. As part of the workshop experience, I asked them to respond in writing to some of the assigned readings. Although my ultimate goal was to get them to come up with meaningful ways to write on their own, I provided options, in case they got stuck. I hoped that this list of options would provide freedom for those who needed it yet model some possible ways of responding for those who felt uncomfortable writing on their own.

All three teachers had just read an article by Don Murray. Quite independently, they decided to respond to the same article in very different ways. I was intrigued by the breadth and scope of their responses. In excerpts of their written texts, and in the process accounts written shortly afterward, you will see that their choice of outcomes greatly influenced their thinking and writing processes.

Heidi: Language for Self

Heidi is a senior high school reading teacher. As a way of better understanding Don Murray's text, she decided to write a "think-aloud" response, stopping at several points in her reading and reflecting in a private, stream-of-consciousness way. More surprising to Heidi than to anyone else, her think-aloud went on for several pages. By the time she finished, she realized that she had "entered into" the text at thirty-one different points. Her first few responses center on her own classroom, as she compares Murray's ideas with what happens in her own classroom:

> 1. I picture the proverbial "gold engraved invitation" — lavish handed out to kids in my writing class....

> 5. Whew! A damning argument against "motivating." I've never much liked extrinsic motivators, but how to reach inside and "draw" the writing "out of the student"?

Partway through her response, her initial thoughts about teaching begin to shift as she wonders about her own daughter and begins to reminisce about her own childhood:

> 6. Fleeting thoughts — does Caitlin feel "an only child in the land of giants"?. Remembering my own childhood fantasies, multiple personalities. Did I ever write any of it? All I remember is poetry — especially one poem about being a middle child.

After a few moments of reminiscing, she moves back to the world of her classroom. Here she indicts Murray for failing to account for the difficulty of trying to provide students with choice within structure:

> 7. Frustration at this point — yes this all sounds well and good, sir, but how am I supposed to allow students to feel their need to write — by sharing writing and giving choices. Is it enough?

> 8. How to provide that quiet time even in my own class, much less my students lives — which often seem completely chaotic. They come tumbling into my class, trailing the chaos behind — the missed breakfast, the slap from a parent, the hall fight with a friend, the hot memory of motorcycles and hunting trips. How can I make them want the quiet time — so it is not imposed by me? ...

As we eavesdrop on Heidi's private conversation, we can guess many things about her thinking processes. There appears to be little self-consciousness about style or correctness in her writing. Sentences blend together; punctuation marks fall in random places. She vacillates between thinking about her daughter, Caitlin, and the students in her classroom. She admits and grapples with her confusion, occasional irritation, emerging insights. Later, in her process account, she extols the value of this self-directed language.

> I certainly wrote more than I ever write while reading — five pages front and back, with responses to thirty-one "think-aloud" points. It felt very different to me than my usual note-taking process in that it

skips the replicating part and goes directly to connecting and occasional extending. I often use the double-entry note system, replicating info. in one column after each chunk of pages and going back later to respond in the other column. In general it felt fine to skip the note taking replication here — no one will test me on it later....

The kind of thinking this process encouraged seemed to be more connecting than extending. I remembered similar things I'd read, seen, or done. I agreed or disagreed. By letting my thoughts run, rather than pushing or leading them, I think I allowed a broader range (more connections) of fairly superficial thoughts. I think this is good for looking at things in a new light, opening up possibilities...

As she wrote privately, Heidi began to look at things in a new light, to discover the possibilities for how Murray's ideas intersected with her experience as a writer, a parent, and a classroom teacher.

Catherine: Language for Intimate Others

Catherine, a twelfth grade English teacher, had met an old friend at a family reunion the weekend before reading the Murray article. She and her friend had spent several hours talking about the importance and enjoyment of writing in their lives. She decided to share Murray's ideas with Jim in a letter. Here is an excerpt of that letter:

Dear Jim,

I have no recollection how it came up but a stray comment you made last weekend has had considerable resonance for me. I know if I really mull it over I can mine this nugget.

It came up somehow when we were sitting on the back porch. Everyone else, gathered for this Brown family 1,000 Islands weekend, was scattered throughout the cottage. You were across the room from me in one of the renovated rockers when, from who knows where, you came out with: "I really like to write." (Wait, I think I may have, in my quasi-field gathering, asked if your job entailed much writing.) This surprised me. In high school, from what I've heard, you were a wild man. Subsequently you've gone into a recondite aspect of computer programming. I sort of suspected you wouldn't be much of [a] writer. But that perhaps, as the stats show of most jobs, you had to do your share. Now, though, to hear that you like it! You explained: "I like to be able to express myself clearly, logically, to make something difficult understandable." You obviously took pride in others finding your reports the most readable.

Your comments were still rocking around in my mind when I read an article for my summer course. They exemplify Donald Murray's theories in "Inviting Writing: Assignments and Demonstrations." I hear your enthusiasm in Murray's "The craft of writing itself can be inspiring." I've long felt this, but when, where, how did it get into you? And how the devil can I foster it in more of my students? This reading, and this course are giving me some food for thought. In class today, for example, we discussed purpose in writing. Murray says, "The strongest impulse to write is to make meaning of chaos." Apparently, Jim, that is what you enjoy doing with difficult computer programs — making them lucid to others. Murray puts it: "Writers need to write. They have an itch they need to scratch." My teacher, Susan Hynds, discusses this writing urge in terms of human purposes. I fancy myself rather good at working up and through writing topics, but this does give me pause for thought. This will be a significant consideration in my future fashioning of assignments. It's obviously a human purpose which makes your writing exciting and rewarding for you...

Interesting, Jim, how your brief comment helped me integrate various strands of thought. We must talk more soon!

Take care,
Catherine

Later, in a note written to me, Catherine recounts her writing and thinking process in drafting the letter to Jim:

I don't know when it hit me but reading Murray, listening in class, and reflections on real life came together like a thunderclap in this assignment. I had been struck by the comment of an in-law; I was struck by your class comments; and I've always felt Murray's brightness. Having to interweave the three strands into this letter helped synthesize the thoughts for me. Without this response I don't think I would have made the connection between what Jim said and the thrust of this reading and course. In the letter form I had to keep the connection clear, point by point.

> *As you can see from the raggedy looking scratch page following this, I had many thoughts, finishing Murray, that I would have liked to include in my response. Unfortunately there were too many miscellaneous points to write into my format. As it is, toward the end, I'm sort of running a list mainly so I can squeeze in and remember more of Murray's points. This form proved quite time consuming, but it was worth it.*

Although directing her language to a close friend proved to be somewhat time-consuming for Catherine, the process allowed her to synthesize information from her course, her readings, and her personal experience in a rather relaxed, casual way. Her letter was an interweaving of quotations from the texts and reminiscences about her conversation with Jim. Crafting her ideas for someone who mattered allowed her to bring her private thoughts into a safe, but public realm, elaborating upon and enriching them in the process.

Kathi: Language for Distant Others

Kathi, a speech therapist in an elementary school, decided to write a letter to Don Murray himself. Here is an excerpt of her letter:

> *Dear Dr. Murray,*
>
> *I would like to thank you for the strategies you offered to writers in **A Writer Teaches Writing**, particularly the chapter on "Inviting Writing: Assignments and Demonstrations." As a graduate student, I have been forced to confront my inadequacies as a writer in learning how to facilitate authorship among my students. I previously viewed writing as something to be done merely to please a teacher or meet course requirements (such as this one, ha ha).*
>
> *As a young student, my written compositions never seemed sufficient — when compared to the works of other students — to be shared with the entire class, so I turned away from writing and pursued areas in which I could excel. Writing became to me a waste of time, belonging to the category of mindless pursuits taken up by those who led very dull and isolated lives. I had much more interesting pursuits, or so I thought!...*
>
> *Your confession that your need to write sprang out from the loneliness and confusion of your home life was something that I could relate to. It was comforting to realize that another person spent a*

considerable amount of his youth engaged in fantasies about other lives. I, too, was addicted to leading "the multiple lives that went on inside my head." But unlike you, I never realized that I could gain satisfaction from "putting words on paper to record and play those secret lives."

I am afraid that I have been one of those "inhibited," constipated, frightened — in no condition to produce good writing — writers" that you referred to in your text. The simple realization that I am not alone in this gives me the courage to try some of your suggestions on how to become a better writer.

Based upon your advice, these are the initial steps I plan to take to develop my writing skills:

1. *I intend to begin my quest by simply writing. I now realize that I have to get something down on paper before I can begin to assess my writing.*
2. *I intend to make time to read quality literature. I began this summer by reading the works of John Steinbeck.*
3. *I am going to share my writing with my students and ask for their input.*
4. *My students and I will write about things that are important to us rather than follow a list of assigned topics.*

Hopefully, my own increased interest in writing will carry over to my students. I view this process as a journey in which we come to realize that our writing is ultimately an extension of ourselves. The journey may at times be arduous, and for many, a road less traveled, but nevertheless a worthy one. I'll keep you posted on the progress of our journeys.

Sincerely,
Kathi S.

Interestingly, although she seems to have gotten a great deal out of what Murray wrote, Kathi is not altogether satisfied with the process. The public and distant nature of the task became so overwhelming that it interfered with her concentration. She reflects:

The letter format forced me to look at the information more closely, which was good. But I found myself getting bogged down in "the correct letter format," which was bad.... These things don't flow down from my hand either, so I find myself spending a considerable amount of time trying to generate something memorable but ending up exhausted, bored, and disappointed. By the time I get to the conclusion, I'm so sick of the thing that I end up writing some trite closing comment. I always wondered why the conclusion was so difficult for me. It's because I'm tired! To me, the letter format was hindering to my learning process. I ended up focusing more on the format of the letter than on the information in the article.

Although Kathi's writing is polished, articulate, and reveals a great deal of careful thought, she appears to have been swept up in a concern for form and a worry about audience that gets in the way of the exploratory thinking she needs to do. Her comments remind us that going public should be a choice and not a requirement. If we expect students to say real things to real people, they can't be overly intimidated by the task. When students have more choices about when to go public, and when they are comfortable with the final product, writing to distant others can become a meaningful and motivating experience. When there is little or no choice, it can be a frightening task.

Inviting Language

As teachers, we take on a variety of roles in accepting and responding to our students' language. In the first few days of a term, we probably begin as distant others, but we can gradually take on the roles of co-learners or trusted adults (Britton, 1978). As we increase the level of intimacy, we increase the possibility for invested, committed learning. This process, however, is not without some risk. What follows in the next section is a story of how a teacher named Janet and a student named Seth successfully managed to strike this balance between risk and investment.

Classroom Closeup: Seth's Story

Dear David,

Thank you for your letter. I enjoyed being with you on Sunday and hope to see you on Saturday. Do you think Janet needs to lighten up? She wants to teach everyone to get along. Not to be mean and undignified. She likes joking sometimes and can be funny too. I want to be like you someday. Janet is lucky to have you. Please write back.

Seth

What seems like a rather ordinary note between a young man and a good friend is nothing short of a miracle. Although it is not immediately obvious in his articulate letter to David, for most of his life, Seth has been labeled autistic. Seven weeks earlier, before he began to work with his tutor, Janet, he was isolated in the narrow world of a special education classroom, often unable to communicate successfully with others or to make his emotional needs known. Janet's recollections of her first meeting with Seth are a mix of contradictions:

> *The first time I met Seth he was at a local hardware store with a Teaching Assistant .... I was surprised that Seth was "in public" because I had heard that the Teaching Assistants had refused to take him into the community.... [O]ne person told me about the time Seth broke her toe when he stepped on her foot.*

That day in the hardware store was an eye-opener for Janet. At the moment they were introduced, Janet remembered:

> *I held out my hand and said, "Hi." Seth took my hand and gently shook it saying, "Hi, Janet, yes." I noticed his blue, acid-washed Levi jeans and couldn't help but glance down at his feet .... He was wearing the largest white sneakers I think I've ever seen! In this brief meeting, I was struck by how very handsome and gentle he was. These were two qualities I would never have imagined Seth to possess given my preconceived notions formed by the anecdotes I had been told.*

In her recollections, Janet describes how this young man with a reputation for violence and antisocial behavior came to a place where he could write this articulate letter to David at the beginning of this section. As you will see, Janet became a willing and trustworthy audience for his first hesitant attempts to reach beyond himself through language. As a trusted listener, Janet gradually drew Seth into new worlds and new relationships.

A First Step

Ironically, when she met Seth at the hardware store that day, Janet had no idea that a few weeks later she would be asked to tutor him in his high school. As she thought about her new job over spring break, she had many doubts and questions: "Would I be able to teach Seth? What if he lost control? What would the faculty think of me?" During the vacation she took the opportunity to visit him at home.

After what seemed to be an eternity of standing there, I walked over to [Seth] and said, "Hi, Seth." ... After about twenty seconds he shook my hand and said, "Hi." I asked him if I could sit down. He replied "Sit down yes." We spent about ten minutes looking at National Geographic. While we were looking at the pictures in the magazine I read the captions aloud. Every once in a while Seth would look up into my eyes .... At one point Seth got up and said, "Would you like to go see Mom?" I said, "Sure." He certainly knew how to let me know he was finished.

At School

After that first encounter, Janet began to visit his school setting. She observed that in his present schedule, "Seth was involved in tracing his name on green primary paper, coloring elementary level dittos, using picture cards to point to or express colors and shapes, swimming for a couple hours each day, and basically being requested to participate in activities meant for preschool students." Believing that all students, regardless of the nature of their disability, "are capable of and have the right to live, work, and recreate in the community," Janet decided to teach him age appropriate and functional skills and to involve him in experiences with students his own age.

After that first day, watching Seth work with his teaching assistant, Tim, Janet was discouraged. At lunch, he was continuously told "Hands down," "You need to get control." Janet recalled:

It broke my heart to see all the students with disabilities sitting together and away from typical students. . . . Thus far, Seth hadn't done anything except appear upset. He hadn't purchased his own breakfast, opened anything himself, or conversed with anyone. What was he learning?

Up to this point, Seth had been unable to attend regular classes because he was not "in control." Janet observed: "There was that word again ... just what did 'control' mean and did Seth know what it meant? It seemed like a vicious circle. Seth was told to 'get control' but nobody assisted him in achieving this." With the help of Tim, Seth's regular teaching assistant, Janet worked out a class schedule in which he was able to attend regular classes and work for the Physical Education Department with a peer named David.

Reaching Out Through Language

One of the most striking changes for Seth came about as he began to engage in a process of journal writing through a teaching method known as "facilitated communication." Janet describes the method:

Facilitated Communication is a means of "facilitating expression by people who either talk or do not talk clearly." Rosemary Crossley, an Australian educator and founder of the DEAL Communication centre in Melbourne, is the originator of the method.

Through the work of Douglas Biklen (1990) and Rosemary Crossley (see DEAL Communication Centre, 1992), facilitated communication is being used very successfully as a teaching strategy in the United States. As part of this method, the facilitator either places a hand over the student's hand or supports the student under the wrist, pulling the student's hand back after each key has been struck on a computer or typewriter. Sometimes students initially need the facilitator to isolate their index finger, to make keyboarding easier, but eventually the facilitator can fade back the physical assistance. In many cases, students can learn to use the method with no more help than a hand on the shoulder or an index finger under the elbow. Interestingly, the students all seem to need some kind of physical touch, as well as a great deal of verbal reassurance and encouragement (Biklen, 1990).

For the past several weeks, Seth had been learning facilitated communication with the help of a speech therapist. However, their language activities had been confined to fill-in-the-blank and categorization activities. At first, Janet continued with these structured activities since these did not require Seth to "invest any emotions." As they worked beside each other, Janet would support Seth's hand pulling it back after each choice on the keyboard to give him time to make the next selection. However, as time went by, Seth needed only the tip of Janet's index finger under his hand, and did not need the pulling back "except when he was communicating something very emotional."

The First Breakthrough: Writing Toward Meaning

Because Seth used "echolalic speech" (continually repeating what he heard others say), it was difficult for Janet to determine whether what he said was what he actually meant. One day, when Tim was sick, Janet decided to type a paragraph, explaining that Tim wouldn't be in school. So began Janet's first glimpse into Seth's world. In their first session, Janet typed:

Today is Friday, April 27. Tim will not be in school today because he is sick. Seth and Janet will work together all day. We will try to go swimming last period if someone is available for the locker room.

Interestingly, in response to Janet's note, Seth began to verbalize, "Seth is very upset." Simultaneously, however, he spelled "I like Janet. I feel happy." Janet recalled, "He continued to say, 'Seth is very upset,' and again spelled: 'I feel happy.'" When Janet asked whether she should pay attention to his voice or the computer, Seth typed "listen to the computer." As Janet continued to probe about the difference between his spoken and his written language, Seth typed:

I feel frustrated when I say one thing and mean another ... People think I am stupid when I talk ... I feel like I am two people ... when I talk ... when I use the board ... use the board.

Thus, in Janet's words, "Facilitated communication provided the bridge between Seth's intentions and his communications." She quickly realized how important it was to ask Seth what he needed: "If I analyzed things by myself, there was a greater chance that I would be wrong. Besides, Seth seemed like the expert here and I could learn from him just as much as he would learn from me."

More Meaningful Outcomes

In the next phase of their work together, Janet decided that the fill-in-the-blank and categorization exercises were juvenile and meaningless for Seth. She began to communicate with him in a journal. In introducing the journal, she explained that it was "a collection of stories or thoughts which are typed on the computer through the use of facilitated communication and kept in a binder." She allowed Seth the option of sharing or not sharing all of his work and tried to create a climate of "warmth and acceptance with a lot of choice." She recalled his first entry:

(S) Hi Janet.
(J) Hi Seth. How are you?
(S) Good Janet.
(J) Is there anything you want to say?
(S) How are you?
(J) I'm great! I'm psyched to do this with you.

At that point, Seth verbalized, "All finished," and Janet said, "Ok, that was great writing!" She later reflected: "I remember feeling so pleased about this entry. He created this text. The stance was one of

Outcomes of Language and Learning

replication and the purpose was probably more social than personal, but that was fine because it was *his* work."

As the days went by, Seth continued to facilitate with Janet but was resistant to communicating with people he did not know well. One day, when he was with Tim, he typed "ystyol." When Tim said that he didn't understand, Seth typed "Tim confuses me because url I feel like he does bnot believe I know whow to spell or rfeaid." In Janet's words, "Seth could sense when people did not believe in him and he would literally shut down.... He taught me the importance of believing that all kids are competent." Later when they were alone, Seth typed "I am happy because I am with Janet alone. I like to write the journal with Janet because I trust you ... I feel better when we talk."

Moving Outward

One day, during a "conversation" with his sister, Seth spelled "me lik to swim. me lern to red." Janet wondered "Why was he spelling phonetically and using 'me' instead of 'I?' It wasn't that he didn't know how to spell or that he didn't know the correct usage of words. What was it?" She decided to ask him:

> Seth, I've noticed that sometimes you spell words correctly and other times you spell those same words incorrectly. Also, the vocabulary that you use changes as well as the length of sentences. Can you help me understand?

Seth's response was telling: "Different people have different expectations therefore I need to live up to them."

Even with Janet, there were times when Seth would purposely sabotage the communication session. On one of her home visits, for instance, Janet tried to get him to write in the journal in front of his parents. He took out his board and began to cry. The next day at school, Janet asked him about the incident. Their written conversation went like this:

> (S) I do not want to talk on the journal with Mom and Dad because that is for Janet and Sally.
> (J) It's to help you better communicate with everyone. Just think about all the people you could share your thoughts and dreams with — How about that?
> (S) I am scared because people will want me to be good all the time.
> (J) What do you mean?
> (S) Stop .. Stop
> (J) Okay, maybe later.
> (S) If people know how much I know they will want me to be good all the time .... no more crying, bumping, hitting, or silly talking.

Janet suddenly understood that through journal writing, Seth was able to change other people's attitudes toward him. In Janet's words, "He could show them he was 'smart.' On the negative end, as a result of using language, in his mind, he may be expected to assume more responsibility. He wondered if people would 'up the ante' and if so, how much?"

The experience taught Janet to "move slowly but steadily" with her expectations for students, "to be firm but fair." By the end of the term, Seth was using facilitated communication with his mother and father. He also found that he could write letters, beginning with one to his sister Susan, who lived abroad. He wrote five letters during the last three weeks of school. One of them was the letter in the beginning of this section, which he wrote to David, his partner in physical education. In her final reflections, Janet observed:

We as educators need to remember that just because we may be unable to communicate with a student, it does not mean that a student cannot communicate. It is our responsibility to find the "key" that will open the door to communication for each of our students.

Learners like Seth need not be trapped forever in their silences, but sometimes we must realize that they cannot or will not seek out significant communication partners on their own. At those times, it is up to us to open the world of our classroom and lead them outward, discovering a variety of outcomes for their talking writing, reading, and listening.

Classroom Connections

Moving Beyond the Classroom.

Perhaps one of our hardest tasks is to get ourselves out of the position of being our students' only audience and to help them to reach beyond the walls of school. It's not enough to ask our students to write artificial letters to hypothetical people in business and politics. If we want our students to read, write, speak, and listen with investment and conviction, audiences and outcomes must be real and responsive.

The postal service often publishes lists of international pen pals. Newspapers, particularly during times of crises, often list addresses of servicepeople who would welcome mail. Students themselves probably have many reasons to send letters, interview community resource people, attend and comment upon lectures and presentations. Keeping track of these learning experiences outside of the classroom in a language and learning log can be a regular part of each students' experience.

Adopting Different Roles.

As teachers, we can wear a variety of hats beyond that of the traditional evaluator or gradegiver. Each of us might begin by looking at the comments we make on student papers. What kind of voice lurks behind the commentary? Do our students view us as a friendly editor, a resident expert, a harsh evaluator, or a trusted co-learner? It is possible to change these roles consciously and to let our students know when we must shift from co-learner to evaluator?

There are many chances for us to adopt these different roles. In dialogue journals and student-teacher conferences, we can become co-learners. By situating ourselves as fellow explorers, rather than experts, we open the way for more intimate, informal conversations, in which our students can feel free to enlighten us. At times we can be "interim" audiences for others who might be more critical and distant. At other times, we may just be content to blend into the classroom community, enjoying a class discussion, a student text, a piece of published music, poetry, or speech. The roles we can take are almost limitless.

Creating Private Spaces.

Just as it's important to seek out more distant outcomes for student language, it's also important to provide private places. In schools, where students' writing and speech are typically graded, opportunities for private learning are scarce. It's crucial, then, to reward and model "irresponsible" writing, listening, reading, and talk. Reading corners for independent pleasure reading, diaries, and journals where some writings can be kept totally private, opportunities to listen and talk for the purpose of exploring ideas without fear of evaluation, are all important elements of a classroom learning community.

Finding the "Expert" in Each Student.

Learners like Seth become invested in using language as they discover its power in social relationships. As we learn how to listen and learn from our students, they develop their expertise. As Janet remarked: "Seth seemed like the expert here and I could learn from him just as much as he would learn from me." When we get out of the role of sole authority we quickly learn that each student has something special to teach.

Don Graves (1983) has suggested that we keep and maintain lists of topics that students might be qualified to write about. I find this to be a particularly good idea, even as I work with adults. After a few weeks of classes, following Graves' idea, I try to recreate a class roster from memory. After I get over the inevitable shock of how few names I can remember, I make it a point to get to know those people whose names did not leap immediately to mind and to keep a mental list of what each of them might be particularly knowledgeable about. I find that by making myself more naive and opening my classroom to a variety of student experts, my teaching becomes more fun, rewarding, and successful for me and my students.

Kathleen has discovered this very same thing. She teaches a course for eleventh and twelfth grade students called "English Through Writing." Most of her students have not been very successful in school. They take her course to improve their writing skills for their regular English classes. Her story reminds us of the need for becoming an inviting audience for student language:

> *Today I received one of those surprises that are preserved in the heart and cherished for a lifetime. I've been working with, listening to, and pulling for Don, an eleventh grader, for three years now. I have him for writing class this year, but he also brings his English writing assignments in during another period of the day and I help him with those assignments as well as with the writing he does in his ETW ("English Through Writing") class. Today Don and I were talking about a story he wanted to write but was just beginning to blossom for him. He decided that he wanted to take a portion of his own life and write it as a medieval fairy tale. We had been discussing this for about fifteen minutes when I asked Don who was going to be telling the story. Don pondered this for a few minutes and then he said he thought the wizard would tell the story.*
>
> *"You know," he said, "there are two kinds of wizards. Some are evil and some are good. I think a teacher is a wizard. Some are, well, you know, they are kind of like the evil wizard. They just say, "Do this or you're out of here!" And then there are other teachers that are like a good wizard. They do like you're doing. They just kind of help the student out until the student finds out what it is that's inside. You know, like you just keep asking questions and getting me to find out the story that's in my head. That's a good wizard — the wizard helps the person be the best he has to be."*
>
> *Wow! And Don went on with his story, not realizing that his teacher had gone into mental and emotional shock! Don generally has a very difficult time articulating his thoughts — he's often told me that his "brain gets a work-out" in my class. I think this time Don's brain and his vocabulary collided!*

As Kathleen has discovered, students have all kinds of stories just waiting to be told. Often, we have only to wait patiently for them to come alive in our classroom. At other times, we must become "good wizards," gently and carefully drawing out the expert in each of our students. As we explore the language outcomes beyond the walls of our classroom and as we shift from the various roles available to us — advisor, co-learner, novice, trusted adult — we find that we become more responsive and less responsible for students' learning at the same time. Learning and teaching become easier, as we discover each student's hidden potential, helping each one, in Don's words, "to be the best he (or she) has to be."

Explorations

1. **Playing With Outcomes**: As a way of learning more about language outcomes, you might want to find a text that you have already written. This may be a response to a class-assigned reading, a piece of imaginative fiction, or some teaching notes from your plan book. Now, change the outcome of your language and rewrite the piece. If you have written a totally private piece, take a few minutes and begin a more public draft (to an intimate or even a distant other). If this was a text you produced for a professor or workshop leader, transform it into a more private piece, in which you allow yourself more freedom to play with ideas. Notice how your language changes. Keep track of the decisions you make, as the outcome of your language shifts from private to public, or from public to more private. Write a "process account" in which you speculate on the ways in which the outcomes for language shape what you learn.

2. **Outcomes For Listening**: Have a partner read a section of this chapter aloud to you. Perhaps you might ask your partner to read the story of Seth (pp. x-x) aloud, while you simply close your eyes and listen. Don't worry about being held accountable for what you hear. Simply open your mind and try to experience the story as completely as you can. Now, have your partner reread the section again. This time, try to remember the exact sequence of events in as much detail as you can. When your partner is through, take a few minutes and jot down the highlights of the section. When you are finished, talk to your partner or write a short piece in which you describe the differences you experienced in both listening situations.

3. **Name Your Own Exploration**

References

Biklen, D. (1990). Communication unbound: Autism and praxis. *Harvard Educational Review 60* (3), pp. 291-314.

Britton, J. (1978). The composing process and the functions of writing. In *Research on composing: Points of departure*, C.R. Cooper & L. Odell (Eds.) Urbana, Ill: NCTE.

Britton, J. (1983). Language and learning across the curriculum. In *Fforum: Essays on theory and practice in the teaching of writing*. P.L. Stock (Ed.) Upper Montclair, NJ: Heinemann/Boynton/Cook.

DEAL Communication Centre. (1992). *Getting the message: Notes on aspects of communication without speech* (Report). Melbourne, Australia: DEAL Communication Centre.

Graves, D.H. (1983). *Writing: Teachers and children at work*. Exeter, New Hampshire: Heinemann Educational Books.

Marshall, J.D. (1989). *Patterns of discourse in classroom discussions of literature* (Report No. 2.9). Albany, NY: Center for the Learning and Teaching of Literature.

Mehan, H. (1979). What time is it Denise?: Asking known information questions in classroom discourse. *Theory into Practice, 28*, 285-294.

Rosenblatt, L.M. (1978). *The reader, the text, the poem: A transactional theory of the literary work*. Carbondale, IL: Southern Illinois University Press.

Rosenblatt, L.M. (1985). Viewpoints: Transaction versus interaction — a terminological rescue operation. *Research in the Teaching of English, 19*, 97-107.

CHAPTER 5

Case Study
Lauren: A Personal Metamorphosis

It occurred to me recently while I was reviewing a lesson on the life cycle of an insect how my own life seemed to fit into the metamorphic pattern that insects follow. The pattern is one of activity and then retreat, then reemerging in a new changed state. My life and my professional growth did not seem to be following the same pattern. Professionally I would say that I am in the cocoon stage of development, just prior to emerging into a new and different stage. Although the cocoon feels as if it is only a temporary state, emergence is inevitable, and unavoidable.

In recent years, the mere idea of change has become something that is so threatening, that I overlook the opportunity to change my thinking and my teaching, rather than risk the consequences. Coping with the death of my husband and a radical career change from parochial to public education has almost paralyzed me from moving forward with my life. Although the majority of these changes have been circumstantial, nonetheless, they have left me with an extremely vulnerable feeling. The person I am forced to be now is far removed from the housewife working at a parochial school I was happy to be then. At times these changes seem so overwhelming that I doubt myself and my abilities. This causes a great deal of incongruity in my life and in my teaching.

Lauren is a fourth grade teacher in an urban elementary school. These words, written in her journal over a year ago, describe how abruptly her life had changed over the course of a few short months. Her husband had died a year earlier, casting her suddenly into the role of a single parent. She soon found it necessary to leave her comfortable part-time job in a private school and move to a public school system, where she had to adjust quickly to the demands of a full-time workload and a very different group of students. As if these events weren't challenging enough, she had recently learned that her provisional teaching certification was about to run out and she had to complete a master's degree within the year or risk losing her certification altogether.

I remember one of my first conversations with Lauren. She had signed up for a graduate course I was teaching. Somewhere in the first week, I was holding conferences with participants about their ideas for a paper. As Lauren spoke, I noticed that she seemed to be experiencing an extraordinary degree of tension and anxiety as she told me of her struggles to find a topic for her paper. It seemed that, no matter how hard she tried, she couldn't get past her own fear of not being perfect.

I soon learned that Lauren was an extremely conscientious adult learner — one who took her work very seriously and who was not able to accept, in herself, anything short of perfection. By the time she had written the journal entry about her own metamorphosis at the beginning of this chapter, she had begun her first fall term in a public school and was again in the midst of another graduate course that had put her in touch with several new, exciting, and admittedly frightening ideas about teaching language.

As the early weeks of school wore on, Lauren came to a difficult realization. Perhaps the fear of change she felt in her life outside of the classroom was beginning to affect her teaching. She wondered if this might be true:

> *I always set very high expectations for myself and those who are close to me. Usually no one can live up to these expectations, including me. That is why I am almost always in a state of frustration and disappointment. Did I set the expectations for [my students] so far from what they could hope to reach that they gave up before trying? Most importantly, was I making them feel like failures because I was feeling that I had failed to motivate them in their learning and growth process?*

Over the next three months, this question, and many others, began to enter the walls of Lauren's classroom and end up in the pages of her journal.

What follows is the story of how Lauren managed the process of change in her teaching. The journal that she kept during those first few months of the fall term begins from a place of initial fear and confusion and moves through a realization of her successes and failures. In the end, Lauren discovered some valuable insights about her students, her teaching, and herself. Eventually she found that change need not be painful, though it is usually accompanied by uncomfortable moments of questioning and self-doubt.

Like most true stories, this one doesn't come to neat resolutions; nor does it move steadily and unshakably toward some irrefutable truth. I've tried to present Lauren's story as it actually unfolded, through a series of journal entries and reflections she wrote during the time of these events in her life. I hope that her story will give you a chance to think about and reflect on some of the ideas and issues you've been encountering in this book thus far.

You can simply read the story if you like or you can stop occasionally to reflect privately or with others. You might want to read over some of the options in the Explorations section at the end of this chapter. These are simply a starting place for reflecting on your reading in more focused and systematic ways. Feel free to modify any of them to suit your needs.

Lauren's story from September to December chronicles her own personal metamorphosis—as a parent and a teacher, and, not least of all, as a writer herself. She begins in the middle of September.

Lauren's Journal

9/12 Thursday —

Today I decided to have the class write something about themselves, a short autobiography, to hang up for open house. First I had asked them to bring in a picture of themselves. What a nightmare! Over half the class has some reason why they couldn't bring the picture in. What a group! Some forgot, some had the picture at Dad's but they live with Mom. One person said "My parents never take pictures of us." One child produced a picture 8 by 10 though, which was not able to fit on loose leaf paper.

I should have learned from that what I was in for with this assignment. I really felt very prepared for this assignment. First we brainstormed about ideas to use. I listed them on the board as they volunteered them, in any random order. Next, I numbered them in sequential order starting with basic information first. I even suggested using the three paragraph form (early years, your life now, and what you might hope to become). The thought struck me that I was the person doing most of the work. I put a word bank on the board of words that I thought they might need to spell correctly. I had hoped this would be an easy assignment for them and would give me some information about how they wrote.

What a nightmare! I was besieged with questions about what to write with, where does my name go, how many sentences are in a paragraph, and do we really have to do this?

I felt like a failure. Where did I go wrong? As I walked around the room, some of the students were writing, but it was short choppy writing with very little variety in sentences or words used in them. We continued for about thirty minutes, then I called in the papers. Only a few were able to come up with three paragraphs. Many of them had only eight to ten sentences written and some less. One girl said she thought it was stupid to love to write. I can see I have my work cut out for me.

Monday — 9/16

While reading Janet Emig's article on presenting writing developmentally in schools I couldn't help but think of myself and my class this year. It was an almost exact parallel. The majority of my students had previously been taught by very "traditional methods," especially in writing. [Emig's] statement about "magical thinking" — the uninsightful notion that what is taught is necessarily learned — certainly seems to fit here. All of these students had been "taught writing" in previous years, but they obviously had not learned what writing is.

My current students definitely were not "risk-takers" nor did they seem to have any driven quest for knowledge. Most of these children are below average to average readers. Over half of them did not have a very large speaking vocabulary. Many of them have never traveled or gone anywhere with their parents except to a store or mall. The majority of their experiences are centered around their home...

Another point that [Emig] made seems to focus on attitude and involvement in the writing experience. She says that only "direct, active, personal experience can be transferred into personal knowledge and that personal knowledge of any process to be presented is a requisite."

Frankly, I hate to write. It makes me feel inadequate (a feeling I am always wrestling with in some area of my life, and therefore I avoid it when I can). I phone rather than write, I memorize rather than write, I converse rather than write. The majority of my writing is to meet specific requirements given to me by someone else. I wonder how much of my attitude shows through when I assign a writing task to my students. The students rarely see me writing except for the assignment and I never use something I have written as an example for them. I wonder if their attitudes are affected by this? I am not known for being a great risk-taker, adapting new methods and *trying new things is very threatening to me. Maybe I will be forced to changed if I plan to move forward with these children.*

9/25

Today my son brought home many papers from school. He's in first-grade. Josh is an inquisitive first grader who has become fascinated with the idea of communicating through writing that people can read. Many of the techniques used in his classroom were unfamiliar to me, especially the use of invented spelling for children who are learning to write. At first I was not sure that I was in favor of this method. However after a few months, I realized how much I have to learn and what a valuable tool this can be for children. [Today Josh] was so delighted to share his work. You could see the pride on his face as we looked at each paper together. He brought home several papers that he said were from Writing Workshop. Some of them were scribblings and drawings with words beneath. He could easily identify each sentence and word he had written. It was thrilling to see him so excited about what he had done. It suddenly occurred to me that this must be how some of my students' parents feel when their children bring home successful papers.... Mrs. B (my son's teacher) has really brought out the best in him.... All attempts at written and read language are celebrated as milestones. She also provides the classroom with a definite amount of structure and routine, but the children don't identify these rules as restrictive. They feel comfortable and eager to learn. This is really exciting watching an emergent writer and reader move forward before your eyes.

9/26

Today we attempted another writing assignment. I really felt I was well-prepared for this assignment. The topic was an assigned topic but I tried not to give to many guidelines so that the papers would be somewhat imaginative. The assigned topic was a silly, somewhat ridiculous open-ended assignment ("if I were a garbage can I would say..."). I really tried to limit and guide the writing and discussion to give some general ideas about the topic but not say anything specific because I did not want them to feel that they had to write to please me.

I was pleased with many of the papers. About one third of the class "dug right in" and started writing immediately. All of the students were able to produce some form of text (This made me feel really good). They wrote uninterruptedly for about forty minutes. At the end of the time I asked them to reread their pieces to themselves and make any changes they felt they needed to. After about ten minutes I asked if anyone was willing to show their writing. Many were obviously nervous. However three people anxiously raised their hands. They read their stories. They were wonderful and funny. I could hear some of the others say "I wish I had thought of that," "I like the way they are making the garbage can talk." This really seemed to be a positive experience. There was no pressure to share, but I noticed that as more people were willing to share, others were definitely trying to take the risk too.

What did I learn? Wonderfully, I learned that I could invite some positive and good texts from these children. They showed me that they did have many capabilities when forced to use them. I also learned that I needed to applaud all the small steps they were willing to take rather than be disappointed because they didn't measure up to my expectations. Perhaps I need to lower my expectations for them. I wonder if my own personal negativity is having an effect on my students. I know it affects my perception sometimes, but I never really thought about whether or not it affected their attitude or performance.

9/27

My son brought home some more of his papers from Writing Workshop today. You can already see the improvement. Words have boundaries. Some even have vowel sounds written in them. While I was working in the kitchen he started "writing." The paper was about fall leaves. As I watched him thinking I noticed how concentrated his efforts were. He was saying each word he wanted to write out loud and then repeating the word but emphasizing the sounds that were pronounced (i.e., t rr e). Then he would write each sound on the paper. This was hard work for him. He continued until the sentence was finished and he marked it with a period (A lev fel uv the tre.) When he finished, his pride was obvious from the wide grin on his face. I asked him how he knew what to write. He said "I just think it in my head and then write the words." That sounded pretty logical and very much how everyone else wrote.
"Well, how do you know what to think about?" I said.

"I just look around, or think of something I heard, or did today," he answered.

Next I asked him, "How do you know what letters to use to write it?"

"You say the word and hear the sound. Stop asking so many questions," he answered.

It made me wonder, if young students could have so much innate knowledge of how to approach a writing task, why doesn't this knowledge grow with them? Why do they come to third, fourth, and fifth grade ready to give up at the mere mention of writing? Even one or two word answers are a chore, let alone a story or lengthy piece. What happens to change these initial eager attitudes?

Week of 10/1 - 10/8

This week, I wondered whether my students were more comfortable with and more willing to write assigned topics or free choice topics.

I had already asked them to write on an assigned topic the week before ("The Garbage Can"). My preparation for the free choice writing topic was brief. They could choose anything they wanted to write on and write a story about it. That approach was met with confused looks and many hands waving and asking "What do you mean?" I repeated the directions but immediately realized that they still had no idea what I was talking about. I decided to give some examples: "You could write about something that happened to you, or a trip you took, or your best friend, or a sport that you play or something you can do well, like dance or play an instrument." Some seemed to get the idea.

Gradually, most of the students did decide on something to write. The writing task seemed much more difficult for them than the assigned topic.

As I walked around I noticed that many had very little written and much of that was repetitious of the same thought or event (i.e., "I went____. It was very fun. I had a good time when we went to ___.). There was very little evidence of the detail I was hoping for (or explanation). I stopped there and said, "I noticed that no one has told me much about what happened when you were visiting some place. When you say it was fun, you need to tell me why you thought it was fun. That will help me understand your story."

I wrote on the board the "five basic elements of a story: who, what, why, when, and how," thinking that would help them. It only confused them more.

One observation that really surprised and baffled me was that it seemed the students I considered to be at the top of the group and the most capable were struggling hardest and seemed the most uncomfortable when making their own choice in writing. They were very concerned about whether they were doing what I wanted them to do. Even though I kept repeating that anything was fine, I wanted them to choose. I would have expected just the opposite reaction from them.

It will be interesting to compare later if this was only an initial reaction or if this continues.

Week of Oct. 8 - 15

I really enjoyed reading Nancie Atwell's "Everyone Sits at a Big Desk." It made me think how much of my own educational experiences had been "dummy runs." I felt a little guilty for all those students I had "taught" in previous years but never really taught them much more than regurgitating what I had described or set up for them in the planning session before the actual writing. I guess I'll have to live with that guilt knowing I did my best at that time and that I am really striving to restructure my thinking and approach to teaching now.

I agree with [Atwell] that topic choice allows students to use their own experiences, but it scares me that they won't have any experiences to draw from. What do I do then?

I found her two suggestions for starting the year off very helpful. I wish I had read this in August rather than October, but it still is not too late to try these ideas. I am now trying to let the students know that I expect them to be writing, and writing actively, not dawdling and relying on me to write the piece for them. I have reduced my help from giving topics and starting sentences down to asking questions about their experiences or what happened next when they are doubtful or confused. This new approach is met in my classroom with little enthusiasm and a little disappointment as I watch students struggle in their attempts to write. I hope it will become easier for all of us as we continue throughout the year.

I am really interested in the thing that my son has been writing. Donald Graves is right. In young writers, their voices do boom forth. I have been collecting his writings and studying them. The progression is amazing, from the undecipherable random letters to now well though out sentences that almost anyone can read (although I am biased because I am his mother). The invented spelling shows how much he has already learned about writing and reading. Some of the words even have a final e on them. (He said that the teacher said when you can really hear the vowel sound that the word has an e on the end). I also noticed that uv is now more frequently written uf or sometimes of, off.

Over the weekend we went apple picking. We found some things to bring for science class (milkweed pods and a bird's nest). When we got home he sat down and wrote a letter to his teacher telling her about this. It actually started "Dear Mrs. B." and continued with the event and was signed "Joshua Taylor."

I can't imagine how he knew to write it in letter form. When I asked him he said "Well you don't want to start just 'Mrs. Bird.' That's not very nice!! You put your name at the end so she knows you're done and who wrote it!" If a first grader can figure this out without any formal introduction to it, why do 4th graders have so much trouble writing letters in the classroom? My suspicion is that they really don't want to write when asked to, so the task and form are not important to them, much less the message. He had something to tell her and the form came automatically to him. He was investing himself in this writing.

It makes me wonder what goes wrong between first grade and fourth-grade. How does this spirit get dimmer or become extinguished altogether? The more I observe, the more important the question becomes to me, not only to help me understand my current students but also to prevent this from happening to my own child (a vested interest again).

Case Study — Lauren: A Personal Metamorphosis

Week of Oct. 22 - 29

What would happen if I gave them a topic but said they could write whatever they wanted about it?

Mon. I decided to tell them to write on Halloween (topic). It can be anything you want, leaving out blood and guts and rewriting Friday the 13th or the movie Halloween. The story can be imaginative but it doesn't have to be. You can make your own characters or use real people. Try not to use characters you have seen in other movies or in television (These were the directions)....

I noticed that many students seemed to be struggling, trying to come up with ideas. I asked them to stop and then I made a story map for a story that I might have written. Starting with Halloween Night in the center, I used connecting circles for main ideas and lines for details about those ideas. I strongly encouraged them to use a similar pattern if they were having trouble deciding what to write.

About half the class used the mapping process. Some of them said that it really seemed to help them know what to write next. Others said that it was too much extra work and they didn't think that they need to use it. Surprisingly as I looked around the room those were the students who were having the most trouble writing anything down on paper. They also are the students whose sentences are the shortest and lack any details or creativity. I was stumped again. I couldn't force them to use this method, unless I almost wrote the story for them.

For the most part, though, things seemed to move along. After about thirty-five minutes I asked them to finish the idea they were writing. We could work on it more tomorrow.

Tues. Today, almost everyone said they were finished. I asked them to read it over and see if they could add any more. This was not what I had expected. Almost no one had anything else to write, or anything they wanted to change. I was at a loss!

Why were they unwilling to continue to improve their stories? I could tell from quickly reading some [that] they had no ending to the story. It just ended because the time was up. I wonder if the kids are ready for this. Or should we go back to using the textbook? They seemed more content with skill sheets than thinking on their own. From the looks on their faces I could see they didn't care. Their attitude seems to be to just get it done, any way possible, and hand it in. The teacher is the one who should worry about whether or not it is correct.

At the end of the time, several students asked if they could read these stories to the class. We spent some time sharing stories and pictures.

When I got back to my desk I found many papers piled on it. "Aren't you going to read them and correct them?" asked Brie.

"Yes, but first we're going to help each other correct them," I said. She made a face and shrugged her shoulders. I guess that told me everything I needed to know about how she felt.

Wed. I am getting discouraged!! Maybe I'm expecting too much? Today we tried a framed paragraph about a pumpkin. (I was desperate. I'll try anything). I wrote it on chart paper and hung it up. I explained what we were writing today and that our purpose was to use describing words to explain what the pumpkin looked like. The blanks in the story were for them to fill in with their own words. "Try to make me really see your pumpkin," I said.

They liked this!! When I asked why, the answers were obvious. "It was easy," "You did all the work," "We only had to think of a few words." Someone did point out that everyone's was the same but yet different. (Pretty much what I expected. Maybe writing isn't the real problem, but lack of motivation and thinking skills?)...

They started editing their own papers. I had thought of having them exchange papers and edit each other's but decided that would probably become too difficult a task. The majority of the class was finished in about 5 or 6 minutes, and they had very few corrections to make. I questioned them, asking, "Are you sure you're finished?" From each student, the answer was a definite "YES!"

Once again, this message told me that they did not see this as part of their responsibility as the writer. I assume they thought the writer writes the paper. The teacher should be the one to correct the mistakes. I think that they also thought that this was taking too long and was too difficult for them to do. Many of them were lying down on their desks as they were trying to read their papers. This told me that they were not concentrating on what they were doing.

At the end of the writing time ... I questioned myself. Is it their attitude, or am I missing an important connection in this process? I don't seem to be able to keep any amount of motivation going for any length of time.

Fri. Today we wrote poems about witches. I read them several poems from a book called *Best Witches* by Jane Yolen (It describes modern day witches in very funny terms). These poems were wonderfully illustrated by Elise Primavera. They loved it. I also gave them a coloring picture of a witch, a broom and a cat. I asked them to write an 8-line poem about a witch.

When I first shared my plan for writing today, the usual amount of moans and groans could be heard, and several students settled into their usual position of lying on the desk and staring off into space. I decided to ignore their behavior, not even commenting on it, and proceed with reading the book. For me that was a very big step. I usually get noticeably irritated and frustrated and make some comment to the class. At times I was beginning to think that they would exhibit this behavior just to see what I would do.

Case Study — Lauren: A Personal Metamorphosis

As soon as I started to read the book they became more interested, especially during the poems with the funny pictures. After a few poems they were laughing and commenting on the strangeness or weirdness of the pictures and the words. At the end of the book, I gave them five minutes to talk to a partner about what a poem should include. With this information we made a list of six basic elements on the board.

Before starting to write, we discussed the placement of rhyming words in a poem, at the end of a line, and to remember to use punctuation marks to indicate the end of a line or a pause in the reading. Their assignment was to write a two-stanza poem about witches. The poem may rhyme but it does not have to. The choice was up to them.

I was very pleased that they started writing and most of it was good. I noticed that almost everyone made the poem rhyme. Many said it was easier to think of rhyming words to go together. As I walked around everyone was busy and no one was complaining. Everyone was busily at work, rather than looking for reasons for not working. After about twenty-five minutes, I asked them to read their poems to a partner and listen carefully to how they sounded. Reading out loud was helpful in listening for the rhyming words and the tone of the poem. Many of them decided they were not happy with the way it sounded, and they needed to make some changes.

When I announced that the time for writing was ended I was surprised that they wanted to continue working and try to finish the poems today. We worked about another twenty minutes. As they finished their poems, I had them tape them to the board in the front of the room. We had a wonderful art gallery to look at for the rest of the day. By the end of the day everyone had placed their poem in the gallery.

This was a very successful project, but I wasn't exactly sure why. How much did setting the tone of the room by reading the book effect it or having the sheets to color make a difference? I wondered if displaying them immediately as they were written was an incentive to others. It was such a simple thing, yet they really liked putting their own up. I had never tried this before. Usually I collect them and read them, then put them up. Could that have made any difference?

However the combination of events worked together, they produced positive results. This was the most successful writing time we had spent together as a class! I asked the students to write me a few sentences about how they felt about his project. Their answers told me that my initial theory was correct. It was a combination of setting the mood with the poetry book and having many examples to model after. They even commented that coloring the picture helped to keep them focused on witches. Mark, a very enthusiastic boy, wrote, "Mine is on the chalkboard with a lot of other people's. It was very fun, there are 13 of them up there." Obviously displaying the finished product was very important to him.

In retrospect, we had done three short focused activities this week and I had increased the modeling of each. They seemed to be more comfortable. Maybe I had been pushing too much at them at once. I wonder if choosing a variety of things to write was helpful for them (I decided to try to use short activities and to vary them rather than try a longer piece that needed to be revised and edited. Maybe they are as insecure and doubtful as I am!

Week of 10/29-11/5

Mon. *I am struggling to find a way to interest my students in revising their drafts.... They still have a difficult time seeing that their written text has missing parts and that the reader will not be able to understand what they are talking about.*

Today, I had planned to do a lesson on placing quotation marks correctly when writing in narrative. I decided not to use the textbook listing of isolated sentences but to use some of the sentences that the students had written in their stories. Three students volunteered to let me use their papers. I put their sentences on the board and we collectively decided where the quotation marks should be placed and what kind of punctuation to use. The students were very interested in this activity. When we had finished with those three papers, Josh read his paragraph aloud. The students were to raise their right hand for beginning marks and their left hand for ending marks. This was difficult on the first try. Mixing up left and right was part of the problem. We tried it a second time with much greater success. They seemed to be getting the idea, and everyone was interested.

Students looked through their own written papers to try and find places where they had written dialogue. I asked them to use a colored marker or crayon to circle their quotation marks or to add them in. During this time, Kristen raised her hand and read a few sentences. She then asked if her sentences needed quotes, because she wasn't sure. Carl answered her, "No, because the person isn't really speaking." I was thrilled they were finally beginning to help one another in a useful manner. The activity sheet they were given next was not as much fun to do. However, everyone completed it quietly, willingly, and quickly.

To the outside observer, this probably doesn't seem like anything very significant. However, I felt we were finally making some progress as a cooperative effort between the students and teacher. This kind of lesson was what I had read about in the articles on writing I had been reading. Students using their own texts to learn from!! This was another small step of the path we need to travel this year, but we successfully accomplished it together.

Although the steps are slow and I have to work very hard at not becoming impatient with them, I can observe they are trying. Trying to keep a positive attitude about the class as a group has seemed to help my relationship with them and has helped me to recognize the things they can do, rather than what they are unable to do. Having a positive attitude about anything has always been difficult for me, especially when I am frustrated with a situation.

Tues *Today I planned a writing lesson to introduce a reading skill, focusing on using and identifying idiom expressions. I wrote three sentences on the board with idiomatic expressions in them. They were:*

> *"Don't pick on your sister, Tom," called Susan.*
> *"Why don't you hit the road," answered Tom.*
> *"Go take a hike," yelled Susan.*

I told the class to pretend that Tom and Susan were having an argument and that these words were part of their conversation. What do these expressions really mean? Many students volunteered to answer. They had heard these expressions before. We discussed the fact that an idiom was an expression that didn't literally mean what the words said. Idioms have special meanings when used in sentences. I could tell by the expressions on their faces that they still didn't understand what I meant.

I had borrowed a book on idioms from the library called In a Pickle and Other Funny Idioms, *by Marvin Terban. I started to read it. They were laughing in a few minutes. The book is written to illustrate the idiom on the top of the page. For example, "Tom is in a pickle" shows a boy in a pickle jar between a sliced pickle. We discussed the fact that it really means Tom is in trouble. We laughed a lot while reading this book.*

At the end of the book, students were asked to share any expressions they had heard or used that could be idioms. Jackie said that she was very moody one day and her mother asked her if she had gotten up on the wrong side of the bed. Michael commented that his teacher last year always said "get your head out of the clouds." Kristen said her mother constantly tells her not to pick on her younger sister. Following this discussion I asked them to think of an idiom that they knew and write it down, then to draw an appropriate picture to go with the expression. As a group we decided not to duplicate the idioms, if possible, so we could make them into a book when we finished.

During the working time, students were busy working independently and sharing in small groups. I was circulating the room, offering help, encouragement, and checking for duplicates. It was difficult for some of the students to think of original idioms. After some discussion, the class decided that some duplication would be acceptable as long as the pictures were different.

At the end of the writing time, I asked them to share what they had written with the students in their small group. There were noticeable giggles and whispers as they shared. Again, I asked them to write me a few sentences about how they felt about this activity. What was difficult, what was easy, what they liked about it, and what was helpful to them?

Their responses told me that they liked doing this kind of an activity. It was fun. The hardest part was thinking of an idiom to use before someone else thought of it. Almost all of the students enjoyed the book and thought it was very helpful in understanding what an idiom was.

This information also reinforces the important effect modeling has upon the confidence of the students when they are asked to complete a task. Time is another important factor, one that I hadn't really taken into consideration before. Students, especially young writers, need to feel that they have time to think before they write. Placing time limits on them adds to their frustration when coping with a new task.

I am beginning to really feel more confident. We seem to be having a successful writing time more often now. I am very much afraid of becoming overconfident and suddenly being faced with failure again. I need to remind myself constantly to be satisfied with small increments and not to look at how far behind we were, compared to the other fourth grades.

Week of 11/5 - 11/12

Would the students react differently to someone else leading them through a writing lesson?

At a meeting I was able to talk with Elaine, the writing consultant in our district. I had taken an inservice from her last January. I explained some of the problems I was having. She suggested that she come into the classroom and help get them started. We set a date on Thurs,. Nov. 7, at 9:30-10:30. She came and talked about choosing topics to write on.

I was thrilled and anxious to have Elaine meet my class, thrilled because I admire her so much. She is always so enthusiastic about what she does that you can almost feel excitement in the air when she walks in. At the same time, I was apprehensive that she might think that I wasn't doing enough with the class. I decided that her visit could only benefit me. She was willing to help and I felt I needed the help. Perhaps she could suggest an area I needed to work on with them that I had completely overlooked.

Thurs. *Today, Elaine bustled through our classroom door pulling her red wagon, heaped with information, behind her. From the looks on the children's faces I could tell they were very nervous and weren't sure they were going to like this at all.*

Elaine introduced herself and told the class about herself and the reason she was here today. She started to ask some questions, but no one volunteered to answer except me! Finally she said she was going to be calling on people at random and that they should be thinking and ready with an answer. After a few more questions that they were able to answer, I could see the class begin to relax.

Next she started to read them a book about a grandmother who is moving from the house she has lived in all her life. She and her grandchild visit each room of the house to say goodbye and reminisce about special memories. Elaine related this to the relationship that the students might have with their own grandparents. The book is entitled Grandma Remembers. *As she read, she stopped after each room and asked who had a special memory about that room. It was wonderful. They actually showed some excitement and volunteered answers. Students responded with funny experiences about events they could remember in their own homes or their grandparents' homes. Elaine listened to the stories and gave each a chatty title and listed them on the board.*

At the end of the story, she had the students open their folders and list at least five choices of true things they had experienced that they could write about. We circulated around the room and encouraged the students to move from broad titles to specific events, from "My Trip to Florida" to "The Day I Met Mickey Mouse." I told them to choose something special about the trip to focus on.

I was surprised at the response from the students. Everyone was actually writing. Many came up with more than five choices. Next, they were asked to circle the one choice they liked the best and share it with a classmate. The students worked in small groups to help each other think of clever titles to use for their topics.

The students obviously enjoyed this. Hands were waving when it was time to share, and their smiles were apparent. They were pleased with themselves about the work they had done. The students responded that they were pleased, happy, excited, and anxious to start writing their new stories.

Although I felt like a failure myself, I realized that I had much to learn from watching Elaine. She is a real professional. She had captivated the students. Her enthusiasm was contagious. She enjoyed what she was doing so much that it was like watching a performer on a stage. The children caught the enthusiasm of what she was doing. They worked to gain her praise. Praise was something Elaine flowed with. Any small attempt was praised. As I watched, I noticed how she built their self-confidence. They didn't need her; they wanted to show their capabilities. I had to be honest with myself. My own lack of enthusiasm and negativism was my greatest stumbling block.

Fri. *Today Elaine came back and gave them a mini-lesson on topic sentences. Her phrases were to grab the reader or hook the reader. Your first sentence has to make the reader get interested and want to read on. She and I took turns reading some passages from authors' books, to give students the idea of what starting sentences should look like (she read better than I at first). I was catching some of the enthusiasm and really started to put all of my enthusiasm into the passages I read. I noticed that the students looked at me, as if to say, "You never sounded like that before." When we finished, the students started to write their own topic sentences. Elaine told them to really try to "grab" their readers on the first line.*

We circulated around the room and helped them think of catchy topic sentences. The students were concentrating on trying to come up with different ways of introducing their topics. The room was almost silent as I walked around. I remember thinking that my heels sounded loud. I don't think I ever noticed their noise before. Most of the students did a great job on their own. At the end of the time several of the students shared their titles and topic sentences with the group. You could tell they were pleased by the anxious way they wanted everyone else to know what they had decided on.

Again, I noticed how the teacher used her own enthusiasm for the task to motivate the students into using their best effort to write the kind of sentence she had modeled for them. I couldn't decide whether they were trying to please Elaine or whether they were really engrossed in writing the very best sentence they could. Once again, I was struck by the powerful tool that modeling was for these children.

Monday and Tuesday and Wednesday of next week will be devoted to writing their stories.

Week of 11/12 - 11/19 — How can I get them to revise?

11/14 Thursday Mrs. G. arrived again. Everyone was glad to see her. She did a lesson on revision. Again, it was wonderful. She brought a story she had written on chart paper. She and actually changed and moved words, crossed out things, rewrote new words above in different colors, and even cut a piece out and retaped it in a better position. The students were fascinated. They watched intently and helped choose new words for the story. They could actually see what should be happening. I had never thought to do such a demonstration for them.

Today, the resource teacher, who usually takes three children from my room during writing time, decided to come into my classroom. Her students wrote along with the other students in the class. The resource teacher is a valuable help with all of the students, not only those assigned to her but many others. The students had the benefit of more than one teacher in the room to help them with any problems. I noticed a real sense of security in the students. Perhaps having so many adults available to them at one time added to their self-confidence. Help was readily available, and they were aware of it.

I went over the revision symbols that we were going to be using, then gave them a sheet with the symbols to refer to while they were working. I also distributed red and green pens to them to make their revisions stand out from the original text. Many started right away. Others needed lots of help, but with three people to help there was much support. The session went well. We will continue to revise tomorrow.

What a difference enthusiasm, attitude and concrete modeling made. There was no way they could not understand exactly what to do. I have learned a valuable lesson from all of this. I own more than half the problem with their lack of willingness to complete these tasks. I am glad Elaine was willing to share her expertise with me.

Weeks of 11/22 - 12/3

The class has been working on the revising stage of their papers for several days. The final stage of the process is the actual editing of the paper. The class was familiar with this technique, as we have been doing it since the beginning of the year, using a spelling sheet. Again, Elaine used her story on the chart paper to demonstrate the method she wanted the students to use. As I watched her, I realized how much of herself she had put into teaching the lesson. I somehow got the feeling I was watching a stage performance, in which she and the students had roles, while I was the audience. I began to wonder whether I could ever be this good.

Elaine also used some of the students' texts to provide examples of the editing skills she was demonstrating. We decided to have the students edit for each skill separately. At this time, they were to edit their own papers for punctuation, capital letters, paragraphing and finally misspellings.

During the editing time the room was very quiet. There was close attention to the details of their papers. The students' concentrated attention was obvious. Those who needed help waited patiently for someone to come to them. I was very pleased when Elaine told me that she thought the class was progressing extremely well and that they had been well-prepared. She suggested that I should look for the things that they can do rather than for the things that they cannot do.

"You're too hard on yourself," she said. "You don't give yourself enough credit for the things you do with them." This made me feel a little better, especially coming from someone that I respected and admired. Perhaps my original question ("Do I expect too much from myself and them as students so that I make it impossible for us to be successful?") is really the source of my problem. This is an area that I will have to do some readjusting in as the year progresses.

When the class was told to edit for misspelled words Elaine wanted them to read their papers backward, from the last sentence to the first sentence. This would make it easier for them to concentrate on each word. At first, they had a difficult time doing this, but as they struggled with the skill, it became easier for them. I asked some of the students to tell me how they felt about doing this. These are their comments:

- *Editing and spelling was fun. I liked reading backwards to find the misspelled words.*
- *I thought reading backwards would be hard, but it was fun and easy once I started.*

- *I was surprised at how easy it was to pick out the misspelled words.*
- *I thought that I didn't have any misspelled words because I'm a good speller, but I was surprised to find that I had many mistakes and some of the words are words I know how to spell.*

As the class continued to work you could feel the low degree of tension in the room. Children were helping one another and working independently as they never had before. I could tell by the manner in which they were working and seeking help that they were self-confident about their ability to complete the assignment. I noticed how much they had grown from the kinds of questions they were asking for help with. No longer were the questions "What do we write with?" but rather task-oriented questions about the kinds of words to use to describe details or the correct way to state something. Again, I attributed this success to Elaine's mannerisms and self-confident ways. This was a very good lesson on the power that unstated attitudes can have for students. Children are often more perceptive than adults give them credit for.

While the students were working I was able to make some observational notes about the class as a group. It is enough to state that during this period of time, from late October through the end of December, the class seemed to take a different attitude toward writing and learning in school in general. They became more independent and self-motivated. The level of self-confidence for completing assigned tasks has obviously increased.

The classroom atmosphere has become one of a quiet buzzing noise while children work cooperatively with each other. The level of frustration for both the children an the teacher has decreased and been replaced with a sense of cooperativeness among the members of the class.

Looking Backward

By the end of that fall term, Lauren had learned as much about herself as she did about her own students. Perhaps the most powerful lesson she learned was that the process of change — for teachers, as well as students — often demands a great deal of support and modeling. In one of her last journal entries, Lauren was able to reflect upon all of the changes she and her students had begun to make:

Change is not something that can happen overnight. It is a long and often painstaking process that a person is constantly searching through. In my particular case, the changes are happening in all areas of my life. At times, this leaves me with a feeling that I am not the person in control of what is happening. This feeling has caused me to lose the self-confidence I once had as a teacher and a capable person in general. Regaining or rebuilding that confidence has become for me a daily struggle.

Change always carries with it an element of risk. Sometimes that risk is very threatening. It is comfortable to remain with the familiar. However, never taking a risk results in not growing. The choice then becomes how much of a risk can you afford to take and still maintain your self-confidence. One of the most valuable lessons I have learned from Elaine is that enthusiasm is contagious. It is very hard to be negative and uninvolved when you are faced with someone who is excited about something. Some of that excitement gets transferred into the audience, no matter how resistant they are.

Another lesson I have learned is that knowledge develops self-confidence, and confidence empowers that knowledge for others.... This is true for adults as well as children. It's almost impossible to build self-confidence in others when you don't have it yourself. In my situation, I may have been forcing my students to be dependent on me for everything, without really knowing why I was doing this, because I was not developing their self-confidence. I was not able to model this attitude for them because I don't possess it myself. I observed for myself how differently they behaved when they interacted with a person full of self-confidence. For many children, school is the only place they can hope to develop confidence and positive attitudes about themselves.

Where do we go from here? I can't promise to become a positive person and self-confident, enthusiastic teacher tomorrow. However, I have gained much insight into the importance of these attitudes in the classroom. I do know that I need to develop more patience with the small gains that students make — to start focusing more on what they can accomplish rather than what areas they are lacking in.

The students have started word processing some of the stories we have written earlier. Many of them are finding this a challenging and rewarding experience. Others are totally frustrated by this. They, like I, find typing the most difficult of tasks. I have enlisted three parent volunteers to come in for forty minutes on three mornings to help these students while they are working at the computers. This will allow me time to conference and work with other students rather than stand by the computers to help students.

We have also made plans to team up with a first grade class in our school to do reading and writing projects together. One of the first projects in January will be a fable story. The fourth-graders will be reading a variety of fables to the first-graders. Then the first-graders, with the help of my class, will write and illustrate an original fable from a topic the students choose together. The fourth grade students will type the stories into the computers and print them. Together, they will illustrate them. We are hoping to have them bound into a book that can be used by future first grade children. Both Mrs. B. and I am excited about this joint project.

Change has affected every aspect of my life in the past three years, both personally and professionally. Some of these changes have been of a profound and irrevocable nature; others have been welcomed and embraced. In changing my teaching style and methods, I hope that I will be able to provide my students with an atmosphere in which they can grow and change to the best of their ability.

ès

Explorations

Perhaps you might want to reflect further about Lauren's story. You might already have a good idea about how to proceed. In case you are having trouble coming up with some ideas, though, here are some possibilities. Feel free to modify any of them to suit your time limits and your interests. For instance, you might want to write about them, talk about them with a partner, or split up the task in some way and discuss what you learned as a group. You can choose one option and stick with it, you can combine options, or you can create options of your own. These are just guidelines and suggestions, not rigid assignments.

1. **Associations and Explorations.** One possibility for capturing your moment-to-moment responses is to agree to stop every so often (for example, after each of Lauren's journal entries or after every few pages) and write down what you are thinking about. Pay attention to times when Lauren seems to be reaching a turning point in her thinking or teaching. What is happening at these moments? Can you tie Lauren's experiences back to anything you've read thus far?

   If you are reading this chapter along with a small group, you might want to take turns reading each journal entry. At the end of each entry, take a few minutes to capture your thinking, then talk with your group about what you wrote for a few minutes before moving on.

2. **Focused Reflections:** Another possibility is to decide to focus your writing on one of the dimensions of language and learning you've encountered in the preceding chapters. If you are working with a group, you could decide in advance which dimension each member will write about. Here are some more specific suggestions to jog your thinking processes.

   a. **Language Purposes**: Keep track of all the different purposes for which Lauren's students seem to be using language. For example, how often do you notice students writing and talking for personal, social, or artistic purposes, or for some combination of these? Do these purposes seem to change as Lauren changes her teaching ideas and activities? You might want to keep track of these different purposes on a chart or list as you read. When you've finished, take some time to write about what you have learned.

   b. **Learning Stances**: As you read through Lauren's story, try to identify writing assignments and activities that seemed to give her students difficulty. Reflect on what kinds of learning stances she was setting up in these assignments and why her students might have had some trouble adopting them. When, for instance, did she seem to set up a replicating, connecting, or extending stance, or some combination of these with a particular assignment? When you've finished, you might want to reflect on the specific things she did to help her students to write and think in ways that might have been difficult for them at first.

   c. **Language Outcomes.** Consider the outcomes and audiences that Lauren provided for her students' writing throughout that fall term. Did these outcomes change as time went on? Did her own roles as a reader and respondent to her students' writing seem to shift over time? Make a chart or list if this is helpful. Then take some time to reflect on what you've learned.

3. **Telling Your Own Story.** You might want to read Lauren's story in its entirety, without directing your thinking in any particular way. When you're through, consider an experience you had in your own or some other teacher's classroom that reminds you of Lauren's story in some way. Write about that experience in any form that's comfortable. If you are working with others, you might want to share what you wrote. When you are done, take a few more minutes to consider what you have just learned.

CHAPTER 6

Choice in the Learning Climate

John is a special education teacher. He teaches in an urban high school where there is a serious dropout problem. Several years ago his school decided to create a special classroom for at-risk students. His students are eighteen to twenty-one years old. Their reading and math levels range from second to sixth grade, and their school-assigned labels vary from "learning disabled" to "emotionally disturbed," "mildly mentally retarded," and "multiply handicapped."

In his first year of teaching, John used journals as a management technique. During the first ten minutes of every period, his students were required to write in their journals while he finished some classroom tasks. He recalls one morning early in his career:

The bell ending first period rang. I quickly packed my cart — first year special education teachers never get their own room — and pushed my way through the crowded hallways heading for the other wing of the school. With preparations for six different classes on my cart, I must have been pretty amusing as I darted in and out of traffic. The second bell rang just as I wheeled through the doorway. The students were spread about the room talking quietly.

"Okay, class, come up to the cart and take your writing journals back to your seat," I explained.

A loud moan resounded through the room.

"Just ten minutes of writing," I scowled. "Tell me anything, how you feel about your day, anything, I don't care."

"Do we have to do this again?" whined Melissa.

"I hate journals!" pronounced John as he had every other day since the beginning of the year.

"You only have to write for ten minutes, but I am not starting the clock until everyone has begun to write," I barked.

I sat down on my desk with my attendance cards feeling like I had just spent three minutes in the ring with Mike Tyson. Glancing around the room I noticed some kids actually writing. Sean loved to write and I enjoyed responding to him. Melissa was staring into space chewing on her pen. She was not into journal writing today. John sat in the back, defiant as ever, with his journal closed. I walked over and asked him to please start writing.

"I have nothing to say," he snapped.

"Tell me in your journal why it is you don't like to write," I urged. I would trick him into this. Finally, he opened his journal and took out a pen. The ten minutes, which seemed like two weeks, were finally up.

"Okay, class, time's up. Pens down, close your journals and return them to the cart," I directed.

We were ready to begin the day's lesson.

Later that night as I sat on my couch with Bob Marley on the stereo, I read and responded to the class journals. Sean wrote me a whole page on why he hated his brother. Melissa had written one sentence. It read, "Mr. C., these journals are fun, but not every day." Finally, I got to John's journal. I was really looking forward to reading it. I was expecting to read why it was he did not like to write. I opened to the day's entry. There in front of me lay a blank page with his first name printed in the upper right hand corner. That was all.

On the average each entry was about three lines long. Most were written without much feeling or commitment, which made it difficult for me to respond.

I scribbled in the last journal thinking to myself, "there must be a better way."

Choice and the Learning Climate

Some time after his experience with journals, John had the benefit of reflection. He saw that his instincts to use journals were well-intentioned. Unfortunately, he had used them for the wrong reasons and conveyed those wrong reasons to his students. He admitted:

My purpose for having the students write journals was so that I could have ten minutes at the beginning of class to take attendance, unpack my cart and organize my materials for the day's lesson. I knew that if I did not keep eighteen "behaviorally challenging" special education students busy at the beginning of class while I unpacked, things might get a little bit crazy. The students saw right through it. They knew it was busy work. Sadly, by using journals as a defense mechanism, I may have turned some students off to writing.

Ironically, John later realized that the impersonal nature of the task restricted his students' choices. Instead of setting himself up as an interested audience, he told his students that he didn't care what they wrote. This set up a climate of distance. As a result, John's students perceived journal writing as a closed assignment, written for a distant authority figure. He remembers,

I thought that I was creating an open assignment, I told them they could write about anything they wanted. Again, by saying I didn't care what they wrote, I closed down their choices considerably. They were not going to write anything personally meaningful to a person who didn't care what they wrote.

John's situation is not unique. As I look back on my own first attempts to use journals with my high school students, I can't help but remember feeling the same way. I, too, had used them without really knowing why. Each marking period, I dutifully assigned them, carted them home, wrote responses in the margins until sleep overtook me, and still failed to listen when so many of my students told me that they hated the experience.

Unfortunately, because I saw journals as just another classroom management technique rather than a tool that could be used for a variety of purposes, I cheated myself and my students out of some great opportunities to use writing in tentative, exploratory, and personal ways —as a gateway to learning. More than this, because many of my students saw journal writing as an activity without purpose, they failed to explore the creative choices for writing that lay before them.

I continue to meet teachers who are struggling with the same issue. Just recently I was talking with some student teachers in a weekly methods seminar. Margaret, one of the women in the group, had just finished her first week of student teaching. When she tried to introduce the idea of using a journal, one of her students moaned loudly, "Why do student teachers always make us write in journals?" She had been hoping to introduce her students to an innovative way to use writing, and her students had treated the idea as just more busy work.

Sadly, the use of journals has been so badly abused by well-meaning teachers that some students learn to detest it. Someone in the seminar that night suggested that there should be a "journal abuse hotline" where adults would be required by law to report incidents where students were being forced to share intimate secrets from their journals or, worse yet, to submit to someone's red pencilling them for grammar and punctuation errors!

Certainly one reason why some students hate journals is that they don't feel they have choices in how, when, or whether their journals will be used. It's easy to assume that all students will be motivated somehow, as if by magic, to embrace our goals, our purposes, and our timelines. This, as John and Margaret discovered, is not always likely.

There have been many persuasive arguments by people such as Don Graves, Nancie Atwell, and Lucy Calkins that students should have choices about what to write and read. Topic and text choice are not the only issues. Beyond choices about what they read and write, students could have choices about the outcomes and purposes for their language, the kinds of learning stances they adopted, when and how they spoke, wrote, read, or listened — even choices about whether they participated in these classroom experiences at all. The options for providing or closing down choice in our classrooms are almost limitless. We need to give the responsibility for learning back to our students while we are providing comfortable structures within which to exercise that responsibility.

Reflections: Choice

At this point, I'd like to ask you to look more closely at the issue of choice in the learning climate. Try to remember a lesson you might have taught recently or a lesson in someone else's classroom. This should be an experience that is recent enough so that you can remember most of the events as they occurred. If you have your plan book, you might use it to jog your memory, or perhaps you have a "teaching tale" that you've already written. In any case, take a few minutes and list every event that you can remember in the course of this lesson. Be specific. No detail is unimportant. Even details like "I took roll" and "Students straggled into class" should be included.

As soon as you feel that you have exhausted your memory, go back and make another list of all of the choices you, or your teacher made, that ultimately influenced student choices in some way. This list might include items such as "Evaluation: Every paper was responded to and graded" or "Seating arrangement: Desks were placed in rows."

Compare your list with this list that was generated by the group of student teachers in Margaret's seminar (see figure 6.1).

Choices about Choice

Here are some areas where student choices can be opened up or restricted:

Topics
- self-selected
- loosely controlled (menus of options)
- teacher-directed

Classroom Procedures:
- independent work stations
- learning centers
- whole class activities
- conferring
- language workshop

Techniques:
- individualized reading and writing
- group activities
- partnered activities

Forms:

letters	diaries	charts	speeches
essays	reports	graphs	debates
stories	lists	drawings	dramatics

Response:
- peer groups
- external response (from adults or peers outside the classroom)
- teacher response

Grading and Evaluation Systems:
- self-evaluation
- contract grading (negotiated grading)
- individualized goal setting
- teacher-directed
- point systems

Figure 6.1

As this list reveals, practically every moment in your classroom you will find yourself making choices that affect your students' learning. One rule of thumb might guide you as you make those decisions: "Whenever you close something down, open something else up." Through the years, I've found this to be a pretty useful idea.

Creating a Climate for Choice

Nancie Atwell recalls the days before she allowed her students choices about their writing:

> I assigned topics because I believed most of my students wouldn't write well without them. I assigned topics because I believed my structures and strictures were necessary for kids to write well. I assigned topics, when it came right down to it, because I believed my ideas to be more valuable than any my students might possibly entertain. So decreeing topics wasn't just a philosophical issue; it was political, too. Writing well became a matter of writing appropriately and convincingly about my ideas, and I chalked up ineffective or perfunctory responses to low ability or effort (1987, p. 178).

Discovering how to nurture and encourage responsible choice-making in our classroom is not always an easy task, and yet it is essential. Most of us were probably good students, but we didn't become that way through tight and total adult control. As young children, we were probably given a lot of room to make mistakes. Parents praised us for our scrawls and scribbles, our childish attempts at words. Gradually though, by the time we reached middle school or high school, we probably learned some painful lessons about the penalties of being too different from "the norm."

It shouldn't be surprising, then, when our students come to us asking for specific guidelines and wanting to know in clear terms what constitutes the "correct response" in our classroom. We struggle against these requests, especially since we know that taking too much control over our students' learning keeps them from grappling with the very concepts they need to learn. As Donald Murray (1985) argues:

> When we give an assignment we cheat the students of experience with much of the writing process. They are not trained in awareness and in limiting and focusing their subject. We, the instructors, do much of the work for the students — and that is why so many students prefer to have specific assignments. They want us to hold up the hoops so they can jump (p. 100).

Rigid standardized testing systems are also part of the problem. Statewide and schoolwide competency examinations are built on the notion of certain normative skills that all students should be able to master at particular grade levels. We can give our students choices about what to read, write, or talk about in our daily lessons, but at some point many of them will be expected to take standardized competency tests. We live with a gnawing fear that our students will not be able to master the standard competencies required of EVERYSTUDENT. We worry about what might happen if we don't bring them up to the same standard or evaluate them on the same assignment.

Ironically, the result is that sometimes, like our students, we become uneasy when we are confronted with the idea of giving too much choice. We shouldn't be surprised, then, when our students seem convinced that they have nothing special to say and look for us to choose the topics and substance of their learning. Donald Graves calls the lack of topic choice "writer's welfare" (1983, p. 98) and argues that most students lose their ability to choose topics by the time they reach seventh grade. They become unable "to put their voices on the line" (1983, p. 98).

However, opening choice doesn't mean abandoning structure. Everyone needs some structure to learn, even if that structure only involves a set of classroom procedures within which to make creative choices. The trick is in providing only those structures that are necessary for student learning, then removing them when they are no longer needed.

Choice, Ownership, and Motivation

It seems logical that when students are given the opportunity to take ownership of their work and to exercise choices they will be more engaged and motivated to learn. Students who take ownership of their work tend to stick with tasks for longer periods of time and to learn more from those tasks. Unfortunately, providing students with ownership opportunities is not enough. How many of us have given our students total choice over an assignment only to be met with moans of protest and demands for strict assignments and grading policies? Some students don't feel capable of taking ownership because they don't see themselves as being competent and in control of their learning.

Much useful work in the area of "instructional scaffolding" (Applebee & Langer, 1983; Spaulding, 1989) supports the notion that what children can learn on their own is only a small part of what they might learn with the guidance and support of a trusted adult. Helping our students to discover things to write, read, and talk about is not as easy as it sounds. For one thing, we are so often the classroom expert. Our students begin from a defensive position, proving to us that they have learned what we already know. Seldom are they able to teach us anything. Yet, every student can be an expert about something, even if it is only her or his experience.

Further Reflection: Pen Pals

For some writers, the hardest part about writing is choosing one topic from a seemingly endless array of possible choices; for others, it's believing they have anything valuable to say at all. Here's an idea that you might like to try, as a way of loosening up your writer's block and discovering some possible topics to write about. For this particular experience, you'll need a partner. If you aren't reading this book as a part of a workshop or class, maybe your spouse or a friend would be willing to do this with you. Or perhaps you'd like to simply read over this idea, considering how it might be adapted for your own classroom.

Topic Exploration.

Begin by taking out a sheet of paper and privately brainstorming a list of everything you feel that you know anything about. Your list might include everything from "how to buy a used car" to "how to plant an herb garden." At this point it doesn't matter whether anyone else will be interested in your ideas or whether you feel that they are creative or unique. The main thing is to find some topics that you feel comfortable writing about.

Now, exchange lists with your partner. As you read your partner's list, try to find that one topic that seems to call out to you the most. Circle this topic and write a note to your "pen pal," explaining why you chose this topic, why it was particularly appealing, and what questions or issues you would like your partner to address. As you write this note, remember that you are not only asking for what you would like to know more about; you are also inviting your partner to write. Your note should be as friendly and encouraging as possible.

Drafting.

As soon as you have exchanged notes and have read what your partner has to say, begin drafting your piece. Feel free to use any form that suits you: a letter, an essay, a poem, or a magazine article. When each of you is done, exchange papers again or take turns reading your texts aloud to each other.

> *Reflecting.*
> 	Now, look back and reflect for a moment on this process of writing. Did you notice that, at some point, you felt compelled to write? You might have lost track of time, or you might not have wanted to stop when your partner was done. If so, what made you feel this way? Were you particularly proud of what you wrote? What made you feel this way? Finally, did you notice that, once you started writing, you knew even more than you thought you did about your topic? What do you think contributed to your feelings of expertness?

I've used this particular writing experience with many groups of people, from secondary and elementary teachers to high school and middle school students, and I find that it's usually pretty successful. Often, I vary it a bit, depending upon the situation I'm in. If I'm working with a group of twenty or thirty people in a one-day workshop, I often ask them to place a pen name, rather than their real name, at the top of their paper. This way, everyone can write without being overly conscious of audience at this early stage of the writing. The anonymity usually helps people to loosen up without worrying about audience too much. Then, I collect and distribute the lists, making sure that no one has his or her own. It's not until later that "pen pals" are revealed to each other. This usually adds one more dimension of intrigue to the experience.

One thing I have noticed is how engaged writers become as they begin crafting their pieces. It usually takes only a few minutes before everyone seems to be drawn into the drafting process. The room becomes whisper quiet, except for the sound of pens moving across paper. It's always a treat to watch people's faces as they read their "mail." If there is time, partners can volunteer each other to read pieces that were particularly intriguing, informative, or funny. Everyone's genuine interest and enjoyment makes this writing experience particularly fun. Best of all, everyone usually feels a bit more like an expert in the process.

I think what makes this particular activity appealing is that participants are gently led and not thrown into the process of topic choice. If I had simply said "write about any topic you like" (often a grave mistake, especially on a first meeting, when group members don't know each other), some people may have felt completely comfortable, but others would have been panic stricken. Giving everyone the opportunity to brainstorm a bit about things they know and then making sure they are invited to write about a topic is a way of creating a comfortable structure within which they can feel free to make choices.

Closing Down and Opening Up

There is probably not a single one of us who, upon looking closely and honestly at our curriculum, won't find occasions for opening up choices and allowing students to arrive at their own topics, outcomes, purposes, and learning stances. At the same time, there are some occasions where we need to close down choice. We may wish our students to focus on the Viet Nam war, the growth of cells, or the hazards of toxic waste. The important thing to keep in mind is that as we close down topics, there are still many ways to open up choice. Is it important, for instance, for everyone to write within the same form? Are deadlines and evaluation systems somewhat flexible? Is there a great deal of latitude for creativity within one general topic, or do students need to stay within strict guidelines?

There are also times when we must close down form. Perhaps we are teaching students to write an academic paper, how to pass a writing competency examination, to write a letter of application for a job, or to give a constructive speech in a formal debate. At these times we can open up the topic and outcome, asking students to find real reasons to use these language forms. We can also offer choices about the processes students can use to experiment with these language forms. Students can engage in peer and teacher-pupil conferencing, make multiple drafts, and select their best pieces for grading. The choices for opening up choice seem almost limitless.

Modeling Choice

If we are serious about wanting students to make their own choices, we must sometimes provide models and procedures for them. In my early years as a high school teacher, I was somewhat disappointed by the lack of investment and ownership I saw in some student papers. I wondered if I was too restrictive in the choices I gave them for what to write about. One day I went to a restaurant that was famous for its hamburgers. The menu included everything from the "California Burger" (with a whole wheat bun and sprouts) to the "Tex Mex Burger" (with guacamole and salsa). At the bottom of the list was the "Name Your Own Burger"—an option that was limited only by your imagination and your pocketbook!

When I got back to school on Monday, I decided to offer the "Name Your Own Burger" option to my students the next time I made an assignment. Their choices still had to be negotiated with me. In fact, I require my students to explain, in writing, their alternative version of the assignment and discuss it with me before proceeding. But opening up choices in this way generally helps those students who are self-motivated or who find it hard to get interested in someone else's topic.

As another way of modeling choice, I often hand out a menu of options for responding to class readings, for instance. Sometimes I'll ask that people try at least four or five different options before deciding on their preferred form of response. After I've been able to model several possibilities or ways of reading, writing, and talking over the course of several weeks, I can fade back my assistance and trust that people will come up with their own useful ways of using language to enrich their learning.

For example, Carol is a ninth grade English teacher who has been conducting a reading and writing workshop with her students. As an alternative to the traditional book report, she designed this list of options (see figure 6.2). Her students keep their written responses in a notebook. From time to time, Carol corresponds or confers with them about their writing.

**Writing Options for Independent Reading Period
English 9**

For each of the books that you read in our independent reading period, you must select one writing activity. You always have the opportunity to create your own activity if you do not wish to use one of the choices below. If you are creating your own activity, please let me know.

Option 1: *Reading Log.* As you read your book, you may wish to record your questions and reactions to the reading as you go along. Simply jot down your questions, hunches and reactions as you read. You would need to stop periodically during your reading and record your reactions.

Option 2: *Diary or Journal.* As you read your book, imagine that you are one of the characters and keep a diary or journal from their point of view. Within the diary or journal, you could write in various forms—freewrite, write a poem, record a letter you "received" or "sent," record how you feel about what is happening, etc.

Option 3: *Adding New Events.* Perhaps you would like to change or add an event to the novel that you read. You may alter the characters or events in any way that you wish. Use your imagination. Use any form you find comfortable and create additional or altered scenes/events.

Option 4: *Create a New Ending.* Maybe you didn't like the ending of a book. If you didn't, change it and write a new ending for the book/novel.

Option 5: *Editorial.* Write an editorial/opinion piece dealing with a subject that your novel addresses. Example: The novel, *The Outsiders* deals with the issue of teenage violence and fighting. You could write about *your* feelings on the subject.

Option 6: *Letters* If you would like, you could pretend you are a character and write five letters from the character's point of view. These letters could be to different characters or just one character.

Option 7: *Newspaper Articles.* If you like to do research or read the newspaper, you could collect articles that relate to the novel/book that you are reading. You could then write a brief summary of the articles that you have read and collected. Example: Many novels written for young adult readers deal with the issue of alcohol/drug abuse. You could collect newspaper/magazine articles dealing with this issue and write a summary of the information discussed in the articles.

Figure 6.2

Modeling choices for writing about reading in this way provides some structure for shy or reluctant students, while it allows more confident students to venture away from the teacher's choices and to create their own options for learning.

Simply offering choices may not even be enough. Sometimes it's necessary to bring in examples of alternative assignments and projects that were created by former students as a way of getting our students to believe we're really serious. The idea is to provide flexible structures within which our students can make creative choices. In the next few pages, we'll see how two teachers do just that.

Classroom Closeup: Language for Learning in Mathematics

I must admit that I am probably one of those adults who falls into the category of "math-o-phobe." When I was in high school, it seemed that my math teachers were more concerned with the answers on my paper than they were with the problem solving strategies in my head. I might have demonstrated many skills in solving a problem, but for some reason I usually stopped just short of the correct answer. I wasn't exactly a traditional math learner, either; in geometry I was always one of those students who took twenty-three steps to arrive at a proof that other students could arrive at in five!

Today, I'm pleased to see so many math teachers giving their students the opportunity to make choices about they way they approach mathematical problems and concepts. In moving away from the one-correct-answer mentality, they help their students to discover a wealth of strategies and skills. Best of all, their students are learning from each other, and not just from their teacher or textbook.

Joan, for instance, teaches sixth grade mathematics in a suburban middle school. Although she was an education major in graduate school, she minored in English and math as an undergraduate. Her philosophy of education centers around exploratory language and student-centered learning experiences. In her words, "You don't simply teach students how to do percentages. You say to them: 'We're going to provide you with tons of experiences, then you're going to figure out how to do percentages yourself!'"

Joan began using writing as a tool for learning math in her classroom twenty years ago. She recalls,

I began by saying to my students, "every time you do a word problem, you have to write your answer in a sentence. When you write your answer out this way, I'll be able to see if your way of solving the problem makes sense."

Joan's friend Fran teaches seventh grade mathematics in another wing of the school. She has taught on the middle school level for the past three years, and for seven years on the high school level before that. Since they rarely teach the same students, Joan and Fran meet routinely to share materials and ideas. For some time now, students in their classes have been experimenting with tentative, exploratory writing and oral language experiences that help them to grasp complex mathematical concepts.

One day Joan and Fran introduced me to the curriculum and evaluation standards for school mathematics published by the National Council of Teachers of Mathematics (1991). Drafted in 1986 by the NCTM Commission on Standards for School Mathematics, the standards are based upon an interdisciplinary approach to mathematical problem solving that makes frequent use of collaborative, exploratory learning experiences, based on real world problems. Similar to many whole language or process centered approaches to language learning, the view espoused by the NCTM is that students learn mathematical strategies and skills not through drill and practice but through the opportunity to wrestle with authentic problems. Furthermore, the commission argues:

> [A]lthough it is often necessary to teach specific concepts and procedures, mathematics must be approached as a whole. Concepts, procedures, and intellectual processes are interrelated. In a significant sense, "the whole is greater than the sum of its parts" (NMSA, 1991, p. 11).

In contrast to the rather rigid view of mathematics that many of my high school teachers seemed to espouse, the Commission argues for giving students exposure to:

> problems with "messy" numbers or too much or not enough information or that have multiple solutions, each with different consequences [that] will better prepare them to solve problems that they are likely to encounter in their daily lives" (NMSA, 1991, p. 76).

As you will see, within the comfortable structures and routines that Joan and Fran provide, their students are able to make many choices about how to solve mathematical problems in the real world. In comparing the different ways that students go about solving problems, their teachers learn a great many things about their learning processes.

Writing to Learn: The Mathematics Notebook

Students in both Joan's and Fran's classes keep a record of their learning in spiral notebooks. Routinely, students are asked to write out their own solutions to problems, which they compare with the solutions of their classmates. In keeping with the NMSA recommendations, Joan and Fran believe that "[s]tudents should be encouraged to explain their reasoning in their own words. Listening to their peers and their teacher describe other strategies helps students refine their thoughts and the language they use to express their thoughts" (NMSA, 1991, p. 82).

For example, Joan has been teaching percentages in her class. On one particular day she handed out the following chart, adapted from an idea by Marilyn Burns and Cathy Humphreys (see Burns and McLaughlin, 1990, p. 149):

50% of $600	$300
25% of $600	$150
10% of $600	$60
5% of $600	_____
1% of $600	$6

After explaining the chart, Joan asked her students to compute the answer to item four ("What is 5 percent of $600?") and to write out their procedure for finding the answer. Their writing reveals a rich array of inventive techniques. Unlike traditional one-correct-answer mathematics assignments, writing in the notebook is an opportunity for Joan's students to make individual choices about the best way to solve problems.

Kevin, for example, has not been as academically successful as some of Joan's other students. Yet the writing in his notebook demonstrates a fairly sophisticated strategy for solving the percentage problem. He writes: "*5% of 600 = 30[.] I got that because for every 100 dollars you would count 5%.*" Impressed by Kevin's strategy, Joan remarks, "Kevin probably would have had trouble passing the writing test. Keeping a notebook like this is a wonderful reminder to students that everybody thinks differently."

Notice, for instance, the varied approaches that Joan's students bring to the same problem.

* Ned says: "Find 5% of 100, which is 20, then you divide 600 by 20 and get 30."

* Ilyana, a student who came from the former Soviet Union, begins by figuring out what the word "percentage" means and using this definition in formulating her answer: "Because % means 'out of 100' 5% of $100 is $5 so I multiplied $5 by 6, because we need to find 5% of 600 (6 hundred). 5 X 6 = 30."

* We can almost overhear Maddy thinking aloud to herself in the exploratory, conversational tones of this response: "To get 5% of $600 I said, 'OK. Well if 10% is $60 then 5% has to be half of $60 because 5 is half of 10. Therefore it would be $30.00.' "

* Paul and Larry word their answer differently, but use roughly the same strategy: [Larry] "I got the answer of $30 by just splitting $60 in half because 5% is half of 10% so $30 is half of $60." [Paul]: "After I found 10% I knew 5% was half of what I had for 10%."

Joan continues to marvel at the diversity of strategies revealed in her students' writing. Often, as students are reading their responses, Joan transcribes them on the board, pointing out similarities and differences. She explains,

> *We might begin by listening to two or three students who have the same strategy, expressed differently, then move on to some that have different strategies. That makes students aware of the variety of strategies available to them.*

In addition to writing down their problem-solving strategies, Joan's students also take turns being "class scribe." She explains:

> *They miss class because they're absent to go to music lessons, to see their counselor, and so forth. To help all these students find out what they missed, we have a scribe each day in each class. The scribe writes the notes from class, the homework assignment, names of absent students, and information about upcoming tests on a scribe sheet. My students have a study hall at the end of the day. Students who missed class come to my room. First they read the scribe book and then see me if they have questions or need help.*

Informal writing and reading allows students to capture their thinking processes on paper and to share them with others. More than this, it allows students choices and the room to experiment within their different ways of learning.

Writing to Explain: Instructions

For the past few days in Fran's class, students have been writing out instructions for how to use a protractor. It's an idea she borrowed from Marilyn Burns and Cathy Humphreys (See Burns and McLaughlin, 1990). She plans to share her students' instruction sheets with a fifth grade class in the same school. Fran's students were very enthusiastic about acting in the role of expert with the fifth grade students. She recalls:

They started asking, "What kind of words would the fifth grade students know?" As we thought about this question, we put a list of words on the board. They wondered, for example, if the fifth graders would know what an "acute angle" or a "vertex" was. Making this list helped them to jog their memories about important terms and concepts.

For this particular activity, Fran's students worked in groups, drafting their tentative ideas before putting them in final form. As students handed in their drafts, Fran didn't make grammatical or form-centered comments but focused instead on the ideas they were trying to get across.

Several of the students chose to combine drawings with verbal explanations. For instance, in their direction, Matthew and Andy begin by defining some terms (i.e., "vertex," "ray," "obtuse, reflex, acute angle," etc.) through visual diagrams. Then, in writing, they describe how to form a 49 degree angle using the protractor (see figure 6.3).

Choice and the Learning Climate

Using a Protractor: Andy and Matthew

House 3

math, 4
May 2, 1991

How to measure Angles

1) First, when drawing angles you have to know some ~~terms~~ terms Now True!

   [diagram: ray, vertex, ray — obtuse angle, acute angle, reflex angle, 180° straight line]

2) When measuring angles you have to put the line that is in the middle of the protractor right on the vertex of the angle.

   [diagram of angle with ray, vertex, ray]

   the point that you are measuring is this

You are off to a good start!

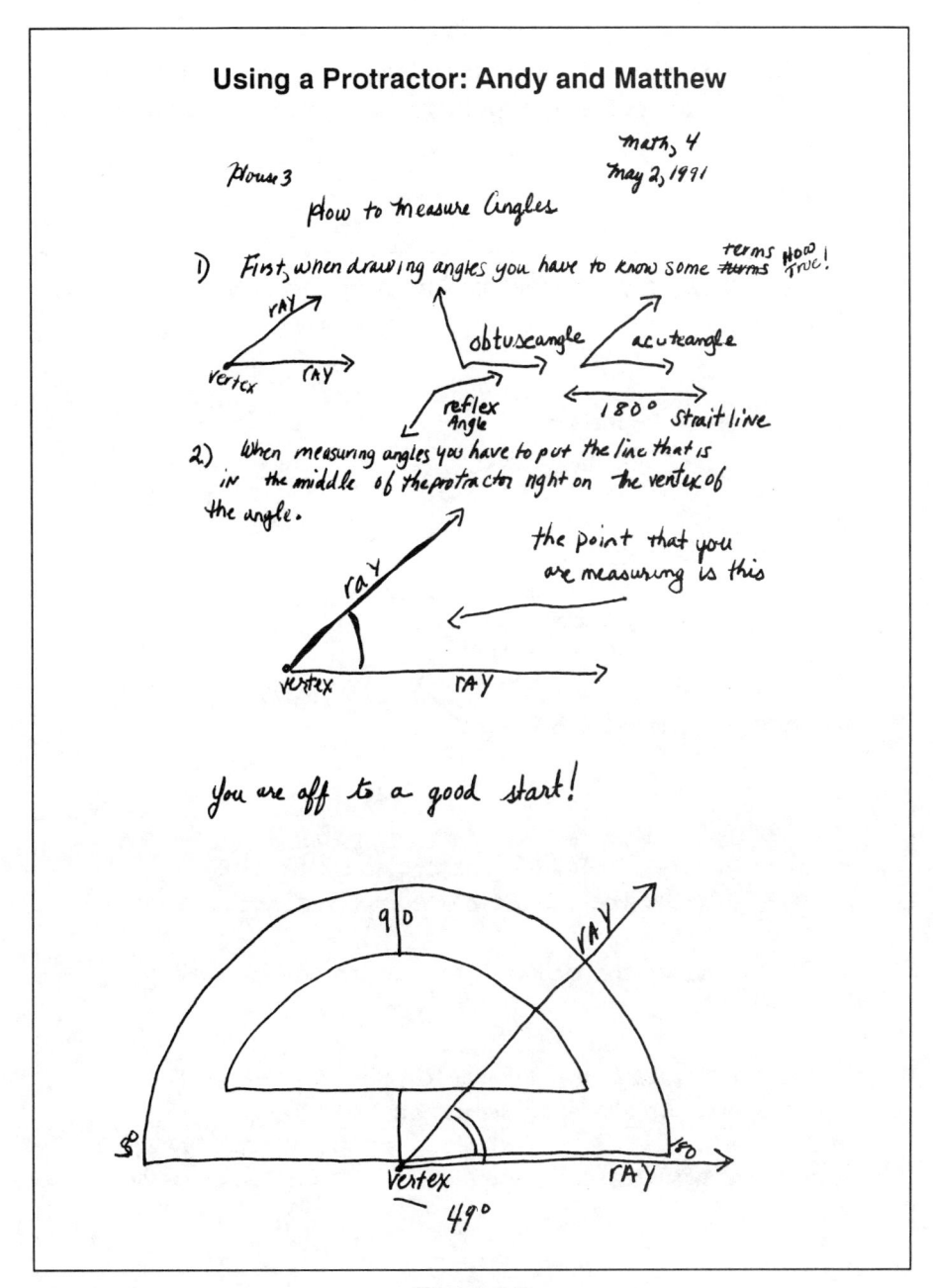

[diagram of protractor showing 90, ray, vertex, ray, 49°]

Figure 6.3

In her comments to them, Fran tells Andy and Matthew that they are "off to a good start." After conferring again with each other and with Fran, they will revise their instructions, adding essential information and detail to their drawings and explanations.

Ann and Zachary take a slightly different approach. They begin by defining the three points of an angle (c, b, a), then explaining how each point coincides with a particular point on the protractor (see figure 6.4).

Using a Protractor: Ann and Zachary

How to use a Protractor

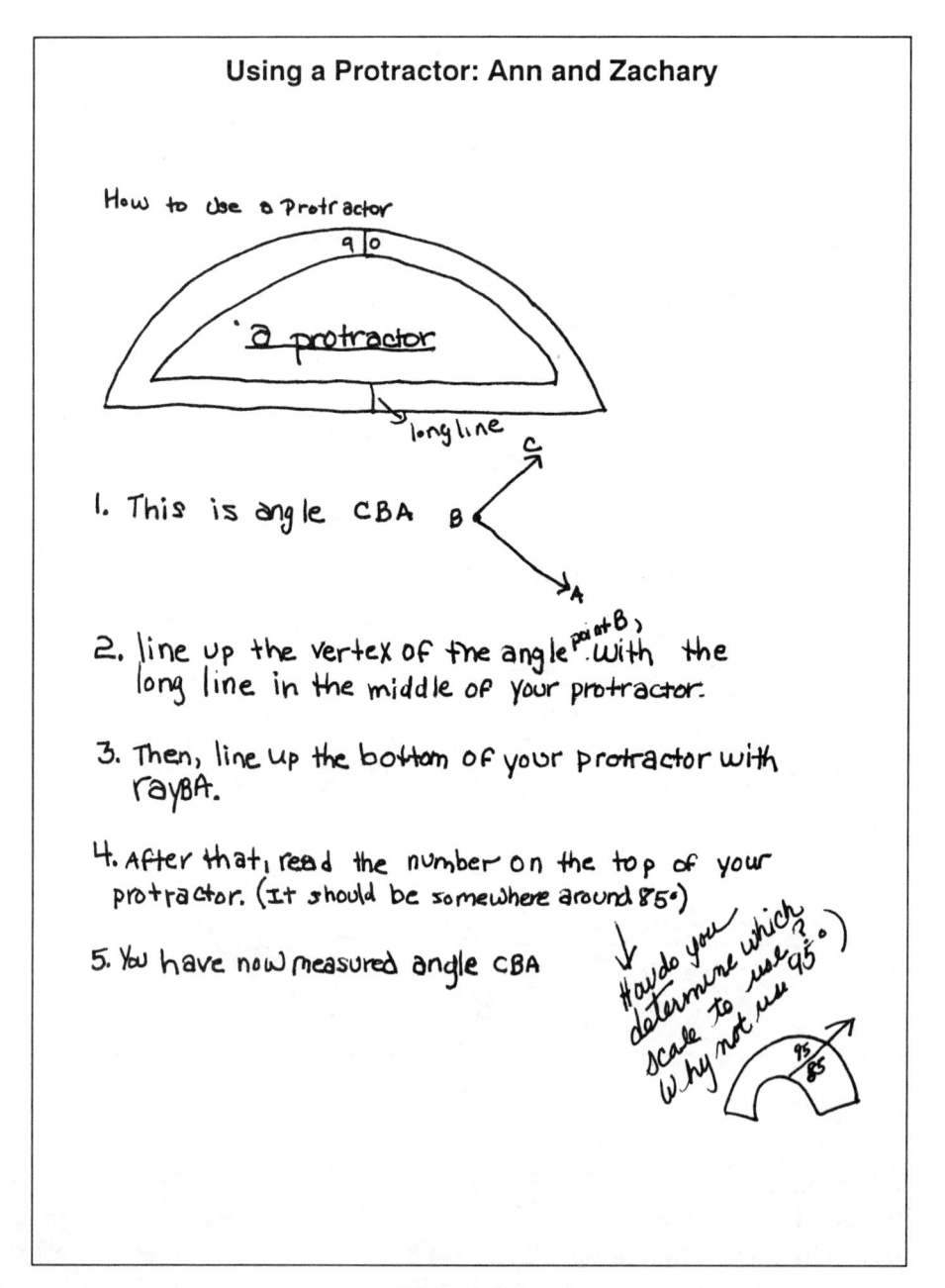

a protractor

long line

1. This is angle CBA

2. line up the vertex of the angle (point B) with the long line in the middle of your protractor.

3. Then, line up the bottom of your protractor with ray BA.

4. After that, read the number on the top of your protractor. (It should be somewhere around 85°)

5. You have now measured angle CBA

How do you determine which scale to use 95° Why not use 95°

Figure 6.4

As Fran points out, Ann and Zachary still need to explain which scale on the protractor to use, depending upon whether their angle is acute or obtuse. They will also need to define some terms such as "ray" and "vertex." Asking them to draft and revise directions in this way gives Fran a window on their thinking processes. Knowing that their texts will be used by a real group of fifth graders keeps them thinking about what terms will be unfamiliar and what parts of their directions may be vague or unclear. This process allows the students to make some potentially difficult concepts more permanent. It also allows them to take control of their own learning rather than being dependent on their teacher.

Drafting instructions in this way helps Fran's students to learn something about language and math at the same time. As they begin to define mathematical terms for other students, they grapple with important vocabulary in a way that makes these terms more significant, meaningful, and lasting. Joan explains that:

We make a big distinction between "kid talk," "teacher talk," and "math talk." We tell them that when they are writing privately in their notebooks, it is all right to use "kid talk," but if they are writing to someone else, they have to use "math talk."

Students regularly keep a glossary of mathematical terms as a part of their notebook. Sometimes they copy definitions from the board or the back of the textbook, but at other times they write down definitions in their own words. "Every time they choose a word to define a concept," Fran observes, "they're grappling with what it is and isn't." In this choice-making process, they develop and discover what they know.

Writing Imaginatively: Story Problems

To get her students writing, thinking about, and exploring different approaches to math concepts, Joan has adapted an idea from *The Mathematics Teacher* (Erickson, 1990). She hands out the first line of a story about Aunt Gloria, a woman who comes to visit with three plum cakes for a dinner with nine people. From this simple beginning, Joan asks her students to make up three story problems using percentages and to write the correct answers on the back of their paper. She explains, "They had to start with the basic information in the first sentence. Beyond that, they could add any information or ask any questions that they wanted to in writing their own story problems." Her students then exchange their story problems with a partner, work out the answer, and write comments to their partner about any problems or difficulties they had in solving or understanding the problems.

Dennis's story problem reveals not only an understanding of percentages but a flair for narrative as well. Notice how he includes some distracting information about the number of people in the Smith family as a way of complicating the solution to his problem:

As Aunt Gloria came through the front door she tripped over the threshold and dropped a pie on Uncle Fred's head. He was so embarrest that he left. Not a moment later the Smith family came to the door with 6 pies, enough so that each member of the family could get their own pie. If the Smith family together, eats 7 pies What percent of the total pies did they eat?

Craig borrows a bit of tabloid gossip in his tale about Roseanne Barr (now Arnold) and her husband:

At a party Roseanne Barr and her husband were at they were serving 3 plum cakes for desert. Rosanne and her husband were currently on nutrisystem so they wouldn't have any cake. There were 9 people at the party including them. What percent of the cakes would each person get if they divided them equally?

The familiar language of narrative allows many students who might have difficulty with abstract numerical concepts to understand and grapple with them in an enjoyable, non-threatening way. Students like Kevin, who are more comfortable with words than numbers, are allowed to bring their own personal talents and learning styles to the activity. Writing story problems is an experience that Joan and Fran provide not only for groups of advanced students like Craig and Dennis but for more typical students as well. She observes: "The writing mirrors the students' abilities. The more tentative the student, the more tentative the problem. The more creative the student, the more creative the problem." Regardless of ability, students of all ages can benefit from learning abstract concepts through writing.

Mathematics Beyond the Classroom

Over the years, Joan has developed several ways for her students to write about and use mathematical concepts, even when they are away from school. For example, before students go off for vacation, Joan asks them to collect brochures from the area they visit, as well as a map and a newspaper article about something of local interest. Students then write five story problems, using some of the information from the materials they have collected. In Joan's view, "It doesn't make sense to give them math worksheets or problems from the book. This way they are working on math that is related to their trip."

Finally, students keep a journal of their vacation, recording important events as well as money they spent each day. When students travel to foreign countries, Joan gives them five dollars, asks them to bring her back something she could not buy in the United States, to return the change in foreign currency, and to figure out how much the item cost and what the equivalent amount of change would be in United States currency.

Maryann and her family, for instance, traveled to Sea World in Florida over spring break. In her daily journal, she records the major events of her family's trip. For example, on day two, she writes:

> *This morning we got up at 2:08 a.m. Around 2:30 a.m. we left for SEAWORLD. It was a three hour ride but it went by pretty quick. When we first got there we saw the fish and flamingos. The fish were huge!! Then we saw the sea otters. They were funny! At 10:00 we saw the whale and dolphin show. It was fabulos! We also saw the Shamu show, the ski show and the sea otter shows. They were good too. At around 4:30 we left. On the way home we ate at Sbbaros. I had pizza. We arrived home at 7:45. It was a fun day!*

She also keeps a record of her finances — what was purchased, on what date, and by whom (see figure 6.5).

Maryann's Spending Record

Money I or someone else spent

Date	Amount	what bought	who bought it
3/20/91	$ 3.00	magnet	sister
3/21/91	50 c	postcards (2)	me
3/22/91	$ 5.00	necklace	dad
3/22/91	$ 8.00	2 stuff animals	dad
3/23/91	$13.00	shirt	grandpa
3/23/91	$10.00	shoes	grandpa
3/23/91	$ 2.00	earings	me
3/23/91	$ 2.00	bracelets	me
3/23/91	50 c	2 postcards	me
3/23/91	39 c	lollipop	me

Figure 6.5

Finally, Joan requires her to create five story problems from real experiences on the trip. One of Maryann's story problems deals with the cost of airfare (see figure 6.6)

Maryann's Story Problem

q: It cost $245.00 for each person in my family to fly down to Florida. There are 5 people in my family How much money was it to fly my family down.

a: <u>1,225.00</u>

$$\begin{array}{r} 245.00 \\ \times\ 5 \\ \hline \$1{,}225.00 \end{array}$$

Figure 6.6

During school vacations, Joan asks students to send postcards, which they can buy or make, regardless of whether or not they traveled out of town. Their colorful cards are posted on the bulletin board along the sides of the room. "Whenever there's a spare moment," Joan muses, "they're over here reading each other's cards and seeing where their classmates went."

There is nothing unstructured about the ways in which Joan and Fran use the math notebook in their classes. Students work within a predictable framework to create their own approaches to abstract concepts. They make a variety of choices within this framework — choices about language as well as problem-solving strategies. Most importantly, they learn to take charge of their own learning, with the guidance and support of trusted adults.

Classroom Connections

It goes without saying that the school day is very hectic. By some estimates, teachers make thousands of unconscious decisions each day. It's easy for all of us to proceed rather unreflectively, limiting student choice for no good reason. The payoff for opening up student choice is in creating a place where all students can become more invested and motivated to learn through language. Perhaps an obvious starting point is to look back over some of the assignments and activities we have provided, questioning the amount of choice we give our students and revising any assignments that unreflectively restrict student choice. Here are some possibilities.

Becoming aware.

One good place to begin is to look back on a lesson you have recently taught or look ahead to some lesson you are planning, with the aim of becoming more aware of all the choices available in your classroom. You might want to consider, for instance, whether students might have choices about topics, about the location of their learning (i.e., in the library, on the floor of the classroom), the people with whom they will work, whether and how they will be graded, their deadlines, and so forth. The point of all this is not to promote classroom anarchy but to become more acutely aware of all the ways in which you make decisions about student choice.

Most times, when I reconsider my teaching in this way, I realize there are occasions when I have restricted choice for no good reason. Sometimes it is really necessary to limit student choice. Becoming more reflective about our decisions doesn't mean abdicating classroom control; it means being more accountable, exploring the reasons behind our decisions to restrict or open up student choice.

Opening the Options.

Once you have looked carefully at the choices available in your classroom, you might want to try deciding how you can offer more choices the next time around. There are so many ways to reconsider what you do. If you use journals, you might ask how much choice your students have about the substance and form of their writing. If it's important to restrict choice to a general topic area, you might consider ways of opening up other choices. For example, in social studies, students might write about a general topic like the Revolutionary War in a variety of ways: imaginatively, by writing journals and letters kept by American soldiers; critically, comparing political conditions in revolutionary times with the political situation in America today; or analytically, keeping a record of important issues and questions.

You might ask yourself whether all students need to read the same texts and write on the same topics. Begin to question some of your taken-for-granted assumptions. Can students choose which pieces in their writing folder can be evaluated, which audiences to write for, which pieces will be carefully revised, and which forms are most appropriate for each writing task?

If your curriculum dictates that students must master certain language forms, such as the business letter and the personal narrative, is it possible to make these restrictions known to students and allow them the personal freedom to choose when and how they will write in each form? On the other hand, if some students are paralyzed by choice, is it possible to provide some rough scaffolding, such as a list of options, for those who need more teacher guidance? More importantly, are you able to take that instructional scaffolding away once your students demonstrate that they no longer need it?

Frightening Freedom

For many of our students, as for us, choice carries a certain degree of risk. In her work as a high school English teacher, Catherine has tried to remember the importance of nurturing in all children the dignity of choice and the integrity of personal preference, and yet, as both teacher and parent, she often worries about the cost of offering her children too many choices in world that is often harsh and unforgiving. In her journal one day, she reflected:

> *"Lady Lovelylocks"*
>
> *Sam looks like any other seven year old boy — missing teeth, messy hair, many bruises, but a look at his expressed preferences in "action figures" is revealing. I knew trouble was heading my way when I picked Sam up from preschool one day around the holidays. A big wish list of all the kids' Christmas desirables was posted on the wall. Looked okay to me. Some of the staff, though, felt compelled to tell me that Sam had occasioned much laughter when he expressed his request. After all the other boys had mentioned trucks, gun belts and Corvettes, Sam had piped up: Lady Lovelylocks! Apparently he was practically hooted right out of the room. That was no toy for boys! That was news to Sam. He loved the adventure aspect of the figure whose hair grows, whose horse is multicolored, who goes off on fantastic journeys with a dauntless prince. On the ride home in the car I probed Sam as to how he felt about all this. As usual he was OK....*

One day we were both at home, I going about my business, Sam seeming busy with something, when suddenly he asked "Mom, can a guy have a Barbie?" Not taking much note I said, "sure." Sam answered, "The kids in school said he can't." My heart constricted, my stomach turned. What else could I say? "Sam, you tell them a boy can have anything he wants."

I worry, at times, that because of the way I'm raising him, because I choose to refuse to constrict him to certain role expectations, he'll suffer. Not "typically boy" he won't "fit in." Then I look at him with his worm farms, his scientific experiments (eight potatoes rotting on the back porch), his love for school, for dancing, for karate. This is a kid for whom the knock-em, sock-em Ninja Turtles have no appeal. His hard shell fantasy figure is Sebastian from The Little Mermaid. I think he'll be okay.

I've struggled for Sam in this way to keep his options open. My wish for his school experience is that it do the same. But do I do this for my own students? Do I trust that they can be given a wide range of choice and still "fit in" to the college board curricula? Am I constricting them in certain roles? How can I give them the frightening freedom?

As Catherine so poignantly writes, choices are never without risk. The "frightening freedom" to try and fail, to live by and learn from our mistakes, and eventually to take charge of our own learning was not something we found in a teacher's directives. Fortunately, for most of us, there were those caring and supportive adults who created comfortable climates within which we could learn to make those choices and, ultimately, to take command of our own learning.

Explorations

1. **Opening Options**: Go back to your old lesson plans and find a writing assignment or a reading assignment that was rather fixed. Turn this assignment into a set of options, closing down only what is necessary and opening up whatever you can. If possible, try these options out on your students and see how opening up choice changes the learning that takes place.

2. **Making a journal guide**: Sometimes it is a good idea to try writing a letter to your students, telling them about how you plan to use journals in your class and laying out the choices they have about how the journals will be responded to and used as a tool for learning. Along with this letter, you might want to offer an array of rather general options for writing in the journals. This list of options gives students who are reluctant the opportunity to create their own topics a comfortable place to start. You might want to have some plan for helping students move beyond your choices and into their own. You might, for instance, ask them to try at least three of your options, but to also write at least five journal entries of their own choice.

3. **Reflecting on choice.** Reread John's story at the beginning of this chapter. From what you have learned about student choice, consider how he might revise his use of journals to be more successful. You can reflect on this in any comfortable form: as an imaginative letter to John, as a private reflection in a journal of your own, or informally, by means of a chart or list that you discuss with one other person or a group of your colleagues.

4. **"Name Your own Burger."** What else would you expect in a chapter on choice?

References

Applebee, A.N. & Langer, J.A. (1983). Instructional scaffolding: Reading and writing as natural language activities. *Language Arts, 60,* 168-175.

Atwell, N. (1978). Everyone sits at a big desk: Discovering topics for writing. In D. Goswami & P.R. Stillman (Eds.) *Reclaiming the classroom: Teacher research as an agency for change.* Upper Montclair, NJ: Boynton/Cook, pp. 178-187.

Burns, M. & McLaughlin, C. (1990). *A Collection of math lessons.* New Rochelle, NY: The Math Solution Publications.

Erickson, D.K. (1990). Percentages and cuisenaire rods. *Mathematics teacher 83* (8). pp. 648-654.

Graves, D. (1983). Break the Welfare Cycle: Let Writers Choose their own Topics. In P. Stock (Ed.) *Fforum: Essays on theory and practice in the teaching of writing.* Upper Montclair, NJ: Boynton/Cook. pp. 98-107.

National Council of Teachers of Mathematics. (1991). *Curriculum and evaluation standards for school mathematics.* Reston, VA: National Council of Teachers of Mathematics, Inc. (Fourth Printing).

Spaulding, C. (1989). The effects of ownership opportunities and instructional support on high school students' writing task engagement. *Research in the Teaching of English 23* (2). pp. 139-162.

CHAPTER 7

Independence and Collaboration in the Learning Climate

Joanne is a fourth grade teacher. During her student teaching experience, she was assigned to a classroom in which several students with special needs were integrated with more typical peers. In this situation, it was important to make sure that children of various abilities and backgrounds learned to cooperate with one another. Joanne remembers, "I felt education can be fun and active. I had plans for cooperative learning to take place and when the time came I was ready!"

Unfortunately, Joanne's first experiment with cooperative learning happened on the same day that her university supervisor was coming to visit her classroom. Joanne had decided to place her students into groups of three or four and to ask them to work together on some math problems involving fractions with unlike denominators. She remembers:

I had broken down the steps and created dittos with columns for each step. Then each step was assigned to a different person in the group. The special education students had use of a calculator, but I arranged things so that wasn't all they ever did.

Given the fact that she was being observed, Joanne was probably more anxious than usual. She recalls, "There was so much to remember: introduce the lesson, show an example, move into groups and get individual jobs, observe, move, help, and discuss the group process." On top of all this, she had only thirty minutes in which to teach the lesson. She had planned to allocate five minutes for the introduction and example, fifteen minutes for students to work, five minutes for the groups to process their evaluation, and five minutes to discuss the group process. She mused, "No problem, a piece of cake! (It looked so good on paper)."

At 10:00, Joanne's students filed in from gym, while her supervisor had taken a seat to begin her observation. As students walked into the classroom, Joanne told them to get into their groups. At 10:05, she realized that she was already behind schedule. In a panic, she told herself:

Oh, oh, there goes my introduction time! Well I can whiz through it because we had done a similar project the day before. I talk about the group goal of everyone doing their own job but helping their fellow group members with their job without doing it for them.

After giving a quick example, Joanne started to move around the room. It was 10:10. She was surprised at the different ways her students approached the task:

Christine's group is working so nicely (like always). They already have one problem done. Nicole and Lisa are still doing all of Ed's work! I go over and work with them for a while trying to get them to balance helping Ed versus doing it for him. Oh, oh, there seems to be trouble in group three (what time is it — 10:15 — okay). Group three has one student who won't work unless an adult stands over him. His fellow members are very patient, but they are only fourth graders. I stand over him for a while helping him work on his job until there seems to be a problem with group four. The body language in group four is unmistakably one of anger and dislike. I walk over and casually ask what the problem is. Jon informs me that he "don't want no girl help"! Well, I explain the virtues of cooperative learning — that you help each other to learn. Jon's response was still, "I don't want no girl help!"

At 10:25, with her students still in various stages of completing their tasks, Joanne realized she was in trouble:

Christine's group had done a beautiful job and had completed all three problems. Ed's group did much better toward the end. Group three did get one problem done. Group four did not complete the first problem. And the last group lost two out of three members to the nurse and psychologist! It was past time to go and I was relieved that it was 10:32!

Independence and Collaboration in the Learning Climate 147

Many months after her first experience with collaborative learning, Joanne had some time to reflect upon the process:

Well, my purpose is easy to see; I basically needed to get through all of my lesson in a thirty-minute period. No matter what transpired during that thirty minutes, I would not sway from completing my lesson in the allotted time period. Heaven forbid someone (might) not understand and I might have to explain a concept for a few minutes! The poor kids must have felt like a tornado came through for thirty minutes!

Joanne had learned a valuable lesson: There's more to encouraging collaboration than simply putting students in groups and letting them go. For one thing, as she admitted, her need to follow her time structure so closely ended up interfering with the very collaborative processes she was trying to foster. For another, some of her students saw no benefit of working in groups. The way she had set up the task, with each student being responsible for a different step of the problem, didn't really encourage collaboration and caused groups to break down when one member either didn't understand or was not motivated to finish the step he or she had been assigned. Joanne reflected:

[I]n some groups each student just did his or her own job and really didn't collaborate with fellow students.... If I ever do a lesson like this one again, I would change things drastically. I would really like the students to understand why they are writing or doing things they do.... Maybe if I had each group figure out how to add fractions with unlike denominators and report how they figured out the problem, they could collaborate and go public with their information for the purpose of helping their fellow classmates. I will surely think out where I'm going with a lesson next time and not be so concerned with a certain format!

How many of us have stories like this? We want to provide a way for students to help each other to learn. We know the value of working collaboratively. Yet, for every student who likes to work with others, there is always someone else who finds group work to be dull or frustrating and without purpose.

Like many beginning teachers, I started using small groups in my first year as a high school teacher. I remember being disappointed at the unevenness of the results. I had learned in my college courses that group work was a good way of giving some of my authority over to my students and making them more responsible for their own learning. I was shocked when so many of them seemed to resent working with their peers and demanded that I get back at the center of the classroom, where I belonged! At the same time, there were students who seemed to flourish in a collaborative setting. I was reluctant to get rid of groups altogether, but I wanted a better way to use them, one that would be successful with shy as well as more social learners.

I've since begun to believe that every classroom needs a balance of experiences that range along a continuum of independent to more collaborative, and that some students will always feel more comfortable at one end of that continuum than the other.

Collaboration can be both constraining and liberating, depending upon the match between our goals for collaboration and our students' abilities to work collaboratively. The same can be said of more independent learning experiences. There are times when students simply need to arrive at their own understandings independently, with no fear of evaluation or public response. Knowing when learning should take place independently or collaboratively is one of our most important tasks as teachers.

Independence, Collaboration, and Learning Outcomes

Part of deciding when learning should take place independently or collaboratively involves understanding how the outcomes of language influence the learning that takes place. Take writing, for example. Whether students write for good friends, more distant audiences, or privately for their own understanding determines the substance and form of their learning. Writing is usually thought of as a rather public way of communicating with others, a medium that requires correctness, clarity, and awareness of audience. Yet, Peter Elbow (1985) has argued:

> However indelible the ink, writing can be completely evanescent and without consequences. We can write in solitude—indeed we seldom write otherwise—we can write whatever we want, we can write as badly as we want, and we can write one thing and then change our mind. No one need know what we've written or how we've written it. In short, writing turns out to be the ideal medium for getting it wrong. (p. 286).

By this notion, writing can take place collaboratively, as students share drafts in peer response groups, or independently, in the private pages of a journal. The same can be said for other language acts. Reading and responding can take place in the privacy of a living room or more collaboratively in a small group or a classroom setting. Spoken words can be muttered to no one in particular, practiced in privacy, or shared for more collaborative purposes. Even listening can have independent or more collaborative outcomes. Sometimes we listen for the purpose of getting information to be shared later; at other times, we listen privately, for pure personal enjoyment.

All kinds of learning experiences can be pursued collaboratively or independently, or at some point along that continuum. The chart in figure 7.1 gives some examples of the ways in which learning techniques can be modified to promote independence or collaboration, depending upon our instructional goals.

LEARNING TECHNIQUES: INDEPENDENCE AND COLLABORATION IN THE CLASSROOM

Independence		Collaboration
Reading and Response		
reading log	dialogue journals	whole class discussion
independent reading	reading conferences	reading response groups
Writing and Response		
writer's diaries	portfolio conferencing	group drafting
learning logs	peer conferencing	collaborative scripting
Speaking and Listening		
"talking to learn"	public speaking	collaborative learning
listening for pleasure	critical listening	discussion groups
practicing	performing	creative dramatics

Figure 7.1

As teachers, we must perform a number of balancing acts every day. One of our most important is preserving the unique responses of individual students, at the same time as we are providing opportunities for collaboration. Often, students need the chance to develop and document their own individual ideas and insights, without being swayed by the ideas of others. Sometimes, forcing learners to go public too soon inhibits important creative processes. At the same time, collaborative learning often produces ideas that are more compelling and complex than those generated by students working alone. Part of the task involves looking closely at how students view "going public" in the first place.

Sharing and Demonstrating

I believe there's a big difference between **sharing** and **demonstrating**. Sharing means giving others the benefit of our achievements, talents, and understandings. Students of all ages love to share. Performing, dramatizing, reading their work aloud in a writing workshop are activities that are popular with students from elementary to high school and beyond. Demonstrating is another matter. In the context of schools, it usually involves proving competence to someone in authority. It means establishing credibility — giving evidence of work done, skills mastered, competencies achieved. For even the most academically talented students, too great an emphasis on demonstration can have negative consequences.

We might conclude, in fact, that sharing draws upon both independence and collaboration, as students allow others to benefit from their unique abilities and talents. Demonstration, on the other hand, often implies dependence on the opinions of those in authority. When students see collaboration as a meaningless exercise in demonstration rather than an opportunity to share and extend their learning with others, they fail to benefit from collaborative tasks. Many less successful students see group work in this negative way. They are timid and unsure of themselves and often sit silently, letting others do the work.

Ironically, many academically successful students also dislike working collaboratively because they want approval from the teacher and see little value in learning from their peers. For these students, sharing is not as enjoyable as demonstrating competence to the teacher or gradegiver. Still other students take great pleasure in learning with peers. Free from the threat of grades, these students enjoy brainstorming and exploring a variety of ideas with the help of a group.

Just as collaborative experiences are viewed so differently by students, opportunities for independent learning are also viewed differently. Consider, for example, the journal — an incredibly flexible tool that can be used in many ways, ranging from collaborative (dialogue journals) to more private (diaries). Shy students, in particular, can benefit greatly from the opportunity to experiment with ideas and feelings in the private pages of a journal. Despite our intentions, though, many students never see journal writing as a totally private experience. It takes a great deal of modeling before students begin to believe that we are serious about respecting their privacy. Even then, we have to build in safeguards before students will see the journal as an invitation to independent learning. One such safeguard is allowing students to remove or staple shut entries they believe are too private to be shared.

Often, more socially motivated students may see little purpose in writing that is totally private. They may be dependent upon teachers' responses and discouraged when their writing is not commented upon or graded. In this case, it's important to model a variety of purposes for writing, from personal to more collaborative. Asking students to write privately for a few minutes before discussing controversial issues and sharing the importance of journal writing in your own life are ways of modelling the usefulness of writing for private clarification of ideas or working out confusing emotions. On the other end of the continuum, teachers can model the benefits of collaboration by periodically encouraging students to share journal entries with partners or with other members of the class.

The journal, then, is a flexible tool that can be used to promote both independent and collaborative learning. One advantage of asking students to share ideas through writing is that they can be free to experiment with their thoughts and feelings before going public with them. Written dialogue has an advantage over spoken dialogue in that students can make choices about when and how to share their ideas with others. They also have the benefit of reading someone else's words several times, in privacy, before deciding on their own response.

Let's consider the example of one middle school student whose reading was enriched through collaborative writing in a journal.

Classroom Closeup:
Collaborative Reading and Response

Daniel is a seventh grade student. Often, as a regular part of his English class, Daniel and his classmates respond to their self-selected reading in literature logs. Although students in his class have many opportunities for writing and reading independently, at one point his teacher decided to make the literature log a more collaborative experience for everyone.

To begin with, his teacher wanted to provide an audience for her students' writing other than herself. She asked her students to keep track of their pleasure reading in a log, modelled after Jana Staton's (1987) concept of "dialogue journals." As opposed to a private diary or learning log, the dialogue journal allows two people to engage in a written conversation about what they are experiencing and learning. As a way of providing an audience other than herself, she arranged for some graduate students at a nearby university to come in at least once a week and correspond with her students about their independent reading.

Thus, although Daniel and his classmates had been reading different texts independently, their reading was not entirely a private act. As Daniel shared his reading processes in a dialogue journal, he engaged in a collaborative response process with his partner, Eva. Since the graduate student respondents had not always read the same texts as the middle school students, the seventh graders were often able to act as experts, helping their adult partners to understand the text they were reading and understanding it better themselves in the process of writing about it.

For several weeks now, Daniel has been reading an historical and political account of life in the Middle East. As we eavesdrop on his written "conversation" with Eva, his response partner, we will see how his reading circle was expanded and his reading process became more collaborative through keeping a dialogue journal.

In his very first journal entry, Daniel reveals that he was born in the Middle East. He begins:

Reading about where I grew up is very refreshing and reflecting. The book I am reading was before the civil war. 1975. Me being born and raised in leabanon, until I was 4 years old I don't have many memories. In this book I can see how Lebanon was before it was torn apart from the civil war. I think I made a good decision about reading this book, So I can learn a little bit more where I was born and Raised leabanon.

Although Eva has not read this book, she is intrigued by the fact that Daniel's family once lived in the Middle East. She encourages him to share his impressions at home:

Dear Daniel — What do you think about what the author says in the book? It might be really interesting to discuss what the book says with your parents and see how their memories compare to the book.

Apparently, Daniel takes Eva up on her suggestion. Some time later, he writes:

Independence and Collaboration in the Learning Climate 153

> *I am still reading about Lebeanon the author is telling about Lebanon's Economy and what religons rule in Lebanon. Half of the people in Lebanon are Moslem and the other Half is Christian. While I was reading in the book My mom notice a picture of a church that church was our church the church we attended.*

Here, Daniel is able to act as the expert, informing Eva about the religions of Lebanon. He also (not surprisingly) has learned to spell the name of the country! Apparently, from this entry, he has begun to share what he has learned with his mother. Thus, the circle of collaboration has expanded to include another participant in the reading process.

In her next response, Eva shares something about her own reading style. She continues to direct Daniel's reading outward, asking whether he can remember anything about his homeland as a result of reading the book:

> *Daniel — "Wow! It's pretty exciting when a place you know is shown or described in a book you're reading. I especially like it when the author describes the place, because then I can compare what he says with how I remember the place. Did you remember the church? I wonder if it's still there now.*

Eva's questions seem to make the reading experience come alive for Daniel. He learns to use reading as an occasion to learn more about his homeland, and in the process, to learn more about his family as well. He writes:

> *Now I am Reading about Jordan pronounced (Orrdon) Now I get to see how my mom's family lived me never been to Jordan I can't really see anything that I have seen before I will continue reading and get back to you. To answer your questions yes the Church is still their and I do like the book.... I like this book because as I am reading it my mom tells me about it.*

At this point it appears that Daniel is no longer merely reading words on a page. He is bringing those words to life as he compares the author's Lebanon with the memories of his parents. In her next entry, Eva suggests that Daniel might want to imagine himself as a character in the book. She writes:

> *Daniel — Thanks for all your journal entries! It sounds like you respond to stories/books like I do a lot of the time. I enjoy "connect-*

ing" them to my life. Sometimes, though, I do the opposite. That is, I imagine what it would be like to be one of the characters... I'm looking forward to reading more of your responses! Til next time — Eva

In one of his final entries, Daniel reveals that his reading has been an opportunity not only to collaborate with an interested respondent but to learn more about his family and his country of origin as well. He writes:

Now I am reading about where my mother was brought up she told she remember going down to that street their was a place where the made the best arabic pastries she had ever tasted.

Not surprisingly, in his final entry, Daniel writes, "The book was great It was very good!" In sharing his appreciation and understanding of the book, Daniel began to build a personal connection with another reader. In comparing the Lebanon in his book with the Lebanon that his mother remembered, he not only deepened his understanding of a subject but forged a connection with his mother's past as well. Connections and collaborations like this will hopefully invite Daniel into other readings and other reading relationships in the years to come.

Thus, the journal, which is often thought of as a vehicle for individual expression, can be expanded and directed toward more collaborative purposes, depending upon a teacher's goals and a student's needs. Rather than seeing techniques like small groups and journals as promoting only one kind of learning, it's important to realize that there are a range of outcomes and purposes — from collaboration to independence — just waiting to be discovered in any of them. In fact, within one lesson, it is possible to provide activities all along that continuum.

Let's imagine, for instance, that you want your students to work on a project collaboratively in groups but you also want to minimize some of the risk of going public, providing a measure of privacy and anonymity as well. It's possible to do both. Consider the following example.

Reflections: Collaborative Authorship

Reading is always, at some level, a private act. In one sense, no one will ever know the ideas, feelings, and associations that float around privately in our heads when we read. On the other hand, reading in classrooms is often brought out of the realm of privacy and treated as a social act. Seldom do our students read anything — whether it's a science textbook or a novel — without having to be accountable for that reading in some way.

Writing is also a potentially private activity, at least as it's taught in schools. Many students have the same anxiety in writing and sharing their own texts as they do in talking about the texts that they read. Somehow, they've gotten the impression that they will be held accountable for everything they write — that every misplaced comma and every misspelled word will count against them.

Interestingly, many teachers find it hard to shake those one-correct-response notions that they learned as students in other teachers' classrooms. As a result, teachers and students alike find it difficult to go public for fear of embarrassment or ridicule. It's no wonder, then, that so many students hate to read and write poetry. Of all the forms of language, poetry is so ambiguous — so packed with interpretive possibilities, that it's often hard to arrive at a credible interpretation, much less to figure out some mysterious interpretation in the teacher's mind.

Some years ago, I discovered a fun and relatively painless way to introduce poetry to my high school students. I've used this idea many times with groups of adults, and it's worked just as well. I'd like to invite you to try this collaborative writing experience. You'll need a group of about four or five other people. You will also need some paper and a pen or pencil for each member, as well as a pair of scissors, a roll of tape, and a recording of some instrumental music. If you are working alone, you may want to consider how you might adapt this particular activity for your own students.

Because the writing of poetry is so often associated with anxious feelings, I'm going to suggest that rather than writing a poem of your own for the next thirty minutes or so you try to write a poem collaboratively. Since your words can remain relatively anonymous, you shouldn't feel nervous about the outcome. Remember that poetry, like anything else, is written one line at a time.

Drafting.

To begin, each person in the group should have a sheet of paper. Someone should start to play the tape of instrumental music. This music *can be rather quiet and evocative like Aaron Copeland's "Appalachian Spring" or rousing and fiery like Rimsky Korsakov's "Scheherezade. As the music begins, write one sentence at the top of your paper that captures whatever the music suggests to you. Don't worry about what other people are writing. You are only responsible for this one sentence.*

Once you are finished, fold this one line backward, so that someone else can still write on the paper, without seeing what you wrote. Now, trade papers with someone else and write a different sentence on the paper you were handed. Follow the same procedure: fold this sentence back and exchange with someone else. You will be passing your papers to other members of your group and folding the line you have written back so that the paper eventually becomes a kind of accordion. Since no one will see anyone else's words, it doesn't matter where papers are passed as long as they move from one writer to another in a steady process.

Sharing.
This whole process of writing and passing the papers around the room usually takes about ten minutes. When the sheets of paper seem to be filled up, stop and unfold the sheet of paper you have in your hand. Take turns reading these "accidental poems" in your best dramatic voice. You might be amazed at how many decent poems you can get out of this spontaneous process. It's fun to see how many recurring themes are suggested by the same musical text.

Revising.
Now, for the next twenty or thirty minutes, take the drafts that you have and generate some new pieces as a group. You might want to add, delete, or move lines around, to experiment with a rhyme scheme or rhythm or to play with forms such as haiku or cinquain. When your group is done, read the "revised" poems aloud. If you are working in a classroom or a workshop setting, share your group's poems with the larger group. Read them aloud with the music, if you like.

In figure 7.2 are some examples of "accidental haiku" that were created by a group of undergraduate students I was working with last year. Although these collaborative poems are rarely of publishable quality, the point of the whole experience is to take some of the sting out of reading and writing poetry and to get rid of some of those negative myths that seem to have grown up around it.

Collaborative Poems

Haiku # 1
She strolled through the past
Understanding the meaning
telling small stories.

Haiku # 2
Always obvious.
The petals of a flower
After a long night.

Figure 7.2

Now, think for a moment about the collaborative process itself. Were there moments when the collaborative spirit among you was at its highest? What happened to promote it? How did you feel at these moments as opposed to the moments when you were working more independently? How different was this experience from the experience of writing poetry alone? What accounted for these differences? Finally, what did you learn from this brief group writing experience about the process of collaboration in your own classroom?

Independence and Collaboration

If this simple little exercise worked for you, it might have been because you began by breaking a big task into manageable units. Since you were only responsible for generating one line at a time, the task of creating an entire poem might not have seemed nearly as foreboding. But perhaps more importantly, in the early stages of writing you could be totally anonymous. No one ever knew which lines were contributed by which writers. The result might have been freedom to experiment without the threat of accountability. If a line seemed too corny or a word was misspelled, no one could point an accusing finger at you.

In a sense, then, everyone worked independently to generate a sentence bank of possible lines. As a result, by the time everyone started writing and revising the original poems into new ones, they were not starting from scratch but had some preliminary texts to work with — texts that had no identifiable author.

Since there were no rules about keeping the original draft, more adventurous groups could create brand new poems if they chose to do so. Even if you decided not to keep any of the original lines, your earlier writing might have acted as a private brainstorming or rehearsal before you began creating final drafts. This private rehearsal may have helped you to take more risks in revising and creating new drafts.

Because your group created the poems collaboratively, there was another sort of anonymity. Let's say you decided to share your poems with a larger group. No one in the larger group knew, as the new drafts were read aloud, who authored individual lines. Because reading final drafts aloud was totally voluntary. those who enjoyed oral performance could have a chance to get in front of the larger group while more shy individuals could simply listen quietly.

So how does this relate to collaboration and independence in the classroom? For one thing, it's possible to provide experiences that allow students to find their own comfortable balance between independent and collaborative learning. Different groups of students will have different needs. Some are fairly shy and need to be led gently into the process of collaboration. Others are more outgoing and perhaps need to be convinced of the value of private exploration and expression. Usually, it takes a great deal of planning and modeling before we strike this balance in our classrooms.

Now let's consider a more extended example. In the next few pages, you will see how one high school English teacher gradually led her students through the delicate process of collaboration and community building in her English classroom.

Classroom Closeup: Collaborative Writing

Kathleen teaches a course that was originally designed by her English department for high school students who need help in composition. Usually, these are students who scored low on local or state competency tests or who have been referred by teachers for demonstrating minimal writing proficiency. Typically, each class has anywhere from six to fifteen students in grades nine through eleven.

Her first period class this particular year had seven students. At the very beginning of the term, she was distressed at what seemed to be a lack of oral communication skills among the class members. She described what she saw as "an underlying tenseness which overshadowed the classroom atmosphere." In her words:

The hidden baggage these students brought to school with them screamed out in many unusual ways. It became part of my agenda to make these students understand each other's value as human beings and to discover the unique qualities that are latent within each one of them.... My first challenge was to get these students to talk. I not only wanted to hear their voices in Room 101, I wanted them to communicate with each other as valued members of the human species. This task would take special tactics.

As part of these "special tactics," Kathleen began one day by asking the students to listen to a BBC recording of H.G. Wells' *War of the Worlds*. Before playing the tape, she discussed what it was like to live in America in 1938. Many of her students had read about the era prior to World War II in social studies. She recalled:

The recording opens with music that was popular during 1938. I requested that students imagine themselves sitting with their spouses and/or boy/girlfriends in their livingrooms. The year — 1938. While the music was playing I suggested scenarios, which piqued student interest. It's difficult not to listen when your teacher is waltzing around the room, talking about a romantic evening listening to the radio in the parlor with a fire crackling in the fireplace!

As she was playing the tape, Kathleen stopped periodically and asked her students to write down their responses to the program in their journals. She asked them questions such as: "How do you feel as you are listening to this program? What questions do you have? Is there anything you heard that made a significant impression on you?" She also asked her students to keep track of what had happen in each segment.

Her students responded to the program in many imaginative ways. One wrote, "I feel scared and mad so I grab my 22 and I'm driving [to] gloversville." Another wrote, "At first I don't believe it and want to hear more and I'm ready to give the police a call." Still another wrote, "It's not actually a terrified feeling, but more like dismayed and disoriented. A simple, enjoyable program has turned into a major event."

After students had listened to the entire program, they examined their notes together, first agreeing on the basic story line, then examining the devices that were used to make the plot believable, interesting, and entertaining. In Kathleen's words:

> *I compared the basic plot to a person's skeleton, and the devices used to deliver the plot attractively to the muscle, fat distribution, skin and other parts of the human body which make a person both pleasant to meet and able to function properly.*

After her students had finished listening to the program and sharing their responses, she introduced them to what would become their final project. Since this particular class had trouble communicating with each other and with her, she decided to ask them to collaborate in groups, creating a scripts for a radio program similar to "War of the Worlds." She asked them to make believe that they were creating these scripts for their school radio station. The challenge for each group was to write a script that would affect listeners in 1990 in the same way as Wells' script affected listeners in 1938. She introduced the project by saying:

> *Can you imagine the satisfaction and feeling of power you would have pulling off a number like this? Ever played a practical joke on a friend, or an enemy for that matter? Can you imagine fooling thousands of people?*

Surprisingly, over a period of several days, the students in this class not only succeeded in writing their own radio plays but learned some valuable lessons about each other as well. The collaboration that eventually grew in room 101 went far beyond the bounds of the assignment as students learned to be supportive and cooperative in much larger and more significant ways. The rest is Kathleen's story. She tells it in her own words.

The Collaboration Begins

They were not enthusiastic writers. To them, the idea was:
DAVE: *okay*
TASHA: *dumb*
JOHN: *really dumb!*
(but)

TED: (could be) fun.
They wanted to know if they could:
TERRY: really record a radio play?
JOSH: choose our own groups?
JOHN: (actually) write a play?

> I assured them that all of these questions could be answered with "yes." And of course there was a major concern:

JOSH: How will you grade group work?

I explained that students would receive three equal grades: one for group participation, one for individual work, and a third for the written product.

Students formed their own writing groups. Josh, Dave and Ted formed one group; Terry, John, Tasha and, by my choosing, since he was absent, Larry, formed another group. I suggested that Tasha and Ted switch groups, but both students gave me a "get real" look and I let the groups stay as they were. Both groups chose to sit at different round tables. Once they sat down there was a moment of silence. They looked to me and I said, "It's your script!" as I placed a yellow stenographer's pad on each table. After the groups started talking, my aide, Brenda, made herself accessible to the group that consisted of Josh, Ted, and Dave, while I focused on the other group of playwrights.

For convenience, I will call the group consisting of Dave, Ted and Josh the "Dream Team" and the group of Terry, Tasha, John and Larry "Terrorists," although we have never used those names in the classroom (the names correlate with the play scripts which each group wrote).

The Dream Team: Shared Responsibilities

I soon heard a lot of laughter from the Dream Team. I was aware that Ted and Josh generated most of the ideas but that Dave was frequently talking and influencing the group's direction. As Brenda noted after one class when the group was deciding on the basic story situation, Ted and Josh had some "bizarre, crazy" ideas. [For example]:

TED: Glue Turf/Blue Smurf
       Blood suckers
       chemical exslopion

>   *killer fly*
>   *attack of the killer teachers*
> JOSH: *World War III*
>   *chemical warfare*
>   *thing imbedded in skin — Ancient Ruins*

In general, the Dream Team shared roles and responsibilities fairly equally. [During group meetings], Josh took the role of analyzer, with Dave backing him up in second place. Ted was the group explorer with Dave and Josh tying for second in this area. Brenda later reported that "Ted and Josh are bizarre — crazy! Dave brings in realism. His dry humor helps bring the group back to the task."

I noticed that this group spent far less time coordinating ideas than did the Terrorists. I suspect this is true because their idea exploration was more evenly distributed. As the group continued working, Brenda became designated recorder, which probably helped all three students contribute ideas equally, since the actual task of writing slows down the thinking process. Brenda reported that "all three students contributed to the writing (composing) and each one made sure the others did their fair share of the work."

As the members of the Dream Team were choosing their sound effects from a selection of recorded sounds, Brenda said they had serious discussions about the appropriateness of the recorded sound. They often made up their own sound imitations because the recorded sounds didn't fit what they want to do. The Dream Team was acutely aware of their own purpose for the script, and they were analyzing various influences the script would have one a specific audience — their fellow students.

The Terrorists: Crawling Toward Collaboration

The onset of the Terrorists' composition process also produced a designated group recorder:

> TASHA (grabbing the yellow pad): I'll write! You guys tell me what to write, this is dumb! But I don't care!

Thus, with Tasha's hostility and Larry's absence, the Terrorists began to crawl along the composition path. [In this group], Terry emerged as the chief idea generator and explorer [while] John was a definite group analyst. Terry generated numerous ideas, most of them so fantastic that Tasha and John were forced to comment on, at the very least, the absurdity of it all. [For example, Terry generated such ideas as]:

> *— what if for just once there was a bomb*
> *— if you were driving and an earthquake occurred*
> *— what if a dog like Cujo came into school....*

John became very interested at the possibility of the school being attacked and some force having the power to "destroy all teachers"! He then began to explore the possibility of creating "a football field in the clouds."

Hence the process of topic exploration and testing had begun. By the end of class, Terry, with a little help from John, had hammered out a basic storyline. By the time their revising and editing sessions were finished several days later, Tasha had decided "Hey, this is good!" [As I look back on the Terrorists' project], Tasha seems to have been the group's facilitator while John was co-facilitator. This seems very interesting since both Tasha and John were originally quite negative about the project, which was "dumb" according to Tasha and "really dumb" according to John.

"Our Classroom"

One day toward the end of the project, the Dream Team had spent the class time in the Radio Room recording their script. When they returned, laughing and obviously happy with the way the period had progressed, I waited with apprehension as Ted chanted: "Our play's better than your play." Ted was laughing good naturedly, but how would John take this teasing? John and his group members responded light heartedly, "No way! Ours is the best!" Thus began a healthy rivalry that provided positive communication between two formerly hostile rivals!

During part of the writing of these scripts, there had been a graduate student observing the class. This observer was present when we decided to tape a practice reading of the scripts. Larry was absent so the Terrorist group members asked the observer if she wanted to read one of Larry's parts. They were very pleased when she accepted the role. Knowing these students as I do, I don't think they would have asked anyone to read their writing back in September! These students were proud of their product, so proud that they didn't mind having another person hear their reading of the script and they didn't feel uncomfortable asking her to participate by reading something they had written.

By this time our classroom atmosphere had become much more relaxed. The tension that overshadowed our activities during September had subsided. Students began to talk with one another both about the writing of the plays and about other daily issues and concerns. Room 101 had become "our classroom" rather than "Mrs. P.s' room."

For example, every so often I let classes take a free computer day. On these days students may choose to work either independently or with others on one of a variety of computer programs and games. Before the script writing, the members of this class either chose to work alone on a computer program or opted to complete homework assignments. Toward the end of the script writing, I offered a free computer day to this class. This time Josh, Ted and Terry played WHEEL OF FORTUNE on a computer next to Dave, who was using a computer design program called CARBUILDER. The three competitors on WHEEL OF FORTUNE were bantering and laughing like friends, while they kept close tabs on Dave's progress in his car designing.

Tasha still opted to complete a science homework assignment, but she did not isolate herself from the other students. She vocalized a general call for help when he could not understand space orbitation and then listened appreciatively while Josh voluntarily explained the concept to her.

At the close of the period everyone, including Tasha, gathered around as Dave's car was put through the test drives. We laughed when the computer declared the model "scary on downhill braking," and we cheered when Dave's car was deemed to have "exceptional cornering." Quite a change in class dynamics!

Members of the class also began to express genuine concern for one another. On October 29th the class members tried to get Larry to consider his options about whether or not to quit school. Ted said, "You'll get used to [school]. It takes a while, but it's okay." Tasha said "Man, what else you gonna do?" John said, "What does your girlfriend think?" And when Tasha came to school with continuing problems that made her consider moving to Dresden with her dad, Josh suggested that it might be better to "stay in Grassland [because] you know everyone here."

About a week after the groups had finished their scripts, tragedy struck at our high school. A ninth grade student was accidentally shot and killed by his friend, who is another of our ninth grade students. The students in this class had different perspectives of the event and voiced different reactions, but the class was a safe and accessible place for each class member to express sorrow, anger, grief, and/or confusion. They evaluated the situation, think-

ing of both its immediate and its long-term meanings. They personalized the feelings of others and expressed personal ideas about death and dying.

I was surprised to realize the anger some of the students directed toward Jerry, the boy who shot his friend. It's normal for people to get angry when tragic, unexpected deaths occur. The students who went through our school suicide epidemic two years ago were angry with the students who had committed suicide. But I guess I just wasn't prepared for the hostility the students, especially those who knew the boy who had been killed, felt toward Jerry.

[I suggested that they] put themselves into Jerry's place for a few minutes. How would they feel if they had accidentally shot their best friend? Could they ever erase the moment from their minds? How could they live with the guilt? I'll never forget the sounds of death that escaped from some baby rabbits that I had accidentally scared from their nest one cold March day almost twenty years ago. I had tried to keep them alive, since I knew the mother would abandon them once they wore that human scent. But one by one they died. And as each one emitted the shrill squeal of death, the guilt was embedded deeper in my soul. How will this child deal with the guilt of killing his best friend? [Their genuine responses convinced me that] finally, the students had stopped leaving their genuine oral language in the hall when they entered the writing lab!

From Collaboration to Community

Last week, we had a very competitive Trivial Pursuit game, which resulted from John's realization that he could influence class direction:

> *JOHN (to teacher): Can we have our donut day on Wednesday? And you know, we haven't played our Trivial Pursuit game in a while. Could we do that on Wednesday?*

How could I refuse? John, who had been so despondent and negative in September actually wanted to initiate a class activity!

After the students had left the room, Brenda asked me if I had noticed all the changes that had taken place in the first period class. Had I! About a month after this collaborative project was completed, I asked the students to evaluate the project with a focus on the effects the writing had on them personally. I also asked them to tell me anything they wanted to about either the group work or the writing which they accomplished. They said:

From this project, I learned that cooperation and organizatin can lead to astonishing results. Working with other persons can open your mind to different ways of interpreting different ideas (Ted).

I thought this project was fun but very time consuming. It was fun working in a group and very intresting. I think creating Ideas and characters was great (Terry).

I thought it was a learning process, for everybody. I thought we learned how to think with our heads. I learned that working with others is very helpful. This ecpirence helped me in many ways. I think we should do this again sometime soon / Otay, Otay Buckwheat (Josh)

I thought the play was not a waste of time. Also I learned to work with other. It also helped me to come up with Better Ideas. Also it helped me with my reading skills (Dave).

While my students may be talking "off-task" (teacher talk for "not included in my planbook!"), they may be talking about cracked gourds and then decide to conduct an experiment and write a report about whether or not the seeds will sprout. Or they may talk about how tired they are, the effects of a deceptive media idea of "normal" families, student rights in an adult world, hospitalized grandfathers, mean librarians, friends who are drug dealers, suicide, or dying. Sometimes students will write about these issues, sometimes they will just talk about them. Whether they write about what they are talking about isn't a problem, you see, because the students have brought their entire beings to Room 101 writing class. They haven't left the most important parts of themselves in the hall and then tried to write genuine, meaningful compositions using just the shell of themselves that exists without the freedom to TALK during writing class.

Independence through Collaboration

Kathleen's story reveals just how important it is to promote our students' independence while giving them the opportunity to learn from their fellow classmates. Our decisions about exactly how to strike this balance depend upon how our students view the act of collaboration in the first place. Not surprisingly, there will always be some students who prefer social interaction while others are more comfortable learning independently in a more private setting.

As Kathleen's story reveals, all of these diverse student needs can be accommodated within the same learning environment. Shy students can be encouraged to take risks and venture into new territory, learning from their peers, while more outgoing students can be shown the value of independent, exploratory learning. An important place to begin is to realize that practically every learning technique can promote independence or collaboration, depending upon the way we use it.

Classroom Connections

Here are some ways to begin building those comfortable structures within which all students can develop their independence, at the same time as they discover the value of learning from each other.

Protecting Privacy. Ask yourself how many opportunities for private, independent learning students have in your classroom. Let's suppose that you have used learning logs or journals in your class with rather mixed results. Perhaps one problem might be that students don't believe you when you tell them that they can decide whether to "go public" with particular entries. It might be useful to develop a system for ensuring that privacy. You might want to offer the option of stapling, clipping, or removing particular entries that students don't feel comfortable sharing. You can, of course, require that each student produce so many "sharable" pieces without demanding that everything be shared. Just as some students may fear a teacher's invasion of their privacy, others may feel uncomfortable speaking or sharing their work aloud with other students in the class. Here again, it's possible to provide a measure of privacy for all students.

As a high school teacher myself, I noticed that some students were always volunteering to share their work while others never raised their hands and asked to share. I decided to create a pack of 3" by 5" index cards for each class with a different student name written on the top of each card. When it was time to share written work or read aloud, I would pick up the pack of cards and call on the person whose name was at the top of the pile. I made it a practice never to force students to share their work. On the other hand, I knew that some students would never go public unless they were gently prodded to do so. For this reason, each student was allotted so many "passes" for the marking period. Each time they elected to pass, I would write a "P" on their card. Students had to exercise some care in deciding when to pass. They seldom abused the system, and I believe they felt some measure of control in deciding which topics and texts would be shared. The point is to see how many ways you can ensure your students' privacy while creating an environment where students are able to learn from each other.

Providing Different Kinds of Response. Once you've done some thinking about your students' privacy, you might then consider how many different outcomes and audiences, beyond yourself, are available to them. You might want to arrange some way for students to share their work with others outside the classroom. If you can't arrange to have graduate students or other adults come into your classroom, you might want to pair your students with those in another teacher's classroom. Same-age or different-age pairs could work together, producing collaborative stories, illustrating and writing books, or writing reports on special topics. Here, the point is to consider how you can provide occasions for genuine sharing and collaboration with people other than you.

Providing Options for Collaboration. Finally, you might consider whether students could have choices about how collaboratively or independently they work. Although there is a recognized body of work, with its own definitions of "collaborative" and "cooperative" learning, I have my own distinction between collaboration and cooperation that I find helpful whenever I ask students to work in groups. I begin by saying that their first task is to decide on the degree of collaboration that feels most comfortable to them.

If groups decide to work totally collaboratively, they can produce one final product and be awarded the same grade. There is usually at least one group in every class that seems to flourish in this arrangement. Often, group members decide to meet after class and on weekends, each taking on the task that best suits him or her. For these people, the collaborative process is rewarding on both a personal and an intellectual level.

Groups that are less comfortable working collaboratively can decide to work cooperatively. Here, I define "cooperative" to mean working with "a helpful and willing attitude" (Webster, 1990, p. 385), as opposed to sharing equal responsibility for a single project. Although individuals are still given time in class to work together, they function as response groups rather than task groups. Members may listen and respond to drafts of each other's papers, help each other with complicated material, or offer suggestions about various aspects of their projects. In this arrangement, each person produces a different final product and is awarded an individual grade, yet still has the benefit of working with others.

Still others may wish to find a middle ground between collaboration and cooperation. These individuals may decide to do separate projects, all relating to the same theme. For example, a group of teachers may decide to create separate unit plans for students of various grade levels on a theme such as such as "the life cycle." Projects are still graded independently, but group members benefit from the help of others, as each member pursues different aspects of the same general topic. I find this system to be relatively easy to administer. I simply ask my students to write a short note to me at the end of the project, telling me how various aspects of the work were divided up and whether to assign group or individual grades.

As a general rule, it might be useful to think back over the lessons you have taught and to decide just how closely and collaboratively you have asked students to work. If no opportunities were available for collaborative learning, you might ask yourself if and how you might have provided these opportunities. You might also want to try offering a range of choices from collaborative to cooperative and see how students take to the idea.

A Piece of the Whole

Ironically, sometimes we learn the most about our students, not from what they write and say on their own but by how they interact with others. Fred is one such student. Meg, his seventh grade teacher, had been perplexed for some time about what seemed to be an inability or a reluctance to read and write independently. Then one day, in observing him with some of his classmates, she discovered his hidden talents. She mused in her journal:

[Fred] pretty much refuses to do anything except draw. When he does write it always has to be illustrated or he will not write at all, and all his reading is about drawing or from comic books. But he has such a creative mind! I really feel that somehow I could tap into that creativity and show him that it can spill into many other areas besides drawing. It happens occasionally but then something always seems to happen that scares him back into his silence. Today, however, he was doing so well and was so involved! His group was working on a horror movie scene, and he was fashioning the characters on paper. What a reader and writer he must be if he can see characters in so much detail! While the others were writing he was throwing in his "two cents' worth" about how the characters would react and what they would say or do in a particular situation. Sometimes kids work so well as a piece of the whole. Don't we all?

Indeed, so many of our students "work so well as a piece of the whole." To many students like Fred, learning is a very vast and confusing thing. It's not easy to accomplish the whole piece by themselves. But when they are allowed to cooperate and collaborate with others, they discover special abilities and talents. Often these talents are best discovered in that essential balance between learning independently and learning together.

Explorations

1. **Essential Elements**. Together with a group of your colleagues, design a way of responding to this chapter that would help you to learn more about the subject of collaboration and independence. You can follow any form or use any combination of language activities in designing the "Exploration" your group feels most comfortable with. You might even design an array of options similar to those at the end of each chapter in this book. Once you have settled on a way of responding that suits your group, take a few minutes and talk about the collaborative process in which you just participated. Ask yourself when collaboration among you seemed to be at its peak and when ideas seemed to get lost or participants seemed resistant to collaboration. As a group, come up with a list of "Essential Elements for Collaboration."

2. **Inviting Independence**. Create an array of options that might be similar to the "Explorations" at the end of each chapter in this book. These options should invite a reader to learn independently more about the subject of collaboration and independence in the learning climate.

3. **Encouraging Collaboration**. Think back to a time when you worked well in a group on some project. Write a brief description of this experience, in which you consider what elements most contributed to the collaborative spirit among the members of your group.

4. **Name Your Own Exploration**.

References

Staton, J. (1987). The power of responding in dialogue journals. In *The Journal Book*, T. Fulwiler (Ed.). Portsmouth, NJ: Boynton/Cook, Heinemann, pp. 47-63.

Elbow, P. (1985). The shifting relationships between speech and writing. *College Composition and Communication, 36* (3), 283-303.

Webster (1990). *The Tormont Webster's Illustrated Encyclopedia Dictionary.* P.B. Devine (Ed.). Montreal, Canada: Tormont Publications, Inc.

CHAPTER 8

Commitment: Exploration and Permanence in the Language Act

Sometimes our most valuable lessons about teaching come to us not in our official roles as teachers but in our other roles as friends, spouses, colleagues, or parents. As a high school English teacher, Kathleen has worked hard over the years to help her students find meaningful uses for reading and writing. This year, her own son Solomon wasn't so lucky. In her teaching journal, she describes how she helped him come to grips with another teacher's task:

> *You know, being a teacher and a parent is sometimes very difficult! .... Generally, I refrain from expressing my personal teaching philosophy to my children's teachers. But lately my son's teacher had tread too incautiously on ground that is dear to my heart! She assigned research reports on assigned topics to each member of her fifth grade class. These reports were to follow her organizational list, which reflects the traditional research paper, complete with bibliography. The report was to be completed by a given due date and was to be accomplished independently. My son, who is a bit more athletic than academic (but not atypical for a fifth grade boy), panicked. "Well there's an F!" he stated as he threw the assignment ditto on the breakfast table.*
>
> *I kept my reservations to myself and told him how much I would enjoy helping him with the project and what an interesting group of people the Navajo are. Would Ms. T. like us to include information about the Navajo people as they live today? No, Mom. Just what's on this sheet. We have to do it this way or we fail the whole thing."*
>
> *So I checked out five books and Solomon and I began a research project on the Navajo Indians (not Native Americans, Mom, Mrs. T.*

says they're Indians). The process we established was that Solomon read the material, then retold it to me in his own words. Then on the sheet that was labeled for that particular bit of information, Solomon wrote down what he had said. Once all the material was read and then written about on the draft papers, Solomon combined the notes into sections, following the teacher's required organization.

I was okay. I felt Solomon had learned a lot, not only about the traditional Navajo but also about the process of research. My heart went out to all those students who have parents who would not, or could not, help their children as I had helped Solomon.... [He] still felt fairly competent about himself as a writer when this report was finished. How would he have felt about himself if he had done the very best he could have done on his own and then received the big red F that he probably would have gotten?

The Research Paper Nightmare

In our years as students, and later as teachers, how many horror stories have we heard about the research paper? How many of us have known (or have been) students like Solomon, who begin the process of research with a teacher's task and topic, rather than a question that they personally want to explore? How many, like Solomon, have someone who is willing to collaborate with them in the lonely quest for knowledge, and how many must do so entirely on their own?

Students aren't the only ones who suffer. A great many of us spend agonizing hours, checking and counting students' index cards, wading through quoted material, and policing papers for correct documentation. The horror stories don't stop once we've graduated from school. Let's think about why the research paper such a demanding task for both teachers and students alike.

Reflections: Reading Between the Guidelines

I'd like to ask you to imagine for a moment that you are somehow miraculously transported back to twelfth grade. You are handed this set of RESEARCH PAPER GUIDELINES (see figure 8.1) and are told that in four weeks you will be handing in a research paper for your high school English class. Take a few moments to read over this assignment. Reflect on the implicit assumptions and goals hiding behind the words. What is your first reaction? What confuses you? For what purposes do you think you'll be writing this report? Toward what outcomes and audiences? If you wanted to do a minimal job, just to get by, what would you do? You might want to take a few minutes to write about your impressions or share them with someone else.

GUIDELINES FOR SENIOR RESEARCH PAPER

Each senior at X high school is required to write a research paper for his English 12 class. This year, the paper will be written during the third marking period. Here is the timetable:

Week of January 29 — Assignment of paper. Topic Selection
February 5-February 16 — Review of process. Library resources. Preliminary research.
Week of February 19 — School vacation: continue research.
Thursday, March 8 — PRELIMINARY DRAFT DAY A draft of the paper will be written in class.
Week of March 19 — Final paper will be due (rotating schedule: Paper is due one week after preliminary draft is returned to student and will vary from class to class.

Length and Format:

a. Paper will be between 2,000 and 3,000 words (5-8 typed pages)
b. Paper will be typed
c. A minimum of five sources, excluding encyclopedias, must be used
d. Style guide is "Preparing the Research Paper" by Dangle and Haussman, 5th edition. Each English 12 student will be given a copy.

Grading:

a. Grade will count as 1/3 of the English grade in third quarter
b. Here is the deduction scale for late papers:
   (1) Papers received in week of March 26—10 points deducted
   (2) Papers received in Week of Apr. 2—20 points deducted
c. A student <u>must</u> complete a paper. However, any papers completed after the end of the third quarter (April 6) will receive credit to meet course requirement only. The zero grade assigned for averaging into the third quarter grade will not be changed.

Plagiarism: Students will avoid plagiarism, that is, appropriating and passing off as their own writing the <u>ideas</u> of another. To avoid doing this, a student should use footnotes to give credit for a direct quotation and <u>to give credit for an original or unusually interesting opinion or interpretation which he has put into his own words.</u>

Return of papers: Research papers will be returned to students in class so that they can read the teacher's comments. Papers will be kept on file by the school for one year, then discarded. <u>Any student who wishes a copy of his paper must make one before submitting the paper.</u>

GOOD LUCK! I anticipate reading your interesting, well-written papers.

Figure 8.1

This particular assignment sheet was given to me by a high school teacher, who got it from a friend. Each teacher in her district is required to assign a research paper, similar to the one described in these guidelines. She tells me that each step of this process is carefully detailed in the districtwide curriculum, along with sample formats for bibliography cards, thesis statements, final outline format, and list of sections for the final paper. Teachers and students have few choices about the process, form, and topic of this particular assignment. From what I've seen, this set of guidelines is fairly typical of those used in most high school English classrooms.

When I first read over this assignment, I was struck by the last line: "GOOD LUCK! I anticipate reading your interesting, well-written papers," especially given what went before about adhering to rigid standards of length and content, avoiding plagiarism, and making duplicate copies of papers that will be read presumably by no one other than teacher, and kept on file in the office for one year before being destroyed! But the potential problems with this research task go well beyond the hidden messages it sends to students about the meaninglessness of outcome and purpose. It has to do with the process that students are required to follow in completing this assignment.

Permanence and Exploration in the Research Process

This assignment sheet, and many others like it, do something that a great many school research tasks do. They lay out a rather rigid procedure, which doesn't recognize the fact that writing is a messy process that rarely proceeds the same way for any two people. Because of this lockstep procedure, assignments like these usually end up leaving at least some students out in the cold.

This is a problem that Pat, a tenth grade English teacher, recently had to grapple with. As a relative newcomer in her department, she sought advice from her colleagues on how to teach the research paper. Her first experience was fraught with self-doubt and anxiety. She reflects:

> As I looked back on my experience teaching the research paper to my tenth grade students, I was initially puzzled. Why did some students complete their papers with a zest that even a doctoral student would admire while others did not even complete bibliography cards and still others wrote papers lacking in depth or conviction? ... The first step in [the district's guidelines] (also the cause of my demise) was The List.... Peggy, the librarian, had a list of topics that teachers commonly used from year to year. She would add or delete topics as

> *they related to current events.... I felt that if Peggy and I already knew that the materials were available in the near vicinity, we would be more easily able to help the students.... I was (also) afraid that if I just said to choose anything, then I would get seven papers on steroids in sports and another five papers on abortion. Not only would I be bored reading these papers, but the kids would be fighting over the limited number of materials....*
>
> *Only now do I realize that my students needed guidance in topic choice. It was too much for the majority of students to veer away from the designated list. Although many students were not interested in topics on the list, they had trouble thinking of something that they could write about.*
>
> *For a long time I have looked at what I could have done differently. I looked everywhere but at the beginning. Giving a too closed assignment with everything lockstep was not a motivating assignment. It was too far removed from [the students'] real lives.*

What's Wrong With This Picture?

As both Pat and Kathleen observe, one of the reasons that the typical research paper assignment is so nightmarish is that "research" in schools is thought of in very narrow ways. Usually it involves several trips to the library and slavish attention to proper documentation. Students are given few chances to do research in some exploratory fashion as they pass through the grade levels from elementary school to high school and later to college.

By the time they get to the research paper, students are suddenly confronted with a task that seems permanent and fixed, right from the start. They are given a couple of days to choose a topic from a list provided by someone else. Yet, how many of us have started to write something and found ourselves changing the topic several times as we learned what we wanted to say through writing about it?

By the time students reach the final draft stage, the language of their report must be unequivocal and certain. No wonder so many students like Solomon, who are treated like novices from the beginning, have trouble enjoying the process of research. Their language commits them to intellectual positions at a time when they feel most insecure about what they know. Yet, as Peter Elbow (1985) has observed, "People can be more careful and get their drafts **righter** when they spend some of their time unhooking themselves from the demands of audience and inviting themselves to get it wrong" (p. 290).

Fortunately, through collaboration with his mother, Solomon learned that research needn't be a lonely process. He discovered that he could play with tentative, exploratory language (telling his mother what he learned) before transforming his ideas into a more permanent form. This freed him up to say what he needed to say and probably saved him from that "big red F" that he was so worried about. In other words, as he spoke aloud to a trusted adult, his language could be playful and exploratory. It required little commitment from him until he was ready to write his final paper. Let's consider for a moment how the notion of commitment plays itself out in the classroom.

Exploring the Issues of Commitment in Language

We often hear about commitment in the sense of ownership. Good teachers find ways to get their students committed to the reading, writing, speaking, and listening that they do. Of course, this version of commitment, as ownership, is crucial to good teaching and learning.

But there is another, equally important definition of commitment, and that is the commitment that various language acts seem to demand from learners. Some language acts are totally exploratory. We don't know or care where they will take us. Perhaps we are making a list of things to write about at some later time, scribbling nonsense words during a meeting, rehearsing an argument with a co-worker as we drive in our car. These language acts demand little from us. They are ephemeral, disposable. Because they are not witnessed, we can pretend they never happened. We can use the ideas we got from them later, as we turn our attention to more formal writing or talking, without ever being held accountable for them. Writing isn't the only form of language that can be exploratory and tentative. "Small talk," rehearsing, pleasure reading, and listening are ephemeral; they don't count for or against us, rarely linger past the moment, are quickly forgotten. They are means to an end and little more.

Other language acts are more permanent. Public speeches and performances, employment application letters, doctoral dissertations, and the legendary high school academic research paper are just a few examples. These language acts demand that we weigh our words, step out of an exploratory stance, and ask how our language is affecting others. We know that we may be judged by our actions and words long after the ink has dried, the tape has stopped running, or the curtain has come down.

I remember writing an essay in high school that was published in the *Chicago Tribune's* youth column more than twenty years ago. Although I was certainly proud of the text at the time, today, I'm mortified when I happen to come across the yellowed newspaper clipping with the essay and a picture of me in black "cat-eye" glasses. I feel the same way about some of the academic papers I've published at the beginning of my career. I can't take those words back, no matter how much I wish they would vanish into the air!

Because I know that some words commit me to a stance, an opinion, a certain self-image, I don't thoughtlessly write or speak them. I think about them for a long time. I create many drafts. I look up words in my thesaurus and try them out on my most trusted friends. Each chapter of this book, for instance, has undergone perhaps fifty revisions, and probably many more in my mind, before the words even hit the paper. There is a review process, in which anonymous readers respond, and chapters are revised again. I meet with my editor and argue about concepts and terminology. Sometimes I win the argument; other times he does.

Even the concepts of "exploration" and "permanence" in this chapter have undergone many changes before being cast in these exact terms. Through several drafts, I considered a whole host of other choices: "temporary" and "permanent," "tentative" and "fixed," "ephemeral" and "permanent," and so on. I tried these terms out on other teachers I was working with. When I got a lot of puzzled looks and questions, I'd reconsider my choice of terms. I'm not even sure I'm completely satisfied with them today. But there's no changing them now, at least not in this edition. The fact is, though, that as I wrestle with these terms, I make important decisions about the concepts behind them — choices that end up teaching me more about those concepts.

A curriculum should have a balance of both exploratory and permanent language acts. Arthur Applebee in the United States (1982) and James Britton and his colleagues in the United Kingdom (1975) have offered some compelling evidence about the lack of tentative, exploratory language in classrooms. Most of the time, according to these large-scale studies, students produce language that is evaluated and judged at every step of the way. As a result there is little chance for exploration, for trial and error. Students become self-conscious and careful, afraid to take risks. In the case of the typical research paper, the task becomes a nightmare rather than the intriguing process of personal exploration that it might be. But, can the research paper be saved? By all means!

Researching Research

People of all ages — from childhood to adolescence to adulthood — can enjoy and profit from the process of doing research as long as they have real reasons for doing so and as long as they are given chances to use language in exploratory, tentative ways before transforming their ideas in the more permanent form of the report or the public presentation. I like to think of "research" in Ann Berthoff's terms — as "REsearch." Berthoff writes:

> It helps to pronounce "research" the way southerners do: REsearch. Research, like REcognition, is a REflexive act. It means looking — and looking again. The new kind of REsearch would not mean going out after new "data," but rather REconsidering what is at hand.... We do not need new information: We need to think about the information we have (1987, p. 30).

Looking at research in this way means beginning with the assumption that learners already have some connection with their topics, even if that connection is only a deep and compelling curiosity to learn more about them. When research begins from a deep and personal interest on the part of the learner, the whole process begins as an exploration and moves naturally toward a more permanent, committed position. Let's consider another example.

Further Reflection: Searching and REsearching

One of the biggest stumbling blocks that people have when they think of doing research is that vision of spending long, lonely hours in the library, documenting what other people have already discovered. The library, of course, can be a marvelous source of information, but there are other sources as well. Interviews, surveys, observations, artifacts, and photographs are all useful sources. Usually, though, they don't find their way into the standard research paper checklist.

As one way of taking some of the sting out of research, I'd like to invite you to engage in a very short "mini research project" that should take no more than one hour. If you're working with a group of four or five other people, you might want to break up the task in some way. If you're not working with a group, you can try this by yourself or perhaps consider how you might modify it for your own students; in this latter case, you will probably want to stretch it out over a few days and change some aspects of the process.

Topic exploration.

Start by considering how many interesting things you might discover more about within a few blocks of where you are right now. Begin with a basic idea, but feel free to modify it as you go. For instance, you might decide to find out something about the quality of service at a fast food restaurant in the area, the traffic patterns on a nearby street, or the varieties of trees or shrubbery on the grounds surrounding the building you are in. The point is to research (as in "re-search," see anew, discover as if for the first time) some place within a few blocks of wherever you are located.

Data Collection.

The sources you can use for information can, of course, include print sources such as those found in libraries, book rooms, or bulletin boards. But there is a whole variety of other possibilities as well — everything from interviews and observations to descriptions and recollections. Work from this list if you like:

Interviews (talk to a shopkeeper, custodian, secretary, librarian, etc.).

Observations (watch carefully and note what goes on for a period of time, say fifteen minutes. Pay attention to all your senses as you observe—sight, hearing, smell, and so forth. Take notes about what you discover.

Artifacts (Collect any materials which might help you and others to understand the topic more thoroughly (pamphlets, objects, etc.).

Recollections (If you happen to know something about the topic already, recall and write about what you know).

Reading: Consider not only books, but other materials as well (pamphlets, notices on bulletin boards, newspapers, maps, and the like.).

> *Research plan.*
>
> *Now decide on some kind of tentative research plan for how you will use your time. If you are working with a group, you can split up the work of collecting data in some way. For instance, one group member might make observations, another may collect artifacts, another might interview people. Don't forget to decide on a time limit so that people will be clear about when to stop collecting data and return to the group.*
>
> *When you're near the end of your time, try to write something about what you learned or prepare a very brief presentation to share the highlights of what you found with a larger group. This doesn't have to take the form of a standard written report but can be a letter, a poem, or a group performance or demonstration of some kind.*

Here's an example. One summer, I was working with a group of teachers in a workshop. We had been meeting every day for two weeks in late July. Although the room had an air conditioner, it was so noisy that we chose to endure the ninety degree heat and the occasional wasp rather than to turn the air conditioner on and suffer permanent hearing damage! One group of three teachers decided to make good use of its sixty minutes outside of class. They each visited a different ice cream establishment within a block of our classroom. Of course, they decided to be thorough and rigorous in their data collection by sampling the offerings at each location! Their eventual plan, though, was to find out something about the menu at each place as well as something about the patrons and their preferences. Here is an excerpt of their final report:

*Mini Report: Ice Cream Establishments
in the Marshall Street Area
This mini-research paper focuses on the three ice cream frozen yogurt establishments in the Marshall Street area: TCBY, Baskin Robbins, and Friendly's. We were interested in:*

1. Which was the most popular establishment?
2. What flavors or items do people order?
3. Who frequents these establishments?

We also wanted to make some hypotheses about why one place would be more popular than another. Our first step was to survey people on Marshall Street. Ten people responded to this brief oral survey, and these people represented a mix of age, gender, and ethnicity. In response to a question about which of the three establishments each person favored, seven people said BR, two had no preference, and one said Friendly's. When asked what their favorite flavors were, only chocolate and gummy bear came out with more than one vote. Three other flavors mentioned included some chocolate (chips, sauce).

We also did a comparison of general characteristics, offerings, and atmosphere of each establishment. Additionally, we observed in each establishment to see what kind of people frequented it and what they ordered [In the next section, each location is described, in terms of its offerings, prices, and clientele]....

With little time to think carefully, we made only tentative hypotheses as to why Baskin Robbins is so popular. We felt that BR was simply better known (a few people didn't know what or where TCBY was). We also thought the variety of flavors figured in as well as the location. We also wondered if TCBY was attracting young women because of yogurt's reputation as being non-fattening. We thought perhaps some people also just don't know much about frozen yogurt — what it tastes like and how it compares to ice cream.

Of course thoughtful, systematic research requires far more time than sixty minutes. However, it's surprising how much you can learn about the process of conducting research from a very brief experience such as this one. I've seen many clever and creative variations — everything from studying the beer drinking habits of patrons in a campus bar to interviewing construction workers about a library remodeling project. There are variations on the "final reports," too — everything from an impromptu readers' theatre presentation to a poem.

Think for a moment about the ways in which this research process differed from the typical academic research task that students encounter in school. If you tried this mini-research project, how did you feel as you explored your topic? What made the process easier for you? Finally, how might you use some of what you learned in your own classroom? One of the most obvious things you might have learned is how much easier the process of research is to manage when you can concentrate on exploring topics of interest and temporarily suspend your concerns about correctness, form, and your final product.

If you were actually going to try some modification of this experience with your students, there might be a point at which you could help them to translate what they've learned into a more formal text or a polished performance for an audience. At this point in the process, it would seem natural to speak to them about documenting sources for the benefit of others and polishing their final products. Whatever the case, you would try to make the process of research a compelling pursuit of interesting questions rather than an exercise in correctness and form. This means leading from an exploratory stance toward one of greater commitment. In the next few pages, you'll read about a high school teacher who helped students to do just that.

Classroom Closeup: Project "Our Town"

Martha teaches eleventh grade English in a rural school in central New York. She has taught in this school for the past thirteen years. She describes the school and her students:

Gordon, New York, is a community of factory workers and professionals. There are also a large number of families on welfare and a great many children who live in one parent homes. The school population in grades seven through twelve is 465. When students enter seventh grade, they are placed in one of two tracks. Track one consists of courses for regents (the New York state accreditation board) credit designed for those who are planning to attend a four-year college. Track two courses generally consist of courses that prepare students to enter the work force or attend a community college after high school. While students may move from track one to track two with ease, movement from a track two to a track one program is rare. Both levels prepare students to meet minimum competencies required by the State Education Department, and, in the case of track two course work, students are often challenged beyond this minimum level. The English department requires all students to write a one-thousand word research paper on a topic of choice in grades nine through twelve.

One of the more interesting features of working in a small rural community is that Martha sometimes teaches the same students during more than one of their high school years. These particular eleventh grade students have been in her English classroom since the tenth grade. As a result, they have developed a comfortable sense of trust and camaraderie.

Martha has always assigned a research paper. In the past, her students would work from four to six weeks gathering information from the library and writing a standard academic research report. According to Martha, the workload for this assignment was awesome:

> *I work two to six weeks teaching the components of research to this audience, and then am often faced with eighty, five-to-seven page papers to evaluate. The grade on these papers is very important since it can count up to 25 percent of a quarter's grade. Students can pass or fail at ten weeks on the weight of this unit alone.*

There are other problems with this assignment besides the demands on her time. For instance, since the students are usually researching eighteen or twenty different topics, she has no uniform topic base from which to present mini-lessons on the process of research. In addition, Martha observes,

> *even though I present the methods of conducting research in whole class mini-lessons, students practice and apply these steps independently. Students work solo, and with only forty-two minutes of class time, I find it impossible to check every student's progress every day. Information gathering is completed in the library. Organizing and writing the paper is done in the classroom, in a workshop setting, over the period of one to two weeks. There are students who are aggressive about getting help, but there are as many who will not ask for assistance or who will state that they do not need help when, actually, they are floundering. This is often not discovered until we are well into the unit and a time for reworking the paper or conducting more research is at a minimum. When the unit is complete, my students breathe a sigh of relief to be done with it for yet another year and we move on to the next unit of study.*

After many years of teaching the research paper, Martha was ready for a change. She reflected:

> *As I look at the class as a whole, it seems evident that the audience these students wrote for was not one they invested in.... [E]ven though they had a personal purpose, learning more about their topic, they had no purpose for communicating that learning to some unknown audience. Such understandings clearly point out the need for a change. In the future, I will ask students to prepare a paper that will teach their peers something about a topic they have researched.... Audience and purpose will move from the vague back seat to the driver's seat.*

From Researching to REsearching

A year earlier, Martha had become interested in the Foxfire network, an organization founded by a rural teacher named Elliot Wigginton, who, for many years, had been helping his own students to conduct research on the many interesting things that happened in their surrounding communities. The student-authored *Foxfire* Books are a great resource for topics of local and regional interest. One can imagine that they are also a great source of pride for the students who create them. A year ago, Martha became involved with the Network of Empire State Teachers, a local affiliate of the Foxfire Teacher Outreach Network, headquartered in Rabun Gap, Georgia.

The previous year, Martha decided the she would involve her class in a collaborative research effort that she would call "Project Our Town." This year's project would be similar to last year's. Students could choose to work independently or in pairs. They would be encouraged to explore topics of local interest through a variety of data. In addition to traditional materials found in libraries, these sources might also include interviews, observations, and films, to name a few. They also had access to a variety of other tools: computers, typewriters, video cameras, and tape recorders. The form of their final project was negotiable. They could choose to create a videotape, a written report, an oral presentation with visual aids and handouts, or any other combination of options for performance or publication. Martha's only stipulation was that they had to have a written component as one part of the project.

Although their final projects could be shared with interested people outside of the classroom, the students also planned to share their projects with each other at the end of the unit. Here, Martha was trying to consciously move audience and purpose to a more central position, giving her students real purposes for sharing the information they found with others who mattered to them. She was also trying to give them some options about how they would be using language, including exploratory, as well as more permanent kinds of reading, writing, speaking, and listening.

Negotiating and Collaborating

On a cloudy day in March during my spring break from the university, I visited Martha's classroom. One look around this very busy, friendly place showed how many things she had done to involve her students in their own learning. She explained that, as a part of her work with the students, she holds regular class meetings. During these meetings, she brings a large easel with chart paper to the circle of chairs where her students are seated in the corner of the room. She remarks: "Sometimes I'm the recorder, sometimes somebody else is." There is evidence of collaborative goal-setting all over the room. On a piece of chart paper on one wall is an agenda for the year. In the early weeks of the fall term, Martha had shared the district expectations as well as the New York State Curriculum with her students and asked them to help her to plan the work schedule for the semester.

She begins by handing out a list of "givens of the classroom." These are things that she considers "non-negotiable." "But within that framework," Martha observes, "there is a lot of room for choice." After students have read over her list of givens, they work in small task groups, generating ideas about how much time they want to spend on particular activities and what kind of help they need. Martha explained, "This particular group felt that this was their third year of doing research papers so they needed more time than they needed teaching about how to do a research paper."

By the time I visited Martha's classroom, her students had been working together for several weeks on the latest phase of their individual projects. On this particular day, I asked the students to sit in the circle in the far corner of the room, the place where all of their planning meetings usually take place. They agreed to talk a bit about how this research process was perhaps different from other kinds of research projects they had been involved in.

Randy began: "Usually research papers are boring, but this is different. Most of us enjoy what we're doing. Miss S. has been one teacher who has dared to explore the outer boundaries of her imagination!" Another student explained how they went about their class project last year, which had focused on volunteer emergency services in the local area:

> We put a big list up on poster board and then we chose our topics, whether we wanted to do ambulance, police, fire, or towing. We got into small groups and researched separate areas and then we combined it all together. We would call or have somebody contact the people who were included in the volunteer emergency services, and we would set up interviews. We asked them to sign releases so we could use their pictures on video. Then we went to certain areas and videotaped a partial interview or maybe a tour of the facilities.

From Exploration to Permanence

The process of conducting their research was different from the research paper assignment that Martha had given in the past. This time, the students began by engaging in a variety of **exploratory** language activities (for example, transcribing interviews, taking observation al notes, talking with experts, writing in task journals, planning collaboratively with peers). At some point, students moved on to more permanent and carefully polished language (for example, letters of request, grant proposals, contracts of work to be done). Martha allowed her students to engage in less threatening kinds of writing and talking before building up to more formal kinds in the later stages of the project.

Although there had to be a writing component in each student's project, they had several choices about the kind of writing tasks in which they would engage. For instance, during the first phase of last year's project, Martha's students were involved in writing a collaborative grant, which she submitted to the regional Foxfire steering committee. If students had been asked to do this kind of writing independently, there would have been many who would have found the task intimidating, if not impossible. Instead, Martha found a way to model the task for them, making it easier for individual students to write grant proposals the next time around. She described the collaborative process she followed in writing this first grant:

> *I stood up in front of class and presented the form we were supposed to follow on the chart paper. I said, "These are the questions we have to answer. What do you want to put in there?" I wrote down what they said. I typed it up, gave them the contract, and said, "Please check. Is everything in there? Is this what you want it to say?" At the end, everybody had to sign off on it.*

That year, the class was awarded $150 for the first phase of their research. Since that time, two other students have received awards from grant proposals they wrote on their own.

In talking with Martha's students that day, I was impressed by the great variety of topics they were pursuing. Jay and Frank were writing a report on police brutality. They had been researching the topic in the library for several days and were in the process of incorporating some information from a recent local newspaper account into their report.

Chris was doing critical reviews of five movies: "Kindergarten Cop," "Home Alone," "The Money Pit," "Blind Date," "Look Who's Talking," and "License to Drive." Rebecca was doing a report on AIDS, while Gwen had chosen to do a library research report on child abuse. Gwen's sources of information included pamphlets and manuals from the local child protective agencies, as well as other library resources. She later prepared a presentation for a group of kindergarten students and their teacher.

On any given day, students work collaboratively or independently in a workshop setting. Martha moves among the tables and gives help where she is needed. On the day that I visited, she helped Jay and Frank to create the first part of their script on police brutality while other students went to the library to find more information on their topics.

At another table, Sam and P.J. were in the process of comparing two local restaurants on the basis of quality and service. They had just finished interviewing students in study hall as part of an opinion poll. Today they were talking about how to write their final report. In the early stages of their project, they visited each restaurant for the purpose of gathering information on the menu offerings, the quality of the food (they compared each restaraunt on the basis of their chicken wings), and the speed of service. Their final project will include a written explanation, a videotape, and some charts that show how the two facilities were rated by their survey respondents.

Randy and Mike: Collaborating and Cooperating

Randy and Mike are both students in a local cooperative education program. Randy is studying precision machining while Mike is studying diesel mechanics. They are reviewing a set of diagrams they have made of gasoline and diesel engines in preparation for their final presentation. Their report will focus on the relative merits of the diesel and the gasoline engine. For the past several days, they have been interviewing an automobile mechanic and a diesel mechanic. They are in the process of writing the script that they will use for their slide presentation to the class, which will be videotaped and saved for use by interested people outside of their classroom and school.

They have decided on a slide presentation and videotape for their final product because they feel that these media will allow them to explain some very complicated concepts through the use of diagrams and other visual aids. As Mike remarked, "It's kind of hard to explain a carburetor to somebody if you can't point to things on a diagram and see where people are confused."

Randy and Mike are not particularly fond of writing. In Mike's words: "I got writer's block and (Randy) hates to write!" Martha explained how the two boys decided to work together:

Because they were in similar programs they gravitated toward each other. They began talking about what they were each interested in. And then, I walked away and when I came back, they said, "You know, we'd like to compare the diesel and the gasoline engine." They both knew, because of their feelings about writing, that they would rather not work alone.

Interestingly, despite their rather negative feelings about writing, their project has involved several kinds of informal and more formal writing tasks. For example, they began the project by writing up this contract, which had to be approved by their teacher (see figure 8.2):

Project Proposal: Randy and Mike

Topic: Comparison of gas and diesel efficiencies

    Why diesel is more efficient.

Design: Written summary of the topic video cassette of diagrams and real motors —go to BOCES — slides for oral presentation / lots of research at BOCES and libraries.

Purpose: Teaching novices the difference between a diesel and gasoline .

Scedule —   2 week section of research on bottle gas and diesel

               3-4 week put information together for proper presentation.

Grading: 60% on finished paper — comparison of efficiency
             20% in-class productivity
             20 % on tape/slide presentaion

Figure 8.2

After completing their contract, Mike and Randy decided to apply for a grant to cover the cost of videotape and slide film. They collaborated on this proposal (see figure 8.3).

Grant Proposal: Randy and Mike

NEST Mini-Grant Application

A. This is an English class of eleventh grade students at Gordon Central high school, a rural school in Central New York.
B. Randy and I are going to compare gas and diesel engines. We will set up a slide presentation of 40-50 slides with charts, diagrams, and pictures of the engines. We will write a prepared script to go along with the slides.
C. We want to show the differences in the efficiencies of the engines and show why the diesel engine is becoming more widely used.
D. We hope to learn how much more efficient the diesel is, and why the diesel motor is slowly taking over the marked. We know a fair amount about it, and we want to learn more. We are both going to be mechanics, so we feel we ought to explore this topic more in depth.
E. We will take pictures of the engines to point out things. We will take pictures of the charts and diagrams. We will take pictures of and interview the diesel and auto mechanics at BOCES to get their opinions on the topic. We will do

Commitment: Exploration and Permanence in the Language Act

---

library research to get a brief history. We will organize the material into a slide show with a script. We will video tape the slide show presentation.

F. Budget

1. Three rolls of film at $6.00 each = $20
2. Developing of film at $5.00 per roll = $15
3. One video tape at $5 = $5

Total = $40

G. Timeline:

Purchase film: 2/12
Take Pictures: 2/14, 2/24-28
Set up interview questions: 2/13
Interview Mr. Sworing 2/14
Interview Mr. Sid Compton 2/14
Get film processed: 2/28
Organize Slides: 3/1-3/4
Write Script: 3/4-3/10
Make audio tape to accompany slides and script 3/10
Present slides show and video tape: 3/16

H. Audience: 7th period English, Mr. Sworing, Sid Compton, and upon request.

I. We'll evaluate ourselves by taking an opinion pole from the people who watch the presentation. They will be asked to write a small paragraph on what they learned that they didn't know before. We will also write a paragraph telling what we learned about these engines that we did not know before.

J. Administrator's Support:_____

Figure 8.3

Interestingly, these two young men who are so negative toward writing have managed to compose some fairly complicated texts. The script for their final presentation will also demand some degree of writing skill. However, for these two students, having the choice about what aspects of their project will be written has made all of the difference in their feelings of confidence and their overall enjoyment of the research process. Furthermore, as Martha observes:

Although Randy and Mike have selected topics that they're experts in, they are becoming experts in other ways too. They've learned how to take slides, how to run a video machine, and how to do a variety of other things.

"Process Grade"

Students in Martha's classroom are given credit for using language in informal, exploratory ways. As part of what she calls a "process grade," students are responsible for handing in all of the informal writing they did in the process of conducting their research projects: transcripts of interviews, research notes, and preliminary drafts, for instance.

In addition, as a way of keeping track of each student's progress, Martha asks her students to keep a daily journal, in which they record how they spent their time and keep track of any problems or questions they encounter. Students are given credit for writing in the journal, but individual entries are not corrected or graded. The project journals are primarily a way for Martha to monitor progress and to offer help or gentle prodding to students when they need it. Martha explains:

> *When they've completed the project, students are asked to write a "one pager," in which they tell me what they've learned. Their journal, together with my classroom observations, and all of their informal writing, accounts for their process grade. When they write the "one pager," I give them a chance to tell me anything else that I might need to know in order to assign their grade.*

A few weeks later, Randy and Mike were able to complete their presentation. The final project took a bit longer than they had originally planned. However, the process of planning and negotiating deadlines was a valuable experience that will hopefully serve them later in their lives outside of school.

Thus, all of the students in Martha's classroom have learned to use language in various ways. Some of their language acts are tentative, informal, exploratory; others are more formal, committed, and polished. In the end, all students are able to work toward the publishing and performing phase with the help of other classmates and their teacher. Martha sums up her experiences with the research projects this way:

> *This is probably one of the most exhausting approaches to teaching that I've ever experienced, but it's got to be the most exciting.... There is generally a sense of self-esteem that doesn't happen in (the classrooms) that I grew up in.... I wonder how many of us continue to teach in the same manner, year after year, sensing that something is wrong but not really knowing how to get at it, how to make a change.... My implementation of this new approach to "The Re-*

search Paper" unit and a subsequent study of the results will help me to know whether it is a better way. In any case it will no longer be the same old way.

As Martha discovered, students will make their own decisions, will take ownership of their work, and will explore their own compelling questions as long as they are helped to strike that balance between exploration and permanence in the process of using language to learn.

Classroom Connections

Martha began her research project by helping students to find their own questions and then convincing them that they weren't starting from a position of complete ignorance. Randy and Mike, for instance, already knew something about gasoline and diesel engines at the start of their research project. Their interviews with experts, as well as the process of selecting and labeling diagrams, creating their script, and explaining their topic to others taught them even more. Here are some ways that you can make the research process come alive for your students.

Expanding the Options.

I believe that students in the upper grades would have fewer problems writing more formal academic research reports if they were introduced to the process of research throughout all of the grade levels. Think about options that exist for exploring questions within and outside of the library. In social studies class, students could conduct opinion polls of their classmates on topics of current interest. In science, they could keep observational notebooks in which they report on everything from chemical reactions to natural phenomena over a period of several days or weeks. They might interview staff in community agencies about real-world topics like applying for a mortgage or buying a new car. They might look through magazines and newspapers for evidence of propaganda in advertising, choose a period or a date in history and analyze newspapers and popular magazines of the day for evidence of fashions, fads, and current events, as part of a literature unit. The possibilities are nearly unlimited. Eventually, students can be led toward more formal research tasks but only after they have begun to see the real purpose for research: looking deeply at something for new evidence it reveals — REsearch, in Ann Berthoff's terms.

Striking the Balance.

There can also be many opportunities for students to engage in more tentative, exploratory language before committing themselves to intellectual positions. They can have choices about the form of their final products — choices that stem from the topics themselves rather than preset notions about style and form. If students have trouble with a particular language task, as Randy and Mike did, they can be encouraged to work collaboratively, helping each other in less threatening situations, before moving on to more challenging ones.

Negotiating the curriculum.

Not all students will be eager to explore their own topics or venture out of the safe world of the classroom and the teacher's assignments. Nor should teachers abdicate all responsibility for classroom procedures and policies. On the other hand, part of our goals should be to get students less dependent on us and more dependent on their own resources.

I've found that there's a difference between controlling the classroom procedures and controlling students' ideas or taking ownership of students' texts. As teachers, we know more about running a successful classroom than most of our students do. It's our responsibility to step in with our best judgments about how long certain activities might take or what topics need to be covered during the school year. On the other hand, our students are the best judges of what is interesting to them, what they need to know, and what they already know.

Martha, for instance, began with certain "givens." She was bound by some obligations within her school system and her state department of education. She felt fine about stipulating, for instance, that the research project would have to have a writing component. At the same time, she accepted her class's request that she spend less time in formal instruction on research techniques and give them more unstructured time to do the tasks that lay before them. The more you can involve students in making their own decisions, the greater likelihood that they will find a topic that calls them forth to greater learning.

From the Hypothetical to the Real

One of the biggest challenges that teachers from all grade levels and content areas face is helping students to find real reasons for investigating, questioning, and challenging the obvious in the world beyond the classroom. When we find ways to do this, we tap into the magical spirit of inquiry that is within each person.

We can probably all remember times when we became caught by the excitement of finding information about some topic we really wanted to know more about. Ruth, for instance, worked as a journalist for a small newspaper before deciding to go back to graduate school and pursue a career in teaching. She describes a professor who did for her what Martha did for her high school students. She recalls:

To fill a core curriculum requirement, I signed up for Introduction to Journalism 101. Here I met professor Robert Cole and my career as a writer began. What was so good about the way he taught writing? I'm not sure. But he made the writing process seem like an adventurous quest for knowledge and information. Men and women — reporters — had been imprisoned for discovering certain true information and attempting to educate the public with their new discovery. Other reporters for the Washington Post discovered Watergate, much to the chagrin of the Nixon administration. I learned that writers seek to learn the truth and that this learning is adventurous. You could find yourself talking to the President of the United States, you could find yourself in a third world country gathering information on how a sunglass company exploits poor Mexican peasants who are living in cardboard shacks, or you could learn about how the world operates and where you personally fit into the grand scheme of things....

My first real writing was for the college newspaper. I still remember my favorite article. It was a piece about the history of my college.... The area was right next to the train station and it was surrounded by beautiful old but dilapidated brownstones.... It was a different world. I savored it and took notes in my little notebook and then rode my bike back to campus. It seemed so real compared to the institutionalized state college I attended where most of the students were of the same age group and race, where no old people existed, no dogs or cats or children, and less than one percent of the students were handicapped. The campus was some mad social scientist's experiment, I felt sometimes, and we were being measured by those hypothetical assignments we had to do .... It was not real.

As Ruth discovered, real research begins not from a teacher's hypothetical assignment but from a student's real questions; not from an objective, impersonal place but from a desire on the part of students to learn about how the world operates and to decide where they "personally fit into the grand scheme of things." From this exploratory place, they can gradually move outward, making the knowlege they acquire more permanently theirs and sharing it with others along the way.

Explorations

1. **Name Your Own Exploration.** Begin with any questions that have occurred to you in reading this chapter. Pursue them in any way that seems appropriate, and document what you find in any form that seems comfortable. If you're stuck, try some of the options that follow, modifying them as you wish.

2. **Create Your Own Project.** You might want to plan a research project for your current or future students. Think of some possible themes or areas of study that they might pursue. Within one general topic area, what smaller questions might be explored? What sources of information might students consult? You can write about this project in the form of a "best case scenario" teaching tale or in the form of a description you might hand out to your students.

    Another possibility is to design a mini research project that your students might pursue. Imagine that you have only one class period within which to work (usually forty minutes to an hour). Design a set of instructions that would be appropriate for your particular students and the possibilities for collecting information outside of your classroom. Consider what kinds of data collecting techniques might be most appropriate for your content area. Try to cast this description in language that invites students to engage in learning that is tentative and exploratory rather than permanent and evaluated.

3. **Revising the Guidelines.** Find a research paper assignment sheet that you have used before or one that is recommended by your school district. Read this assignment sheet for the underlying messages it sends to students. After you've thought about, and perhaps written about these hidden messages, revise it. Phrase the guidelines in such a way that they give students more options, and invite them to pursue their own interesting questions. Do this with a partner or group, if possible.

4. **An "object lesson."** Think about an object that you use every day, something you are very familiar with. This might be something in your own back yard or something you carry around with you, like an appointment book or a wallet. Take a few minutes to note everything you can remember about the object you have chosen. Make a list of all of the questions you have at this point. Perhaps you might not remember its exact color or what is inside. Now find the original object. Take a few minutes to explore the questions you have and to make notes about things that hadn't occurred to you before. Try to get down even the most minute detail. When you're through, think about how this process of REsearching sharpened your awareness about something with which you were already familiar.

References

Applebee, A.N. (1982). *Writing in the secondary school: English and the content areas.* NCTE Research Report No. 21. Urbana, Illinois: NCTE.

Britton, J., Burgess, T. Martin, N., McLeod, A. & Rosen, H. (1975). *The development of writing abilities (11-18).* Schools Council Research Studies. London: MacMillan Education.

Berthoff, A. (1987). The teacher as REsearcher, in *Reclaiming the classroom: Teacher research as an agency for change.* D. Goswami & P. Stillman (Eds.). Upper Montclair, NJ: Boynton/Cook. (pp. 28-39).

Elbow, P. (1985). The shifting relationships between speech and writing. *College Composition and Communication, 36* (3).283-303.

CHAPTER 9

Case Study — Rebecca: "A Leap of Faith"

I knew from the start this school year would be a time of tremendous growth and change. This year all my students would write, take part in the process, and hopefully come to know the joy of writing. My priorities are different this year. In my plan book under "language," I simply write "Writer's Workshop." There are no page numbers, no exercises to assign, just a sense of where I want to go and what I want to see my students doing. I've learned the value of flexibility. I try to let my students guide me, to sense what they need and then take them in that direction.

Like a ship sailing in uncharted waters, I have changed my course many times. It has been a year of ups and downs as I struggle to develop my teaching. I've had successes and failures. I see myself learning and changing. But, it has not been a smooth year and I don't expect it will be. Learning is change and that sometimes means suffering a little along the way.

— *Rebecca*

I remember the first time I saw Rebecca, or perhaps I should say the first time I noticed her. She was taking part in a summer workshop I was teaching. Actually, she hadn't intended to take the course at all, but when another required course for her master's program in elementary education was unexpectedly cancelled, she managed to convince her adviser that a workshop on language across the curriculum would be something that might come in handy in her fourth grade classroom.

It took me a couple of days to notice her. I remember being surprised at her first comments in class because something on that first day had given me the impression that she might be a little shy. I also remember thinking that many times people who seem to be shy are usually the ones that end up saying the most provocative things, proving, of course, that they weren't shy at all, just waiting for the right moment to be heard. Rebecca signed up for another graduate course I taught during the following fall. I was amused and delighted when, later in the term, she reflected upon her early experience in the summer workshop.

> *July 29, 1991. As I reflect on the experiences and events that led me to conduct this research project, that date stands out in my mind. On that day I began an eight day "spiritual experience" that radically changed my perspective about writing...*
>
> *During the workshop I listened to discussions about purpose, choice, audience, stance, and much more. I talked about how to better handle writing instruction in my classroom. Articles by Atwell, Murray, and Graves allowed me to absorb what the experts had to say. I soaked up the "risk-okay" classroom climate that had been created, almost wishing I could bottle it and take it back to my own classroom.*
>
> *However, the most powerful aspect of the workshop was the writing. Throughout the workshop I wrote every day. It was difficult at first, but slowly I rediscovered the power of writing. As I wrote about different topics, for different audiences, I experienced again all that writing could do for me. A letter written to a close friend brought me to tears and to terms with her death. While struggling to write a twenty page paper I began to understand the meaning of "writing to learn." I had forgotten that there was a whole range of purposes and audiences for writing. By engaging in writing, I rediscovered all the possibilities it brought to my life.*
>
> *When I left the workshop on the last day I was not the same person. My brain had been filled with new ideas for utilizing writing in my classroom. My heart was filled with joy at the thought of having writing back in my own life and being able to share its power with my students. I had the courage to return to my classroom and try what I had learned. Yes, after eight days, I was heading home. As I thought of the road I had traveled, I knew that I would never be the same.*

Rebecca has graciously allowed me to print her story in the pages of this chapter. During that fall, she conducted a research project in her own classroom. As part of her work, she agreed to keep a journal, in which she would reflect upon her successes, failures, experiences, and feelings as she tried to create a writer's workshop in her classroom for the first time. After three months of keeping a journal and learning about her students, she was able to reflect on all of the changes she had made since that summer. She describes her classroom and her students:

My classroom is one of three fourth grades in a K-5 elementary school which serves about 500 students. It is located in a suburban area. I am currently working with twenty-five students, who are heterogeneously mixed with a wide range of abilities. In addition to my own students, two boys from another fourth grade classroom come into my classroom for forty minutes each day as part of a "push in" resource program. The concept of the push in program is to provide services for learning disabled students within the regular classroom environment. Each afternoon, Robin, the special education teacher, comes into my classroom to provide six learning disabled students with additional support. Her primary responsibility is to those children with a learning disability in written expression. However, she interacts with all the students, just as I also work with the learning disabled students.

Sometimes I feel unsure, threatened by all this. At those times, I try to let my students be my inspiration. In my teaching log I see times when I have turned to them for support... It is a wonderful sense of give and take. As they experiment with new types of writing, I support them, too.

The sense of authority has been altered in my classroom this year as students and teacher learn together. As Stephen (one of my students) said in his interview, "She's going to classes and she's learning what we're learning." The students see me not as a fearless leader but as a fellow traveller. That's not such a bad thing, is it?

As you read the pages of Rebecca's teaching journal, you will find that her story is not always neat or orderly; like most true stories of teaching, it has loose ends, false starts, unexplained leaps, and momentary steps backward. As you read her story, though, you will begin to see all the ways in which she created a climate for learning in her classroom.

Again, as with the case study about Lauren in Chapter five, you might want to read Rebecca's story and stop every so often to note your reflections in writing. If you want to engage in more systematic reflections, alone or with a group, I've included some suggestions in the **Explorations** section of this chapter.

Rebecca's Journal:
The "Rollercoaster Ride"

Wednesday, October 2nd

I am beginning to realize that this is going to be a rollercoaster ride. When I talked to Robin, the special education teacher, in late August, we decided she would work with my students who were labeled disabled in written and/or oral expression. I told her about my plans for this year and that they were sketchy. She knew I would be trying things on a trial-and-error basis. Luckily, this did not frighten her away. She was more than interested in the idea of kids actually enjoying to write.

I was a little nervous about having Robin in my room. After three years of having a classroom all to myself, I wasn't sure how I would adjust to sharing my room. As I reflect over the past few weeks, I am oh so grateful that I have had Robin's help. It has been so helpful to be able to talk to someone about what's working, what's not, and how we can improve the program.

The first week was more structured. We talked to the kids about topic sentences and sticking to a topic. But before we let them start writing, we sat down and hashed out our goals and purposes, etc. We spent two hours after school, but we came up with a lot of great ideas. For example, we decided to have author day. This will be a day when kids can share their pieces with their classmates. We have a special rocking chair for them to sit in, and it should be interesting. We are also having each student make an "About the Author" card, complete with photograph to display with their finished stories. Each piece will be put together as a book with a cover, title page, etc. We are also having the kids select at least one piece each marking period to submit for publication....

Some days are good and others aren't. Today was a bad day. The kids are finishing their first rough drafts and getting ready to conference. It took us forever to get started this afternoon. Robin was working with several learning disabled students who come to my room for the language instruction, and I was going to begin conferencing. The class had several options if

Case Study — Rebecca: A Leap of Faith

they were waiting to conference (they could read, write in their journals, or proofread their story with a friend).

At the end of fifty minutes I felt like I had accomplished very little and so did Robin. I had only managed to conference with two kids. The boy Robin had been working with had done nothing but fool around and distract others. Last of all, the kids didn't seem to be using their time constructively. They were noisy, and it wasn't writing related.

By 2:30 I was glad to see writing time end. I felt frustrated. As I drove home I wondered if this program was going to fly. That night, I talked on the phone to Robin. We decided that [we] would try to sneak in a few more conferences during S.S.R. (sustained silent reading) after playtime. This would mean more kids ready to work on their final copy during language. We were ready to march on to another day.

Thursday, October 3rd

Today was such a wonderful day. I got some more serious conferencing done with my students. I ate lunch with two of them and we went over their stories. It is so time consuming and yet so worthwhile.

By the time 1:50 rolled around I had about seven students ready to start final copies. I was determined that we would get started right away. Robin quickly introduced the forms she had made for the kids to put their stories in. They loved them and eagerly started. Robin grabbed the small handful of students who had not finished their stories and took them to one corner of the room.... I headed hesitantly to the front of the room.

I called a student who needed a conference. He and I began to look over his story. After a few minutes I glanced around and was pleasantly surprised. I saw three boys at the middle of the room at a small table discussing their stories. I saw other pairs reading their stories to each other. The group at the back of the room was quietly working on their final copies. Robin's group, including Jeremiah, were on task. To hell with conferencing. I just wanted to sit back and savor the situation. At the end of the fifty minutes I felt great (yes, this year is going to be a rollercoaster ride).

I took a few minutes to chat with the class. We talked about how hard it was to wait for conferences. But we also looked at how we could improve the situation and why today had gone so well. I told them that they knew a lot about writing and could help each other as opposed to waiting for me. I told them that I really wanted to continue doing writing this way but that I needed their help. We felt great about the way we had worked together.

I have to admit that conferencing is absolutely the best. I really enjoyed meeting and talking with the kids. Well, who knows what tomorrow will bring. But, with days like this I think I'll be able to survive.
October 6

"We read many fine things but never feel them until we follow the same steps as the author."

— John Keats

I put this quote up on my bulletin board last week, and as the days go by I see how true it is. The enthusiasm I see from my students makes every bit of work worth it. I have one boy who is very gruff and tough. But he just turns into a real softie when it comes to writing. His enthusiasm is uncontainable and I can't help but smile even when his spirit gets him into trouble. For example, the other day I had just gotten the kids' voices at an appropriate level when Alex yells out at the top of his lungs, "I need a conference!" Then the next afternoon I called Alex up and he said, with a smile on his face that was ear to ear, "Me? You're going to conference with me?" I replied, "Yes, before you drive me nuts." While we were conferencing he said, "Well, neither of these are my final piece." It made me smile to hear him using these words like "finished piece." Then there is the writing he started the other morning. He has been asking me at least three times a day, "When am I going to get my balloon story back? I'm not finished." He is just not going to rest until he gets that back.

When I was walking around the room the other day, he heard a girl say she really liked what she was working on and would like to put it on her computer. He turned around and said, "Ah — she had a good idea! Can you do that for me?" Then a few minutes later he was still thinking about it. I heard him saying, "I know! I can have my neighbor do it, he's got a computer."

Alex is just one example of the enthusiasm I am seeing from my students. Their enthusiasm feeds me every day. When I am sitting there conferencing with them it is exciting. They are so proud of themselves, and they feel important. I wonder if it is because they are getting to discuss their work with the teacher. I wonder if it changes the way they look at me? Do they see the concept of teacher in a different light?

I know I see them as very mature when they sit and talk about their pieces. They are, at one minute, unsure, saying, "I don't think this sounds *right," and at the next moment confident, making suggestions for changes. "What if we..." "Could I say..." "How about..."*

But, the important thing is that they are making decisions. They are realizing how difficult writing is and at the same time learning how to improve it.

10/6

I tried today, something like [Nancie] Atwell does at the beginning of each class — where she sets goals for what the students will be doing that day. I have strips of paper on my chalkboard and they have all the possible choices students can be working on. For example, "rough draft," "proofreading," "conference," "publishing," etc. I then have a magnet with each student's name. Right at the start of writing, the kids let me know what they are planning for that day. At a glance, Robin and I knew who should be doing what and who needed to see us. If a child finishes with one task, he/she simply moves the magnet to the appropriate place. Will this help? I'll have to wait and see.

Tuesday, October 8th

The class is still working on their first stories so today I continued to conference. It is just so time consuming. I think when everyone gets through their first story I'll feel better.

I did get an interesting look at one of my students today. We were discussing his story and I encouraged him to expand on what he had written. I was amazed at how he immediately began to do so. It was wonderful — he just rambled off a few descriptive sentences that really added to his story. We wrote down the additions on his rough draft.

As we continued to talk about his story, he played with words and phrases. He didn't seem to have a lot of confidence in himself though. At one point when I suggested something, he said something like, "You can say it right but I can't."

I wonder how much suggesting I should be doing? Am I doing too much? I have a hunch that if I wasn't worried about time, I'd be doing a lot less suggesting. I would like to ask the kids more questions and let them play with their story. This would probably be more time consuming and require several conferences to get the kids through a piece. I'm not really sure where to draw the line.

Wednesday, October 9th

Another day of conferences and another day of questions, failures and successes. Today I spent a lot of time with Brent. He was working on a murder mystery. The main character was Friday and his partner was Tuesday. It was quite a long piece. It didn't have any paragraphs but it was full of wonderful sentences.... At one point he left out the scene of the crime. As he was thinking about where it could have happened I got a glimpse of his thinking process. At first, he suggested "the mall." But then he said, "No, what would he do, kill everyone there?" After another moment he said "the dairy!"...

Each time I conference with students I continue to be amazed. The incredible range of diversity in their topics is very interesting. But I am also surprised by individual students and what they have and have not accomplished on their first piece. Some of the more interesting topics have come from my "average" students. Hmmmm...

Thursday, October 10th

As I continue to conference with students I see some patterns developing. When I read something that totally confuses me I ask the student, "Tell me what you wanted to say here." I like this approach because it allows me to help the student clarify his/her writing, but it is not seen as negative. I take on the role of the "audience" and ask questions where needed....

When I ask the students about their text, my concern is that they correct the error. If they come up with an alternative to what they have that is acceptable I let it go. I do not push them to come up with the "perfect" solution. My focus seems to be on getting them to play with the text and be comfortable with that. Is this all right?

Friday, October 11th

Well, today was our first official "author day." Our goal was to have each student go through the publishing process. We still had a small handful of students that weren't there yet, but we felt it was important to continue anyway.

We formed a circle and the special "author chair" was in place. We had a little talk with the kids about their role as "audience." We wanted them to understand that everyone had worked very hard to get to this point. We made it clear that it was time to enjoy and appreciate the efforts of their classmates. I think they appreciated Robin and I making the author's chair a "safe" place to be. It was really interesting to watch as they shared. Some felt quite comfortable and others were nervous.

As they shared their pieces it was interesting to see that the students were their own worst critics. As they heard other stories they were sure that theirs weren't quite as good. Especially Alex. He was quite verbal about the fact that he didn't want to read his. In his eyes it just didn't live up to the others.

At one point a student read about visiting the "confession" stand at a football game. Robin and I had to hold back our smiles.

When it came time for Robin to leave, there were still stories to be shared. The kids wanted to continue, but Robin assured them that she really didn't want to miss a single story. With some gentle persuading from the kids, Robin and I decided to continue author day on the following Tuesday.

After the room had been returned to order I had the kids take out a sheet of paper and answer the following question: "What did you think of the first author day?" I got some interesting and insightful responses. The kids reported feeling afraid, nervous, and embarrassed when reading their stories. But they also reported that these feelings went away once they got started.

Two students who read their stories felt that they were awful, compared to the others. Those that didn't get to participate were mixed in their reactions. One little girl was disappointed and couldn't wait to have a chance to share her story. Another little boy hoped he never got a chance because his was "stupid."

I learned a lot from this informal survey. I think most of the kids care what their classmates think and they want to write something they will enjoy.

Wednesday, October 16

Tonight I realized something. Throughout this entire first story, not one single student asked me about evaluation. The subject of grades is very high on kids' minds and so this struck me as odd. Did they want a grade? Did they expect a grade?

I thought back to the beginning of the entire writer's workshop. I remembered that when we began, Robin and I talked about "author day." Right from the start, the kids knew we were having this. Had this influenced their expectations about what was going to happen to their work? I decided to do a survey the following morning. I asked three questions:

1. What have you learned as a result of writing and publishing your first story?
2. What do you think you will do differently next time?
3. Now that you have completed your first story, what would you like to see done with it?

Their responses were extremely informational. I won't go into all of them right now. But what I did find out in response to question number three is that not one student said they wanted their story to be graded. They did respond that they would:

1. Take it home
2. Show parents
3. Try to get it published
4. Laminate it
5. See it read again by classmates
6. Type it
7. Read it to other grade levels
8. Put a hard cover on it
9. Do nothing at all — we already did everything
10. Combine it with other short stories to make one big book.

Thursday, October 17

Today the class worked on author cards. After looking over some novels in our classroom we came up with a list of information to include in our "about the author" cards. They worked on a planning sheet first. Then they took their responses and roughed out a paragraph. After proofreading it, it was written on their "About the Author" card, complete with photograph. These will be displayed with their stories.

Already I can see a few students who are really playing with word order and sentence structure. One student, Erin, just kept moving things around. She was determined to start her sentences in a variety of ways. Others were not quite as diligent, but I still saw a change in them.

I'm also trying something new with their journals. I have a little podium and each morning I am allowing the kids to get up and read from their journals. Some are reading short stories and others are simply reading summaries of their day. Of course, I have a few kids who can't get enough of this and others who are more hesitant. At this point, I'm not forcing anyone to share, but I would like to see everyone get up there at some point. They enjoy it and ask me about it if it slips my mind. I think it is great for them to hear each other's ideas and modes of presenting information.

I also hope it will take the fear out of getting up in front of a group. I know that I wish I had been encouraged more when I was young. To this day, the thought of getting up and speaking in front of a group of adults scares me to death. So I hope I can make things different for my students.

Friday, October 18

I would like to record a few observations about my students' attitudes towards writing.

First there is Alex, who asks me continuously if he can write.... Alex actually went so far as to take his story off my desk because he really wanted it back and I wanted him to wait until 1:50. I guess I can see why I call him "Anxious Alex." But, I walked by and there he was working on it. And I said, "I didn't give that to you, did I?" He had this grin on his face and the rest of his group knew he had taken it. Still, I have a hard time punishing that kind of enthusiasm.

The rest of the class has been doing a lot of writing too, besides our workshop time. Many of them have come to me and said that they are also writing at home. This is all in addition to what they are doing in class.

Even one of my most reluctant writers was bitten by the writing bug. Christine is learning disabled in reading and math, but writing is difficult for her, too. When we were working on our "About the Author" cards, she came up to me and said, "Look how I wrote this." In her hand she had her planning sheet and it said, "and of course my red headed brother Adam." She was so damn proud of this! She went skipping back to her seat. Now, let me tell you, Christine is a real negative kid because school has been so rough for her. When I saw her skipping, I just about fell out of my chair.

The other day, one of my students from last year brought me a Halloween poem he had written (I used to call him "poetry man" last year so he knew I would enjoy seeing it). Well, I read it to my class. I mentioned that maybe they would like to try writing some poetry. Poof! All of a sudden, somebody has a poem to read from their journal the next day. Then, Friday afternoon, two of my students came up to me and said that they had written a poem together. It was in Allison's journal but they had collaborated on it.

I just continue to find myself amazed and intrigued by what is going on with my students.

Monday, October 21st

This morning one of my students approached me with something she wanted to share. She had a small notebook covered in fabric, the kind you buy in stores. She opened it up and showed me the contents — two poems that she had written this weekend. She told me that she was going to continue recording poems. This really blew me away. I know that some really exciting things are happening. My class is turning into a room full of students who write. But they are not writing because they have to. They are writing because they want to! Later, during the afternoon, this same student decided that she would collaborate on a book of poetry. They had already put together a little booklet to record some of their writing....

Today the kids were going to begin their second story. Robin was eager for them to do a "Halloween" story. I was not as anxious for them to do such a topic, but I decided to go along with it. When I told the students that they were going to begin a new story I told them that we were going to focus them on a topic. I told them they were going to write a Halloween story.

Well, right away, a look of disbelief came over one little boy's face. He said, "But you're going to... you can't tell us what to write about." I explained to him that he would still have some freedom but that I was going to give him and the rest of the class some direction. I was surprised that he had reacted so strongly. "Choice" is obviously very important to Michael.

I turned it over to Robin who talked a little bit about the concept of a scary, mystery type story. She told the students that she wanted the story to be short in length.

Again, Michael let out a complaint. Why were we now telling him how much he could write? I could tell he was truly upset. Robin told him in order to finish up for a special Halloween sharing session, the stories would need to be short.

We introduced a worksheet that we had designed. It contains a planning section for characters, setting, and plot. It also contains a section on revision. The idea is that the sheet will be completed as the story progresses and follow the student through until publication. There are areas for the teacher to check off after conferences. In this way, Robin and I will be able to see if she or I have met with a student at any point during the story....

I noticed Stephen sitting quietly in a corner by himself. This is a pattern with him. Later, when I conferenced with him about his topic sentence, I said, "You like to be by yourself when you write, don't you?" He replied, "Yes," and I let it drop at that. But I would like to pursue it more at a later time. When

I commented on how much I liked his ideas for his story he said, "Well, I'm a really special boy. I was made that way." I was surprised to hear him talk this way because he had not been that confident during his first story. Changes are taking place so quickly....

Tuesday, 10/22

The students are continuing to work on their Halloween stories. Today I had four writing conferences. I was surprised at the improvement Sara made between her first and second story. This one was twice as long and she took more risks. She used a lot of quotes. When I conferenced with her I noticed several places where she had used "a" instead of "an" before a word that started with a vowel. I asked her to go back and re-read in these spots. I asked her what she noticed about these sections and she replied that they didn't sound right. I then explained the rule to her and will look to see if it "sticks" with her. She admitted she was unsure about her paragraphs but they were actually quite good.

I really noticed a lot of interesting things when I conferenced with Janelle. I could see that she is using vocabulary from her reading (basal stories that is). But more importantly, I noticed that she really does not want me to write on her rough draft. When I first started the conference I made a few spelling corrections. She was one letter off in her spelling of "Stephanie," and I changed it. Well, she went back and went over my mark with her pencil. Definitely some ownership going on here. Then I noticed that she was jumping ahead, making this correction throughout her story.

Also, some kids seem content to let me read their story, but Janelle takes a very active role in her conference. She wanted to read it and she was jumping ahead trying to make corrections. This was especially evident when I pointed out how she could get rid of some "garbage words" like "then," "and," etc. She was cruising along making changes along these lines in no time at all.

I was pleased to see with all four of these students that proofreading had improved on this story. Perhaps it was because we had asked them to mark up their papers a little. The kids were to use green pen to underline capitalization, circle punctuation, and so on.

Wednesday, October 23

The kids continue to do a lot of writing on their own — stories, poems, journal entries. I am intrigued by the changes I see in Matthew (I mentioned him earlier. He was a reluctant writer. His mom is extremely ill with cancer). He has been writing an incredible amount in his journal every day. He has been trying some poetry and also some stories on his own. He didn't have as much difficulty getting started on his second story. He was one of two or three kids who needed a topic sentence conference. Today during the break after playtime when I let my students read, write, or catch up on assignments, he said, "Mrs. Stevens, maybe you could have my conference with me right now." I said, "Sure." And we did. I also noticed him at the front table with one of his friends writing a story together. I could hear them saying, "So, what do you want to write about?" So, I most definitely see a change in Matthew's attitude toward writing. I still think that it is difficult for him. During our topic sentence conference, I said, "Just try something. Throw out an idea." (I was trying to get him to develop a topic sentence). I could see that this was hard for him. He is very hesitant and I think he has a hard time seeing writing as tentative.

During the opening of today's workshop, I tried a mini-lesson. I pulled out five sentences from the first stories the students had written and put them on the board. I reviewed why we use quotes and how. Then, I had the students correct the other sentences on the board. They were quite pleased to see that their sentences were being used. I encouraged them to try to use quotes in their current piece. I liked the idea of the mini-lesson because it is quick and to the point, but hopefully effective, too....

Friday, October 25

Today I did my second whole class mini-lesson. Since the students were using a lot of quotes I wanted to encourage them to use other words besides "said." We brainstormed a list on the board that I am going to put on chart paper so they will be able to refer to it throughout the year and hopefully add to it too. The outcome of this lesson was immediate. As I conferenced with the kids they would cross out "said" for more appropriate choices. Ideas from writing continue to be borrowed and shared. I noticed today that Lisa's ending for her Halloween story was identical to Bridget's ending from her first story. I am curious to see the students' reaction when they hear Lisa's story. Will they remember and how will they view it?

The students are also looking at the structure of stories, too. I read them the book *The Relatives Came* as part of my social studies lesson. They picked up on how the end of the book used almost the same words as the beginning of the book. I suggested they might want to try this themselves sometime....

Monday, October 28th

Today, I introduced a new activity to my students that will be used primarily during language time.

On a small bulletin board at the front of the room I hung up the phrase "You're invited ... to Write." Then I fastened up three envelopes each with an invitation inside. Each invitation contains a writing activity that the students can work on when they have free time (for example, when they are waiting for a conference). I hope to add to and change the invitations as the year progresses. One invitation asked the students to write a letter to a friend or relative. It also said that I would provide the stamp. The second invitation involved a series of books by D. Alexander. They have words on the first and last pages. The students' task is to create a story for the illustrations. The book involves the adventures of a baby and a dog named Carl. The students can write from the perspective of either character. They will then share the book and their story with younger students. The third invitation was "name your own burger."

The students were enthusiastic about the board. Several pairs of students began to work on the Good Dog Carl invitation.

Tuesday, October 29th

...One of the students that comes to my classroom for language made an interesting comment today. He said he had "chair fright." He was not looking forward to sharing his piece on Thursday. It seems that either all the students need to meet with us at the same time or nobody needs to (as was the case today). There has got to be a way to reach some sort of happy medium.

Wednesday, October 30th

Today was a crazy day. The windows in my classroom were being replaced as part of the renovation our school is undergoing. So my class was put in another room for the day. We had to drag all the books with us. Robin was at a workshop and did not come to help today.

Author day is Thursday, so the kids finished publishing — putting the last little details on their books. The spirit of cooperation continues as kids help each other stencil on titles and offer suggestions. Matthew is leaving for Washington tomorrow to visit his mom, who is having a bone marrow transplant. I asked him if he would like to share his story today. He didn't seem too eager so I didn't push it. I know he has a lot on his mind.

Thursday, October 31st

Today was author day. We put up black paper on the windows, turned off the lights, lit our jack-o-lantern, and sat in a circle on the floor using a flashlight to read our Halloween stories. The kids were eager to share, all except the two students who came over from another classroom. When we asked Jesse to read his story he was very hesitant. The student sitting next to me (Stephen) leaned over and said, "Why are they afraid? It's not like we're going to laugh at them or anything." I thought this was a really interesting comment. Jesse and Jeremiah do not seem to feel the sense of community my students do. They do not view it as a "risk okay" environment. I was interested at how much vocabulary the kids are pulling in from reading (shrieked, whirling, shrill, hauling) and even more that I can't remember.

Another interesting theme also came up today. I am amazed at how many stories involve the class as characters, including me. I would be interested in seeing how many kids used classmates in these stories and why. Also, several stories (at least three come to mind) involved the same characters as the first story. For example, one student wrote "Ho Ho the Flying Squirrel" on his first book, and this time he wrote "Ho Ho's Scary Halloween." The kids continue to seek out audiences for their pieces. Two students who had to leave to go to math lab brought our stories with them to share with their teacher. When Michael returned, he reported, "Mrs. Kemp loved our stories." Robin asked Tom (the author of the Ho Ho the flying squirrel series) to come to her classroom to share his stories with her first, second, and third graders. Robin's room is decorated like a rain forest, and that is why she took a special interest in those particular stories.

Friday, November 1st

Today I was alone again. Robin took a personal day. I decided to have the kids start a writer's outline for their next story. They immediately asked me about length and topic. They seemed relieved that choice had been returned to them.

For some, a topic came immediately. Tom knew right away he was going to write "Ho Ho's Thanksgiving." Others sat and sat and couldn't come up with one. I was pleased that their friends were there to support them, offering suggestions and encouragement. They really do want to see their classmates do well. There is no sense of trying to out-do someone.

One group of four boys came up with an interesting idea. They have a club and they call themselves "the masters." They decided to write a story

Case Study — Rebecca: A Leap of Faith   215

called "The Masters on Vacation." But what they decided to do is have each person's story build on to the next. For example, Brent will write part one and Stephen will write part two and so on. They decided that they want to put all four parts together in one book. They even asked me if they could have an extra planning sheet so they could work out the details over the weekend. I'm eager to see how all this works out, but I have a feeling that letting these four friends work together is better than keeping them apart.

I found out after school today that Matthew's mom passed away at noon. I'm glad that he had the opportunity to see her one last time.

But my thoughts also turned to how to deal with this tragedy. Perhaps the kids will hear about it this weekend. But we still need to address it. I'm wondering if writing notes to Matthew would be appropriate. I will have to talk it over with Robin on Monday. I feel good in knowing that I have built a "community spirit" (where my students) will be understanding and ready to help Matt deal with this.

Tuesday, November 5

Today Robin and I continued to talk about evaluation, a topic we can put off no longer with report cards and conferences right around the corner.

Yesterday we talked about guidelines for giving A, B, or Cs. Basically, they consist of the following criteria:

> C - Follows class guidelines (Fills out outline, topic sentence, rough draft/conference/final copy)
> B - Proofreading/Self-correcting
>   Organization — details stick to topic — refined through conference. More sophisticated topic selections.
> A - Well-developed story (Self-developed) Beginning, middle details, End. Refined proofreading, mature topic selection, vocabulary and punctuation

We also realized that we need to look at the individual's attitude and effort over the past marking period. A grade of C would crush some children who have been writing their hearts out and giving it their best. Others who are probably capable of much more will receive Cs because of a lack of effort. It's never black and white when it comes to evaluating writing. Today we decided to design a checklist that could be completed for each child, using the portfolio we have begun. This way we can see at a glance what skills each child has been working on and what they have mastered. These can be shared with parents at conference times.

The past week has been really difficult. Robin has been absent for several days. I've really come to depend on her energy, enthusiasm, and support to keep this writing workshop on course. I've had to take on a lot of extra responsibility in terms of the learning disabled kids because Robin has been gone. I hope everything works out okay because I really need her back....

Thursday, November 7

Yesterday something interesting happened. I have four boys who have formed a club called "the masters." ...They called me over to their group to get my opinion/permission on their idea. They decided to write a four-part story about their vacation. Each member would write a story but they would be called part one, two, three and four. I said that it was fine with me and they were off....

Alex, one of the boys in the group, keeps calling me over. "I'm dying for you to read this!" he says.

Brian said to me, "This is a very important story to us. We will get it published someday."

I can't get Stephen to put his writing folder away at the end of the day. He just keeps telling me "I'm into this."...

One other thing I noticed in talking with the students about story # 3 — they have really begun to think about perspective in their stories. I think this is due to two things. One — "the invitation to write" I introduced, using the book Good Dog Carl. I talked about how the story could be told from the perspective of the dog or the perspective of the baby. Two — I read the class a book called The True Story of the Three Little Pigs, by A. Wolf. They loved hearing the tale retold from the perspective of the wolf.

Since then, I have noticed several students talking specifically about perspective. For example, Lisa is writing about Thanksgiving from a turkey's viewpoint.

Open House went well — parents were positive about the writing workshop.

Friday, November 8

Several of the kids asked if we could have a mini writing workshop. I said that we could and was impressed with their dedication. I mean on a Friday afternoon it is hard to get kids to do much, but they were very eager to write.

Case Study — Rebecca: A Leap of Faith

At the end of the day Brian (one of the boys who is working on the four-part story) came up to me. He said, "When you started passing back papers I said to myself, 'It isn't Friday,' but then I realized it was. I can't believe how fast the time goes." I said, "Well you know what they say — time flies when you're having fun." Then Brian said very seriously, "Well, I don't want time to fly. I like being in this class with the masters and I like writing and I don't want the year to end." I was surprised at how upset he seemed. I said, "Brian, it's only November. Just relax." I told him he shouldn't spend the year worrying about that.

Well, then Brian asked if he could bring his rough draft home to work on. At first I said, "No." But then I said if he really has all this enthusiasm for the story, then I might as well let him take it home. I mean, after all, I am trying to develop a love of writing in my students. I told him he could bring his folder home.

Well, then all four of the boys had their stories and they told me they were going to meet at Brent's house to work on them. I must admit, I was pretty impressed with their dedication.

Wednesday, November 13th

I was worried about report cards. They went home yesterday. I wasn't worried only about parents' questioning language grades but about the kids too. I was afraid that some students might be discouraged if they received a C+ or a B. But, I'm happy to report that I didn't receive any complaints—from students or parents.

The "writing frenzy" continues. The kids' attitude towards writing is very positive. My kids are very honest about their feelings. Yesterday, the kids had just been working on their stories. I looked over and saw four students doing health. I said, "The masters" (that is what they call their group) "aren't going to work on their story today?" Brian said, "We want to, but you're making us do this lousy stuff." He held up his health workbook. I said that health should be done only if they were waiting for a rough draft conference and had nothing else to do. They quickly put away their health, grabbed their writing folders.

When I called Michael up for his conference, he sat down and said, "Let's get down to business." I guess it was his way of letting me know that he wanted my full attention....

Robin and I have been talking about some ways to continue to improve the workshop. I'm thinking about breaking the kids into groups of five to help facilitate conferences. The students would be assigned a specific day to conference with me. I would meet with five kids on Monday, five on Tuesday, etc. Each child would get a ten to fifteen minute conference. This would guarantee that I got to meet with each kid during the course of a week. As it stands right now, some kids want to conference every day and others go seven to eight days without ever talking to me about their progress.

These specific conference times would help me keep better records of student progress, too. I could jot notes and set goals during this time. Robin and I also want to start utilizing more mini-lessons. We also want to start doing some writing with the students. We have also been talking about how we can better utilize areas of the classroom. We are thinking about grouping kids according to what they are working on. For example, everyone who is publishing would sit in one area and rough draft writing could be done in another area.

There are many things we want to do — but so little planning time. But, we keep reflecting, thinking and changing. I believe we are doing the best we can.

Thursday, November 14th

The students are working on their third story. As I conference with them, I am trying something new. After I read through their draft, I ask them to select several areas of their story where they think they could expand what they have written. I then send the student back to write more on that particular part of their story. I really want them to see that they can play with the story and expand what they have said. I guess I want them to begin focusing on a quality story rather than quantity....

November 19

As I look over the past several weeks, I realize how much I have GROWN! (as a teacher and a writer). I have rediscovered how much can be learned if I look closely at my own teaching and my students' development. I have gained insight into how and why they write. I have also seen the importance of looking for competencies rather than deficits.

I realize that in watching my students I have become more aware of my own composing process (how I compose and what I concentrate on). I can't help but feel that I have grown and changed. Both my students and I will benefit from this reflection.

November 22

Yesterday, one of my students said that his brother told him he should be an author. He told me he was considering it. Today, he came in and said he had told his mom about his interest in becoming an author. She called his grandfather and arranged to have Brian get an old typewriter from him. Brian was really excited about this and asked me what he should write that weekend. He went on to say that he was going to dedicate his first book to me, because without me, he wouldn't be doing all this writing.... Later that day, I conferenced with Brian on part of his eighteen-page story. He is still working with his three friends on "The Masters on Vacation." Each boy has about eighteen pages and they are planning on continuing. They are already making a list of places they can go in their next stories. At the end of the day I heard Brent reminding the others to make sure they had their stories. They were all planning on going to Brian's that weekend to type. Pretty neat, huh?

November 26

Today I was talking to my friend who teaches fourth grade with me at East Valley. As I was leaving her room, I saw seven or eight manilla envelopes lined up on the counter. They had sheets of paper attached to them, on which she'd written something. I said, "Hey, Barb, what are these for?" She said that they were topics for reports on Iroquois Indians that she'd created. Each topic had a little sign-up sheet attached so that kids could "pick" their first and second "choice." She told me I was welcome to borrow them if I wanted to. I politely said, "OK," but I knew that this assignment wasn't for me or my students. In allowing kids to sign up for "first" and "second" choice, Barbara had left out the most important choice of all — "free choice." I almost said something, but I didn't. But if I had, I would have advocated for self-selected topics. After a thorough study of Indians, why not let the students generate a list of topics they would like to know more about? Let the kids pore through books to come up with topics that they are really interested in. After all, when kids write about things they care about to people they care about, motivation is there.

I do talk a lot about my writing workshop and how it's set up and what worked or didn't work with my colleagues. I know that I still have a lot to learn. For now, all I can do is share my ideas with them and hope that at some point they'll begin to try some themselves.

November 30

The other day one of my students approached me with a novel from our class library and said, "Remember how you told us about using things in our writing like 'I was as cold as an ice cube?' Well, here's a good one." He read a sentence from the book: "They slumped on the grass under Twig's father's cherry tree on an August day hotter than the inside of a basketball player's sneaker."

This incident reminded me of the reading-writing connection mentioned in the articles by [Frank] Smith and [Nancie] Atwell. Smith talked about "reading like a writer." But he also stated the importance of perceiving oneself as a member of the club. Brian — the boy I mentioned before — was doing both of these things in reading that particular novel. He saw a technique used by a writer that he might like to use himself.

I have to admit that the more I read and find out about language — the more I realize how much I have to learn. When I was getting my undergraduate degree, I took one "language arts methods" course. While I enjoyed the course, I realize now that it simply wasn't enough to cover all we needed to know about language instruction. It just wouldn't have been humanly possible. But now that I have become intrigued by this area, I would like to continue on and take some more courses. Perhaps when I finish my degree in the spring, I can think more about continuing on with some studies of language because my research and reading has really interested me. I want to do so much for my students, and I think that means continuing to learn myself.

December 3

I just got home from my graduate class an hour ago. Usually, I'm exhausted and I want to flop down on the couch and relax. But tonight I felt like I had to reflect on tonight's class.

Tonight, I learned how difficult it is to share writing with others. When we got into writing groups, I was planning on sharing some of my paper that I had written for class. I was working with three people I feel very comfortable with, all friends from previous classes. I even thought my paper was pretty good. I liked it. I didn't think it was going to be that difficult to read them a brief passage — boy, was I wrong!

I was terrified to read it. I was afraid they wouldn't like it or understand what I was trying to say. This experience gave me so much insight into how my students sometimes feel. Despite the fact that they too feel comfortable with their classmates and have worked to develop a story they like — sharing is sometimes difficult. There is no "safe" environment, just "risk-okay."

In asking myself why this is so, I think that it is because our writing is so much a part of us. We develop it, create it, and nurture it. In sharing it, we are sharing a part of ourselves — and that is scary. I know that I must continue to work on developing more self-confidence. But, I also know that I will never minimize the fear of one of my students ever again. I have experienced that fear — and it is very real.

December 9

As I wrote the last entry in my log, I realized that I did not want it to be my last entry. Over the past few months, this log has become an important part of my routine.

It has allowed me to record my growth as a teacher of writing. I have used it to reflect on successes, failures, frustrations, and moments of joy.

My students' growth has also been recorded, along with their successes, failures, joys, and insights about writing. So I have decided to continue to keep a log, at least for the remainder of this year. I want to capture this year of change and growth. I have learned a great deal from my observations and reflections and I just don't want that to stop.

Explorations

If you would like to reflect more on this case study of Rebecca, here are some ways to proceed. Feel free to modify these options in any way you like, depending upon how much time you have and whether you will be sharing your insights with someone else. Most of all, don't be afraid to create your own opportunities for exploration and reflection. Don't feel constrained by these choices.

1. **The Learning Climate.** As you read Rebecca's story in her classroom log, you might want to keep track of all the different ways that she was able to build a positive learning climate in her room. What did she say to students, what choices did she give them, how did she make it safe to take risks, and how did she bring them toward greater collaboration? You might want to stop at several points in your reading of this chapter and freewrite or talk with a group. Or, you can simply take some time to write about your thoughts at the end of your reading.

2. **Dimensions of Language and Learning.** In previous chapters, you were asked to consider three dimensions that relate to the learning climate: choice, collaboration, and commitment. Choose one of the dimensions and look at this story through this lens. If you are working with a group, you might want to split up the work in some way. You can simply make a list as you read, to be discussed later. Or if it is easier, you might want to write a narrative, focusing on the dimension you have selected. You might want to use these questions as a sort of framework for thinking about each one:

   a. **Choice.** Look for occasions when Rebecca takes control of her students' learning in some way, as well as times when she relinquishes it. Speculate on why this happens. Try to become aware of the ways in which she leads her students to greater and greater independence throughout the course of the term.

   b **Collaboration.** Trace the influence of sharing writing and working together in Rebecca's classroom. Are there times when "going public" is threatening and times when it's motivating? Speculate on why this is and what Rebecca does to influence the situation. Think about how the "double-edged" aspect of going public applies, not only to the students in Rebecca's class but to Rebecca herself.

   Reflect on the growing relationship between Rebecca and Robin. Consider the importance, of collaboration, not only among students but among teachers as well.

   Notice the occasions when students in Rebecca's class learn through the example of their teacher or other students. Speculate on the importance of modeling in developing student competencies.

   c. **Commitment**. Keep track of times when you see Rebecca giving her students opportunities for tentative, exploratory language and times when their language becomes more permanent and committing. What does she do to make the process of polishing and rewriting less threatening to her students?

   Notice when students seem to become invested in producing a finished product. What influences seem to be operating when this happens? What different ways do Rebecca's students show that they are developing a sense of investment and commitment?

3. **Reflections on Change.** Keep a running record of each time you notice that Rebecca or her students seem to be experiencing a change or transformation. After you have finished reading this case study,

look at each event on your list and speculate in writing about what you think may have brought about these moments of change.

4. **Reflections on Success and Failure**. Look for problems and occasions of success in Rebecca's journal entries. Make a list of what she seems to see as "successes" and "failures" in two columns as you go. After you have made your list, go back and speculate on what contributes to Rebecca's feelings of failure and success. Notice how she resolved each difficulty. You might want to conclude by writing for a few minutes about what you have learned.

5. **Through Students' Eyes.** Take the vantage point of one or several students that Rebecca mentions in her journal. At several points in your reading, you might want to stop and write an imaginary journal entry as one or more of those students. Talk about what your teacher and other students are doing and how you feel about the changes that seem to be taking place in your classroom.

6. **Reflections on Technique**. Keep a running list of all of the different classroom techniques that Rebecca discovers (For example, putting a chart in front of the room with magnets for each student to indicate what he or she will be doing each day). Speculate on why these techniques work for her. Here are a couple of more specific examples:

   a. **Conferencing**. Trace the development of Rebecca's conferencing skills over the course of the term. Do her perceptions about the goals and purposes of conferences seem to change as time goes by? You might want to keep track of the problems that she encountered and how she solved them.

   b. **Journals**. Trace the different ways that Rebecca comes to use student journals in her classroom. Analyze these different purposes and uses in terms of the choices that students had, the degree of exploration or permanence in their language, and the private or public nature of writing.

CHAPTER 10

Evaluation

Ryan cannot sit still for more than ten minutes so he writes for a little while then walks around. I usually have to find him and practically sit him back down. He also has really bad asthma and the computer room is small and stuffy so he never likes to be there. Anyway, Ryan worked for a long time today on his piece — a long time for Ryan, that is. He called me over and said, "I'm done, take in or leave it. I ain't changin' nothin'." Well, I probably should have left it at that for today, but when I read his poem, I saw that it was just a few steps away from being perfect. His imagery was wonderful, and the poem had so much power and insight. However, every other word was misspelled, and none of his writing had any kind of line logic or punctuation. That doesn't usually bother me, but today it did. I felt as though I was always bringing him just so far, and then he would reach this state of, "I DON'T CARE" (only he doesn't say it quite that nicely). So I asked him to sit down and talk to me about his poem. I really praised the ideas and then started on some of the form problems. Well, he lost it. He stood up, and pushed the table — "I ain't staying' here to get ragged on. You leave my writing alone. If you want me to write, then you keep your hands off it, or you know what you can do with it." I didn't agree with his attitude, but I think he was partially right. But how do you know when it is time to move in and actually teach some writing, and when it's time to just keep praising until they get some kind of appreciation for what they are doing? I felt bad all day.

— Meg

I have yet to meet a conscientious teacher who doesn't struggle with the issue of evaluation. How many of us have spent hours grading and responding to student papers only to have them tossed into the waste basket when the bell rings? Who hasn't agonized over the one student who has worked harder than ever but who just didn't do as well as some of the other students in the class? To this day, I remember the dread I felt whenever a parent would call or visit me to discuss a student's marks. When students like Ryan react so negatively to what we feel is only helpful criticism, we can't help but wonder what we did wrong.

There are no simple rules about response, evaluation, and grading. In fact, I delayed writing this final chapter for the longest time. I wasn't sure how to write about this very complex topic without giving the impression that there was one simple way to do it. I decided finally that it might be best to present the issue in the context of some mini case studies of actual teachers and how they each solved the evaluation and grading dilemmas in their particular classrooms. Rather than a set of fixed techniques, I hope to provide some issues to think about in designing the exact evaluation and grading system that's right for your particular classroom.

I find myself continually adding to my repertoire of evaluation strategies even to this day. My hope is that you will continue to do the same thing — learning new things with every new group of students. First, let's consider the differences between response, evaluation, and grading.

Response

The purpose of response is to give inspiration and guidance to students as they are in the process of learning, not just at the end of the process. There should be frequent opportunities for students to receive response, not just from teachers but from peers and other interested people outside of the classroom as well. Response need not always be written; it can be in the form of informal conversations between you and your students or between students and their peers in small groups. It's important for your students to discover that they can find other audiences besides you. Soon, with a little gentle nudging, even the most reluctant students can learn to value each others' responses as much as they value yours.

Evaluation

Evaluation moves us a little closer to a judgmental stance, but it's a different kind of process than grading. There are times when your students' work must be judged against some kind of standard. These judgments can be made during the learning process (formative evaluation) or at its conclusion (summative evaluation). Evaluative judgments made during the learning process need not be as final as grades; they can be a sort of progress report that helps students to identify their goals or lets them know how close they've come to those goals before the final grade is given.

The problem with many evaluation systems is that they treat student work as some kind of practice exercise rather than a meaningful experience in the present tense. Some time ago, Stephen Tchudi observed: "approaches to evaluation have always been *future directed* rather than directed at writing as something for the *here and now*. Evaluation has emphasized getting students ready for 'the next time' instead of helping them to find success in the present" (see Judy, 1981, p. 209).

When student work is treated as a historical artifact, when texts are autopsied for what they can teach about "the next time," students can fail to learn much of anything at all. That's perhaps the reason why so many of those texts that we and they spend so much time on end up in the waste paper basket once they're handed back.

When evaluation is directed toward the present rather than the future, students see the immediate impact of their ideas on others and are allowed to shape and reshape those ideas. The appropriate time for summative evaluation comes after students have had the chance to bring their work up to acceptable standards with the helpful responses of teachers, students, and other interested people.

There are several ways of conducting formative evaluation. Of course, it's possible to compare students to each other by grading on a curve, or setting up numerical scales. But often, a more effective strategy is to compare students to **themselves** at several times in the year. Better yet, you can teach students to make these kinds of evaluative judgments on their own. Here are a few possibilities.

Self-Evaluation.

One of the fundamental goals of teaching should be to get students to the place where they can make independent decisions about the quality of their own work. It's a good idea to ask your students to review their progress at various points in a marking period. You might work with students in creating an evaluation sheet or set of questions to which students can refer in evaluating their own work or in preparing for a goal-setting conference with you. If students keep logs or portfolios, they can periodically review their contents and evaluate all that they've done to that point.

Even very young children are capable of self evaluation. A few years ago, I had the delightful experience of visiting a first grade classroom. The teacher had asked her students to take their first piece of writing out of their portfolio along with a more recent piece. As I went around the room, each student talked with me for a few minutes about how he or she had grown as a writer from the first draft to the latest.

I was amazed at the degree of insight these young people had about their own growth as writers. Some children told me that they were writing longer pieces; others told me that they were using longer words, were spelling more words correctly, or that they were trying new topics. In the real world, we have to evaluate ourselves all of the time. There's no reason why self-evaluation can't be a part of every student's experience in schools.

Peer Evaluation.

There also should be opportunities for students to evaluate each other. Peer evaluation can be a successful way of getting students to learn critical skills. Although I believe it's unfair to ask students to assign actual letter grades to their classmates, you might ask each student to confer with another student, complete peer evaluation sheets, or write informal notes to each other. You can use these student responses as another source of information when it is time for you to assign grades. Students can be required to seek a certain number of peer responses before they hand in their papers and projects to you.

Program Evaluation.

In addition to evaluating your students' progress, you should be frequently evaluating the success of your own teaching methods and curriculum. In some senses, teaching is a fundamentally political act. If we can't justify the worth of our methods to administrators, parents, and other interested people, we shouldn't be using them. Even if administrators or parents don't ask questions about the success of our program, as conscientious teachers we should be asking these questions all of the time.

I don't believe that program evaluation needs to be a separate process from the ongoing evaluation of student growth. We should be constantly evaluating our program in terms of the positive changes in our students — not just in the skills they can master or the knowledge that they have accumulated, but in the positive attitudes they have developed and the learning strategies they have acquired. The quality of our program should be something we think about every day, not just at the end of a semester or year. The important thing is to design a system of evaluation that is sensitive to all of your curricular goals, not just those that can be easily measured in numbers.

Grading

This is the final step of the evaluation process. It has to be. Grades have such an air of permanence to them. Once they're assigned, they have a way of closing down discussion. Deciding on a fair and sensitive grading system — one that reflects your actual teaching goals — is perhaps the hardest thing you'll ever have to do. Sometimes it takes me a good five years before I come up with a grading system that I like. And even then, I'm still tinkering with the system from year to year.

There are all kinds of questions about grading that need to be considered. First, what should you grade? Is it possible to grade learning processes as well as written or spoken products? Can class participation and effort be taken into account? Who should select the products to be graded: you or your students? Is it even necessary for every text or product to be graded? Is your system easily explained to students? Does it offer them some choices? Is it fair to all students or just a privileged few?

Like teaching, grading is also a political act. Your grading system will in a sense "teach" a set of priorities to your students. If your curriculum goals center around students' knowing how to produce and understand whole texts of language in meaningful circumstances, yet your grading system is based on "particle" assessments of isolated facts, you are sending contradictory messages about what's important in your classroom. Your students will pay more attention to parts than to wholes. They're remarkably adept at figuring out your priorities and values.

If you are interested in developing in your students a set of learning strategies and processes or a certain set of attitudes about learning, your evaluation and grading system should include some way of assessing these strategies, processes, and attitudes. In addition, you should find a way for students to be graded on their efforts and attempts as well as their final performance.

Assigning a "process grade" is one way of doing this. Students can be graded not only on their final paper or presentation but also on all of the more informal language acts that got them to that final product. They can be encouraged to hand in all drafts, notes, freewritings, tapes of group discussions, and other evidence of the learning processes they followed in arriving at their final product. They can keep these "process artifacts" in a notebook, index them, and perhaps write a short note or confer with you to explain all of the work that they did and what they learned at each stage of the process.

The important thing to remember is that your system for grading student work sends powerful messages about the things you value. The priority you give to various learning tasks in your grading system should match the importance you place on these tasks in the everyday world of your classroom. If you allow students a lot of room to make mistakes and to get feedback from others in your daily routine, then you shouldn't place them in contrived conditions and test them on piecemeal information at the end of the term. Furthermore, if you want your students to look upon you as more than just the final judge of their work, you have to consider carefully the roles you assume in responding to their work.

Response Roles

When I was in school, I don't think that my teachers experimented much with the ways in which they responded to my work. Teachers in those days seemed to have fairly defined roles. They gave the grades, and by virtue of this position of authority, they responded in pretty prescriptive and authoritarian ways. I suppose I grew to expect this kind of "in-charge" response. Sometimes, I must admit that I appreciated it.

Today, our thinking about students and their individual needs has led to the idea of empowering students to take charge of their own learning. No longer do teachers have easily defined authoritarian roles. Sometimes they can be interested co-learners; at other times, trusted experts or friendly critics. It's kind of tricky to step out of the role of gradegiver, but you can eventually convince your students that your job isn't only to assign grades and to monitor behavior — that you actually enjoy sharing in their work and that you don't know everything there is to know. Convincing them of this means learning to make "I" statements, rather than "you" or "it" statements, saying "I felt like this when I read that," rather than "You need to..." or "Your text is..." Often, it means being able to take your students' perspective and understand how your comments come across to them.

Reflections: Response Roles

For the next few minutes, I'd like to invite you to engage in a little bit of creative role playing. First, imagine that you are a middle school English teacher. Jeremy, one of your eighth grade students, has just written this first draft of a story and asked you for response. You realize that this is just a very first draft. There are many things that Jeremy might eventually do with this piece. You want to encourage him. At the same time, you want to let him know some ways in which he might revise this first draft. What might you write to Jeremy? Take a few minutes, read over his draft and try writing out your response.

Jeremy's Draft

Once upon a time there was a boy who had lost his mother and father when he was younger and ever since then he has swore to find out what had happened to his parents. He thinks a man named Jasper killed his parents and he has been looking for this man all his life and today he will find him. "Looks like were goin have a big storm," the boy said has he was walking down the side of the river bank. "I think I'll go over and ask that man if he knows where theres a place I can bunk up for the night."

So the boy goes and asks the man if he knows if theres a place he can stay and the man says sure I know you can stay at my house, but it will cost you 10 dollars. So the boy gives the man his money and starts to walk to the man's house with him. Has there walkin the man says "Buy the way kid my name is Jasper whats yours". The boy says "I've been looking for you all my life." Jasper says why and the boy says I think you know something about my mother and father because the day my parents disappeared I food a ring with Jasper written across it. So I've been looking for you ever since. The man (Jasper) pulls out a gun and says "Sorry it has to end like this kid".

To Be Continue.

After you've finished your response to Jeremy, it might be interesting to see how others have responded to his text. If you're working with a group, you might try passing each of your responses around in a sort of "round robin" arrangement, taking a few notes as you go. As you read over the responses of others, try to notice all of the different kinds of responses people seem to be making. Listen to the tone of each response. What voices seem to be lurking behind each one? The point is not to decide which response is best but to look closely at all of the different possibilities for responding to this student's work.

Role Switching

Now, I'd like to turn the tables for a few minutes. This time, imagine that you are Jeremy. In the next few pages, you will see the responses that three different teachers made to your draft. As you read them over, think about how each response makes you feel. What comments would make you eager to write more or to revise your current draft? What comments might make you angry or defensive? Are there any that would make you want to throw your draft into the waste can? Are there any that would make you feel good about yourself and eager to revise your ideas? The point here again is not to decide on the best response. Each of them has strengths. The important thing is to begin understanding the ways in which teachers' responses can make students feel about their work.

❧

Response Number One

Dear Jeremy,

I have just read your story and I must say, I really liked it. You have created very interesting characters in the boy and Jasper. The reader needs to know a little more about them. I sympathize with the boy about the loss of his parents, but if I knew more about him, for instance, his name, how old he was, what he was like, then I would be better able to understand his anger and his need to find Jasper and seek revenge. You show an excellent use of suspense at the beginning of the story. You have the boy state his suspicions about Jasper, but you don't say why he is suspicious until the confrontation. You have a good, strong plot so far. You need to tie up a few loose ends with your ending. You may want to think about why Jasper killed the boy's parents, why he must kill the boy, and how it will all be resolved. Keep up the good work!

Mrs. J.

Response Number Two

Jeremy,

Good use of dialect.
Nice introduction to the story.

Questions to consider

1. What does Jasper look like? Describe him. What is he wearing? Is he tall? Is he mean looking or does he look friendly?
2. What is the boy's name? How old is he?
3. What does the boy look like? Is he a fancy dresser? Is he tall?
4. Why was the boy walking down the river bank?
5. Describe the setting. Where is the river? Is it cold or hot weather? Is it in the city or the country?
6. Who is the boy talking to? A friend? To himself?
7. Where do you want to go with this piece? Does the boy find his parents? Are they dead?...

Jeremy, I think that you have the beginnings of a nice suspense and mystery story here. I am curious to find out what happens next. I would also like to know more about your characters and about the setting of your story. This is a great idea for a story. How did you come up with it?

Response Number Three

Jeremy,

Your story was very interesting because you put a lot of suspense into it. As I was reading, I kept wondering what was going to happen

> *next. It has a good beginning: You tell about the boy and his life, including why he's looking for the man named Jasper. I think you could definitely tell more about how the boy feels. What's his name? Does he miss his parents? How strongly does he feel about Jasper? Does he hate him? Is he scared about talking to Jasper? What would you do if you were in the boy's situation? How do you think the boy feels about all grownups? Think about adding a few things to your story about questions like these... I would suggest adding a few details about the feelings of the people in your story. That way, your audience will be able to understand what your characters are going through and why they do the things they do.*
>
> *Mrs. S.*

Isn't it amazing how the tone of the response, the phrasing of questions and evaluative statements, even the way a teacher's comments are arranged on the page signal different things to students? For instance, take a simple linguistic form like the question — one of the mainstays of most classroom discussions. Think about how all of these questions made you feel when you took the perspective of Jeremy. Now think about the compliments these teachers gave out. Did these comments seem to open up or to close down the chances that Jeremy might revise the text?

Needless to say, there is no one correct way to respond to a student's work. It is possible, though, to become more conscious of voices behind our comments to students and the roles we can choose to adopt when responding to them. There are times, it is true, when you must step in as evaluator and gradegiver. But there are also times when you can give up some of your authority and become a trusted adult, or, better yet, a fellow learner, someone who doesn't have all the answers.

In the next few pages, you will read about some teachers who wrestled with questions about evaluation. More than a set of hard-and-fast principles, I hope their stories will give you some frameworks within which to make decisions about response, evaluation, and grading.

Evaluation Problem Number One: Evaluating Student Growth

Sarah is a first grade teacher who was looking for an evaluation system that would help her to identify important aspects of her students' growth. She wanted a way to become more aware of specific goals might set for individual students. At the same time, she needed a system that could help her to explain her goals to her principal and answer questions about individual students for parents and other interested adults.

That fall, she decided to keep track of her students' learning processes by means of a portfolio system. In her students' portfolios, she would keep a series of anecdotal records from several weekly conferences with them as well as all of the texts they had created throughout the year.

At first, Sarah was a little afraid of how her principal and her students' parents might react to her system of evaluation. After all, this qualitative record-keeping seemed to lack the credibility of the numerical scores on standardized reading and language assessments that she had relied upon in previous years. Eventually, though, she concluded: "The more information I gathered from different sources, the more insight I gained about each child in my room." Throughout the year, Sarah continued to keep track of each child's progress by means of short, descriptive notes that were placed in their portfolios. As she observes, these informal records played a very big part in her classroom structure:

> *(In) previous years I would rely on my memory or the children's pieces to remember where each child was .... This new recording technique is very helpful to me in several ways. First it helps me to remember exactly where each child is when I meet with them for a conference. Second, it provides written proof of the growth or lack of growth each child is achieving .... These written notations have helped me to show that my writing program is working and also helps me to show the parents what their child is working on and how they can help at home.*

By the end of the first nine weeks, Sarah had met with each of her students in brief conferences for a total of eighteen times per student. Her procedure was very simple. In short conferences roughly twice a week, she and her students would meet to talk about the texts they were writing and places where they having problems. Take, for instance, the case of Hanna, one of Sarah's first grade students.

Hanna: from Reluctance to Risk-Taking

In her anecdotal records, Sarah describes Hanna as:

> *a writer who is just now becoming aware of the benefits of invented spelling. Hanna has been writing stories and using print in her stories*

since beginning first grade, yet she wasn't willing to take the risks needed to use invented spelling. If she couldn't spell it correctly, she wouldn't use that word in her story or would ask someone to spell it correctly for her.

Through a series of conferences, Sarah was able to gently lead Hanna to a place where she could take more risks in her writing. Here, for instance, is a transcript of one of the early conferences Sarah had with Hanna:

S: Hanna, what is your story about?
H: I like it when it snows!
S: You do? Don't you get cold and wet?
H: No, I play in it.
S: I like that you wrote "I" and then used blanks and drew the snow.
H: Thanks. I couldn't spell the other words.
S: That's why we use blanks. Some of these words that you couldn't spell are your sight words, aren't they?
H: Yes. I know, but I can't spell them.
S: Do you want me to write them for you?
H: Yes.

In this very brief exchange of a few minutes, Sarah manages to ask Hanna some questions about her story and to get her thinking about other things she might write about ("Do you get cold and wet?"). She also gives her a bit of praise ("I like that you wrote 'I' and then you used blanks") and helps her with the words she is not sure of.

Moving Toward Independence

Through the next several weeks, Sarah realized that one of Hanna's strengths was becoming a potential weakness. As soon as she learned to leave blanks for words she was not sure of, Hanna became very tied to Sarah and reluctant to experiment with invented spelling. For example, one of Hanna's stories in her writing portfolio for September was about picking flowers with her mother (see figure 10.1). Notice how she wrote only two words in the text of her story and put blank spaces for the rest of the words. She seems to rely on Sarah to transcribe most of the story on the bottom of the paper as she tells it aloud. Nine words of the story are left blank. At the same time, though, it is clear that Hanna's picture corresponds nicely with the story that she composes.

238 Making Connections: Language and Learning in the Classroom

— *She is writing more letters and words on her own. She knows all of her readiness sounds and is starting to use them.*
— *She needs to write her recognized sight words — she can read "like" and "the," but she doesn't write them.*
— *I am working on getting her to write in the correct space and to try to sound out her words.*

Gradually, Hanna became more comfortable with invented spelling. For example, in her story about her sister, Bobbi-Jo, she continues to place blank spaces where she isn't sure of the words. However, she begins to draw pictures in place of some words. Notice, for instance, how a picture she has drawn of the rain acts as a sort of pictograph in the text of her story (see figure 10.2). She is developing the sense that words stand for things in the real world.

Hanna's story: October

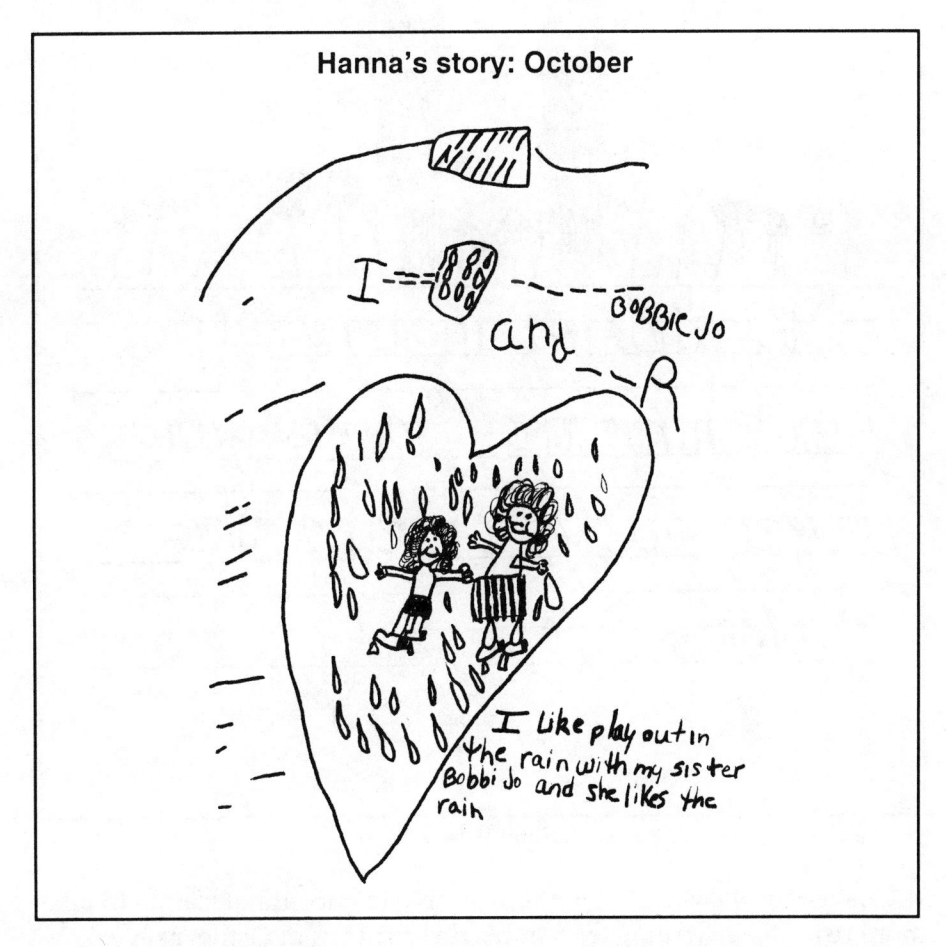

I ___ ___ and Bobbie Jo ___

I like play out in the rain with my sister Bobbi Jo and she likes the rain

Figure 10.2

> **Hanna's story: September**
>
> — and — mommy — — — — —
>
> *[drawing of two figures among flowers]*
>
> Me and my mommy are watching the flowers grow And we're picking the flowers

Figure 10.1

As the weeks wore on, Sarah was able to encourage Hanna to take more risks in her writing, as Sarah's three entries in October reveal:

Growth Spurts

Sarah's records reveal that by November, Hanna was still using blanks for words she wasn't sure of, but she was slowly beginning to add new words to her texts besides the words she was learning each day. Sarah noticed that Hanna hadn't ventured away from her family in topic choice, however. Then, suddenly, around Thanksgiving, Hanna seemed to leap forward, as revealed in Sarah's four entries for the month of November:

> *— Hanna is still using blanks for most of her story words. She is only using her sight word list.*
> *— Hanna is adding some new words to her story this week. She is still focusing her stories on her family.*
> *— Today was the first day Hanna didn't use blanks in her piece!*
> *— Hanna's thanksgiving story was amazing! No blanks! She used invented spelling throughout the piece.*

As Sarah's notes reveal, Hanna made much progress in the short span of time from September to November. In her Thanksgiving story, she has not only spelled many of the words such as "Thanksgiving" and "turkey" correctly, but she has also ventured to try spelling other words, like "have" and "someone" that were not as immediately obvious to her (see figure 10.3). Ironically, this risk-taking is as much a sign of progress as her correct spelling is.

240 Making Connections: Language and Learning in the Classroom

Hannas story: November

On Thanksgiving we hav Turkey and we hav sum 1 un tocl/M ovr and hRwer and The TuRkey wus Tom and wer Givin Hows

On Thanksgiving we have turkey and we have some one to com over and here the turkey was Tom and were giving thanks

Figure 10.3

At the end of the fall term, Sarah reviewed her portfolios and reflected on Hanna's progress:

At the end of September and the beginning of October, Hanna started to use some of her sight words regularly in her stories. She was slowly starting to trust herself and her ability to use the sounds she had learned in her stories. Once this progress started, Hanna's reading and writing seemed to take off together.... Her reading ability has improved two levels since entering school in the fall. Her writing pieces at one time contained only a few words and the rest were lines that stood for words that she couldn't spell. Hanna relied on me to tell her how to spell them and not on herself. Today Hanna is writing more and more words herself and asking me for less help each day! I feel that her confidence arises from the fact that she wasn't pushed into doing something that she wasn't ready for — that with time, patience, and a lot of different experiences Hanna was able to see the benefits of invented spelling and then experience the pleasures of writing herself.

Needless to say, this kind of qualitative record keeping enables Sarah to do several things that more standardized numerical assessment systems fail to do. For one thing, she is able to recognize and keep track of many of the more subtle aspects of Hanna's growing competence, and not just at a few points in the school year but every day.

It's interesting also that Sarah's records contain very little reference to Hanna's deficits. Most of them center around goals that Hanna might work toward and her achievements. Many of these subtle competencies would not have shown up on a standardized assessment measure; they appear not only in Hanna's texts but in her behaviors and her conversations with Sarah as well.

In short, the eyes of Hanna's teacher are far more sensitive than the quantitative assessment measures administered outside of the classroom setting. Sarah can notice the times that Hanna tries to spell words she is unsure of, offers or accepts help from other students, and ventures from the world of her family in her choice of topics. In other words, this assessment system allows Sarah to track the development of writing processes, strategies, and attitudes, as well as Hanna's ability to compose texts.

Evaluation Problem Number Two: Evaluating Groups of Students

A good many tests and assessment measures focus on deficits rather than competencies. As a result, we can often be blinded to the vast array of strengths our students actually master each year. It's a good idea to review your students' work periodically for evidence of these competencies. You can keep an ongoing list of them to help you decide on grading criteria or respond to individual students. Even if only one student can demonstrate a particular competency in your classroom, you can help other students to work toward this goal throughout the school term. Not everyone needs to be in the same place. Growth doesn't always occur in a neat, linear sequence.

Discovering Competencies in Students' Texts

For example, recently, I was working with a group of elementary and secondary teachers. I had asked a few people to bring in some sets of texts that their students had created. We placed teachers into groups, according to the grade levels that they normally teach. First, the teacher who had brought the students' texts took some time to explain how they were produced, whether students had choices in topics, and roughly where they were in the process of drafting and revising.

Each group then began to pass the texts around in a circle and take notes on all of the competencies they could see beneath the words of each student's text. The only rule was to focus on positives and to ignore negatives. Group members were encouraged to be as specific as they could be. In other words, rather than saying "good organization," they were encouraged to make statements like "understands cause-effect organizational pattern." Rather than looking for deficits ("many misspelled words"), they might phrase the items on their list as competencies ("95 percent of words spelled correctly").

When everyone was finished, we placed each list on the board and tried to draw rough conclusions about the kinds of competencies that seem to develop as students proceed through the grade levels. In figure 10.4 you will see the lists of competencies that two groups came up with. They are based on analyses of two different sets of texts: one produced by a group of fourth grade students and another produced by a group of eighth grade students. As you read over each list, you can probably make some guesses about the development of students' writing abilities from fourth grade to eighth grade.

Competencies: Fourth Grade

1. Can use "ed" ending
2. 90-100% spelling accuracy
3. Uses correct word boundaries
4. Uses capital letters for proper nouns
5. Uses periods at ends of sentences
6. Uses quotation marks correctly
7. Is able to create complete sentences
8. Uses commas correctly
9. Uses compound words ("playground")
10. Can show cause and effect
11. Expresses emotions and feelings
12. Uses simile, metaphor
13. Good variety of word choice
14. Uses descriptive, narrative form
15. Can use correct story sequence
16. Good use of adjectives
17. Can write compound sentences
18. Draws appropriate picture for story
19. Can use possessives
20. Attempts new words (even when unsure of spelling)
21. Evidence of revision on the word level

Competencies: Eighth Grade

1. Can use possessives
2. Can correctly use quotation marks
3. Can produce complex sentences (dependent clauses)
4. Is able to make a personal connection with the real world in responding to literature.
5. Can follow a cause-effect organization
6. Is able to give supporting examples for arguments
7. Can use topical organizational scheme
8. Good sense of paragraph boundaries
9. Demonstrates variety in sentence structure
10. Spells 97% of words correctly
11. Can draw inferences from concrete details
12. Can use imagery to describe ordinary events
13. Can use literary terms (such as "foreshadowing")
14. Can use analogies, similes, metaphor
15. Uses commas correctly
16. Evidence of revision on the paragraph level

Figure 10.4

The best part about analyzing students' competencies in this way is that you can set tailor-made goals for your particular students at each point in your school year. The criteria will come from their own texts or portfolios, and not from some absolute ideal or standard set of skills. Of course, this particular assessment technique is an attempt to define competencies evident in students' writing. You can do a similar kind of analysis, generating criteria that are relevant to your particular content area as well.

Evaluation Problem Number Three: Assessing Student Attitudes and Beliefs

Jan is a sixth grade teacher in a small parochial school. She has been teaching at this school for six years. Before that, she was a teacher on the high school level. Jan began the fall term, wanting to know more about her students as writers — not only in terms of their abilities but also in terms of their attitudes toward writing, their beliefs about what writing is, and the kind of writing tasks they prefer. Her sixth grade class that year had only seventeen students, nearly equally divided between boys and girls.

That fall, Jan decided to engage her students in a series of informal writing and speaking activities, designed to give her information about their attitudes and beliefs. Through these informal means, Jan was able to learn a great deal about her students — their beliefs about writing, their composing processes, and their attitudes toward writing in their lives. She began early in the fall term, by asking each student to write her a letter, describing themselves as writers. From these friendly letters, she hoped to glean some initial information about her students' underlying assumptions and attitudes toward writing. Take, for instance, the example of Corey.

Corey: "an author when I grow up, that's maybe."

Corey was a bright child who was very concerned about doing well in school. Early in the fall, when Jan asked her students to write her a letter, describing themselves as writers, Corey wrote:

Dear Mrs. R.

> This is how I think of myself as a writer. I enjoy writing alot, and I may become an author when I grow up, that's maybe. I think writing takes time, and I also think writing is fun.
>
> I always write with the radio on because it helps me think things out. And

I think of myself as an all right writer. And when I'm finished with my work I'm usually proud of it. I like writing when someone gives me a topic because it gives me something to work with. And that is how I think of myself as a writer.

From
Corey M.

From this short note, it was evident that Corey had a positive attitude about writing. In fact, he had even considered becoming an author. On the other hand, it seemed as though Corey might still be a bit tied to the teacher in selecting his topics. Interestingly, Jan discovered that, like many of his classmates, Corey enjoys writing while music is playing. To accommodate students like Corey, she often plays soft music in a corner of the room, where students who prefer to can listen to music during writing time without disturbing the others.

For her next informal writing task, Jan adapted an idea from Alan Purves (1990). She asked her students to write a letter to an imaginary fifth grader explaining their views on how to succeed as a writer in the sixth grade. In these letters, she was able to gather more valuable information about her students' beliefs about the process of writing. For example, Corey wrote:

Dear friend,

The way to become a better writer is by thinking up your ideas and getting them on paper as best you can.

And some of the ways that you can get your ideas is by brainstorming, reading other books, and just by discussing it with someone helps you out.

Another way to become a better writer is by writing a few bad copies first and then write your good copy. And when you write your bad copies skip lines and use a pencil.

I hope these tips help you to become a better writer.

Your friend,
Corey M.

This letter is very revealing. It is interesting, for instance, that Corey is aware of several useful strategies for brainstorming topics. He obviously sees the social potential of writing and seems to see the benefits of sharing his writing and generating ideas with others. However, his description of "writing a few bad copies" indicates that he might see revision as a simple process of changing "bad" copies to "good" ones. This is in line with much research on young writers that indicates that many see revising as merely recopying, not substantively changing a text.

Notice that Corey tells his imaginary pen pal to skip lines and use a pencil, but does not explain why. In talking with Jan later, I discovered that although she asks students to use a pencil and skip lines for editing purposes, writing a few "bad copies" is definitely not a procedure of her classroom. At this early point in the school year, Jan surmised that Corey was relying on his memory of former writing English classes and seems to lack a complete sense of all that goes into the revising process.

After she had collected this anecdotal information, Jan gave out a short questionnaire, asking her students to comment upon their specific writing processes. From this brief questionnaire, she discovered that Corey read his first stories in kindergarten and wrote his first story in first grade. He seemed to believe that he has written a lot in school and that only two of his teachers (Mrs. M. and Jan) had praised his writing in school. She also discovered that Corey doesn't mind sharing some writing but finds other writing too personal to share. When asked if his writing had improved since the first grade, Corey replied: "Yes, I think it has because I have more ideas. I learned more on how to write and I have a better vocabulary." Corey also mentioned a reluctance to comment on other people's writing, because, in his words, "I usually don't know what to say."

After gathering this preliminary information, Jan decided that her students might feel more comfortable chatting with a partner rather than filling out a questionnaire. She asked her students to pair off and interview each other about how they felt about their writing at this point in the school year. On the day of the taping, she had set up tape recorders in two stations in separate parts of the room. Students conducted the interviews in pairs while others worked independently. Prior to the interviews Jan talked with her students about what makes a good interview, and modeled an interview for her students. The tapes of these interviews were then transcribed. Corey was interviewed by a classmate named Kathy:

K: Hi, I'm Kathy S. I'm going to interview famous sixth grade writer Corey M. Corey, what do you think was your best piece of writing that you have ever done?

C: I think the best piece of writing that I have ever done was in creative writing class this year when (Tom) and I wrote a mystery story about me and some of my friends.

K: Can you describe this piece of writing?

C: Yes, well we went up to the, some of my friends and I went up to the gorge because there's a mystery that some kids were, that some kids got killed and we were ready to solve the mystery.

K: Why did you write this story?
C: I wrote this story because the teacher asked us to, and I like mysteries.
K: Explain why this is your best piece of writing.
C: I think this is my best piece of writing because I like the way I write it. I like the way I wrote it, and I'm proud of it.
K: Did you share it with anyone?
C: Yes, I shared it with the class in writers' workshop.
K: Why did you share it?
C: 'Cause I raised my hand.
K: Do you have anything else to add?
C: No.

It's interesting that Corey chooses his best piece not on the basis of its quality but on the basis of how he felt after writing it. He doesn't seem to talk in very much detail about what makes a piece of writing good. It's also interesting that in the course of their interviews both Kathy and Corey admitted that they wrote their pieces because they were asked to do so by their teacher. Interestingly, Corey wrote his favorite piece in collaboration with another student. Neither Kathy nor Corey seemed to share pieces with others outside of the writers' workshop. When Kathy asked Corey why he shared his piece, he replied rather naively, " 'cause I raised my hand." At this point, both students seem to write and share their writing under the guidance of a teacher rather than independently. However, they both seem to like writing and to find personal purposes for doing it.

From these simple pieces of informal writing and talk, Jan was able to gather useful information about her students, the kind of information that wouldn't show up in their letter grades or their scores on achievement tests. Knowing more about student attitudes and beliefs is an important part of planning and program evaluation. For instance, if you are a history teacher, you might want to know if your students see the study of history as a series of meaningless dates or a meaningful search for knowledge of the past. If you're a math teacher, you might want to know if your students see mathematics as a series of drills and computation formulas or as a tool for solving real world problems. Science teachers would want to know if students see science as a set of remote experiments, conducted by people in white lab coats, or as a personal exploration into the many mysteries of the world in which they live. A competent assessment system is sensitive not only to students' knowledge but to their assumptions and beliefs about the nature of the content area they are studying as well.

Designing a Grading System

During the first several weeks of a school term, our goals are bound to be different from those at another point in the year, when students have grown more familiar with us and are more likely to work well together.

Of course, your grading system will depend on the particular group of students with whom you are working and the concepts you are trying to teach. For example, when you are working with a fairly complicated set of information, you might want to pare down the options somewhat, focusing students' learning specifically on a few important concepts and principles. If you close down the topic of their learning in this way, you might want to open up other aspects of the classroom situation, allowing some choices in the form in which they grapple with those concepts (in writing or in speech, for example) or whether these concepts will be learned independently or collaboratively. While there are no easy formulas for designing evaluation and grading systems, you need to consider whether you have been able to design a system that supports and does not undercut your classroom goals.

Classroom Conections

As a way of better understanding some of the issues you wrestle with in designing a competent grading and evaluation system, let's go back to those six questions that were posed in the first chapter of this book.

1. For what purposes are my students using language? It's a good idea to decide on whether grading, evaluating, or even responding are necessary, in light of the purposes for which your students will be using language. For example, language for purely personal purposes should not be graded or evaluated. This is because evaluation by outsiders gets in the way of the privacy that is so essential for highly personal language acts. Language for personal purposes can be "counted," however. That is, you can give students credit for their expressive or exploratory language by means of a contract system. You might, for instance, devise a point system in which students can get credit for producing a certain number of journal or log entries.

Language for social purposes is, by definition, intended to get a response from someone else. Sometimes students are directing their language to an evaluator; at other times, a trusted friend or a co-learner. As a teacher, when you place yourself in the role of a fellow learner, you move from a superior position to one that's on a more equal footing with your students. Evaluating or correcting your students' punctuation or grammar in a dialogue journal, for instance, would be as inappropriate as red penciling the letter of a friend! Once you step in as evaluator or gradegiver, you cut off the possibility of friendly discourse.

At still other times, your students' language will take on an artistic dimension. Let's say they are writing poetry in their journal, for no other reason than their own personal pleasure. Here, unless you are invited to respond, your evaluative comments would be inappropriate. On the other hand, if a student is trying to publish a particular entry or asks for stylistic feedback, your honest evaluation would be appropriate. Still, even in this case, a grade wouldn't be called for. Thus, whether you choose to grade, evaluate, or simply respond to particular aspects of student work shapes the kind of social relationships that are possible in your classroom.

2. What learning stances am I asking them to adopt? Ask yourself whether your students' graded projects evoke the same kinds of learning stances as do their day-to-day experiences in your classroom. In other words, if your classroom activities often involve a replicating stance — if you have your students write simple reports or answer literal questions in the daily routine of your classroom — don't expect these replicating activities to transfer over to activities that require connecting or extending stances in a formal test situation.

Similarly, if students have been encouraged to read simply for pleasure or write for personal discovery, quizzing them on textual minutiae or knowledge of grammatical terms (pure replication) will seem contradictory to the way you have conducted your classroom activities in the past. It's important to balance the kinds of learning stances you set up in activities that are evaluated or graded. Ask yourself if all evaluated tasks set up roughly the same learning stances, if the daily activities in your classroom are congruent with graded activities at the end of a unit, or if students can have some choices about which stances to adopt.

3. For what outcomes are they using language? Many times teachers function as intermediate audiences. Part of our job involves making educated guesses about how strangers or future evaluators will judge our students' reading, writing, and speaking. But, as we've seen, there are many ways for students to get response from audiences other than you. After all, in the world beyond the classroom, we are seldom "graded" on anything. We are often evaluated or responded to, though. At some point, it's important to put your students in touch with respondents and evaluators beyond the classroom — to get yourself out of the position of being sole arbiter of student work. At the same time, you need to give students the opportunity for some purely private, ungraded, and unguarded reading, writing, and talking.

4. How much choice do students have? If your daily classroom routine provides students a good deal of choice, your evaluation system should also provide a measure of choice as well. Can students, for instance, have choices about who will respond to their work or whether certain pieces will be responded to at all? Can they select some of the pieces that will be responded to or graded? Can they decide how many drafts a piece of writing will go through or whether it's worth revising at all? Can they choose the texts they'll read, the forms of writing they'll produce, the other students with whom they'll work? Can they even select the grade they will work toward?

Personally, I like to keep at least part of the grade for each class in my own control. I usually have at least one major project or assignment that I will evaluate and grade, although I try to give students a chance to revise that graded project or paper before that grade is awarded. Other aspects of my grading system are negotiated, and still others are in the students' control. I may, for instance, ask for help in setting up the criteria that I will use for grading projects and papers. Or I may base some of the grade on a mutually agreed upon contract. The contract allows me to focus on giving helpful feedback and not to worry about the devastating effect of assigning individual grades on something that's personal or potentially anxiety-producing.

Of course, the balance between teacher-controlled, student-controlled, and negotiated grading depends upon the particular students I'm working with and the particular demands of what I am teaching. If, for instance, I'm teaching something that has a fairly high degree of performance anxiety associated with it, I might not grade it at all but instead give students plenty of opportunities for response.

I decide what percentage of graded projects will be in my control and what percentage will be in the students' control on the basis of what I know about my students. Classes that are fairly independent and require less external guidance usually work best when much of the work is graded on a contract basis or is negotiated with me. Other classes that seem to be less able to make independent decisions need to be led gradually into taking control of their own learning.

I also try to offer some opportunities for self-evaluation. I personally believe that we put students in a double bind if we ask them to assign actual letter grades to themselves. Usually, this situation just results in grade inflation among less motivated students and false modesty in more motivated students. On the other hand, students can be given choices about which texts they'll be judged upon, which they'll polish, and what criteria will be used to evaluate their work. The point is that if choice is a constant and important part of your daily curriculum, it should be a central feature of your response, evaluation, and grading system as well.

5. Do students work independently or collaboratively? So many grading systems are based on the notion that getting help is inappropriate. Students are segregated from each other and asked to demonstrate performance on final examinations and projects independently. Yet, as Vygotsky (1962) and others have shown, what learners can achieve with the support and guidance of someone else can far exceed what they might have done alone. It's often helpful to rethink your curriculum and decide whether some graded tasks or projects could be pursued collaboratively or if the process of collaboration itself could somehow be graded.

For instance, a group of students could decided whether they want to produce a totally collaborative final product and be awarded a single grade. In this case, you could grade them not only on the final product but on their behaviors in the group as well. You might require groups to make tape recordings of the process. You could listen randomly to the tapes for evidence that groups stayed on task most of the time. Or you could ask each member to keep a daily log, writing for five minutes at the end of the period about what each member contributed to the group's effectiveness. These logs could be compared for evidence about the contribution of each student at the end of the grading period. If certain students are contributing little, this will become obvious by what their fellow group members mention or fail to mention in their daily logs. If one of your goals is to help your students succeed in a variety of social settings, there are ways to evaluate their collaborative as well as their more independent efforts.

6. How much commitment do evaluated activities demand? Most tests and other kinds of end-of-term evaluations are thought of as permanent and committed. This, however, need not be the case. A sensitive and responsive grading system should allow for all kinds of language — from exploratory and tentative to more permanent. Perhaps it's best to decide on where you see your students actually using the kinds of skills, attitudes, or knowledge that are at the heart of your curricular area or academic discipline.

For instance, let's say you are a teacher of literature on the high school level. What happens when you base students' grades on their performance on in-class objective tests? Chances are, you'll be sending a message about how you think literature ought to be read. Students may start taking notes as they read, underlining parts of the text they think might be on the exam, and memorizing trivia — behaviors that hardly encourage creative thinking or aesthetic appreciation.

On the other hand, imagine that you are teaching drivers' education. Here, it's probably not a good idea to allow students to consult their "rules of the road" manuals or experiment with different shifting patterns while they're negotiating a busy interstate. In this case, your students will be judged on their immediate reactions, and their thorough knowledge of traffic regulations. There can be little room in this case for messiness or revision.

As a rule, then, it's best to think carefully about how the particular concepts, skills, or strategies in your content area will be used by students in their daily lives. Would students benefit by having time to experiment with exploratory language in the process of arriving at their eventual destination? If so, you can build these kinds of exploratory experiences into your grading and evaluation system.

In reality, we are very seldom placed in a room and asked to write or talk on command with no opportunity for revision or outside help. When we are applying for a job, for instance, we have given ourselves the benefit of much time, many revisions, and a great deal of response from trusted people in preparing our cover letters and resumes. Even the interview itself may have been something we prepared for in advance, practicing from a list of possible questions with a spouse or a friend.

Some tasks are simply too foreboding and complex to require students to perform them on command. It's been said that in our very complicated and fast-paced world, the skill of being able to know what resources to consult is probably more vital than the memorization of facts or rote knowledge of information that is likely to become outdated by the time that print meets paper. An evaluation system that allows for collaboration and for opportunities to revise along the way allows you to give students credit for persistence and for knowing the proper resources to consult. Ultimately, the real skill is in creating a response, evaluation, and grading system that suits not only your curricular goals but also the unique blend of students in your particular classroom. There are no simple rules to follow in doing this.

Final Reflections

I must confess to being a bit of a dewy-eyed idealist about why I teach. The longer I do it, the more my teaching philosophy boils down to one simple goal. It has little to do with the shaping of minds or the imparting of knowledge and skills. I teach so that the world will be a better place. It's really that simple. I teach in the hopes that some day, there might be a few more people who can use the gift of language in authentic ways: to respond to others, to learn new things, and, ultimately, to positively influence the world in which we all must live. Everything that I do must reflect these goals, especially the way in which I respond to and evaluate my students' work.

Some time ago, I realized that teaching is no longer what I do; it is what defines my very identity. I try to make sure that my techniques or idiosyncracies don't intrude on the essence of what is being learned in my classroom. My aim is to become more transparent, more in the background, to bring my students' ideas and talents to the forefront. This means creating an evaluation system that supports and doesn't intrude on student learning, that brings my students gradually to their own independent decisions, that recognizes their competencies and not their deficits.

A friend of mine once said, "If it's too hard, you're not doing it right." And that's true. When my back aches from dragging boxes of student journals home every week, I need to get out of my central role as respondent and create opportunities for my students to respond to each other. When I labor over comments on student papers that just end up in the wastepaper basket, I need to reconsider just how effective all of those marginal comments are and change my way of responding to student work.

There's a corollary to my friend's statement that's just as true: "If it's too easy, you're not doing it right." If it were possible for me to give you **"THE TEN EASY SHORT CUTS TO BETTER TEACHING,"** I would have just done that and saved myself and my publisher all those printing costs.

We've all seen those educational fads come and go, those textbooks with all of the overhead transparencies and objective tests neatly printed out. They look pretty tempting, until we try to use them with our particular students on a particular day in a particular classroom within a particular school. There are no teacherproof activities. If somebody tries to sell you something that's too good to be true, it probably is. There is simply no substitute for your good judgment; your constant reflection about what went wrong, what succeeded, and what will work for each unique group of students you encounter.

Perhaps that's the reason that I couldn't write this book with hypothetical examples. It had to come out of real reflections about the successes, the failures, and the eventual triumphs of the many teachers with whom I've worked over the years and a few experiences of my own. Every time I tried to change someone's story just a little bit to make it conform to some point I was trying to get across, I found that I was distorting something too vital to tamper with. That's because real teaching happens in particular circumstances. There are no fixed techniques that will work in any classroom.

That's the bad news, but it's also the good news. It means that learning to teach will be a lifetime challenge. This book leaves you not with a set of answers but with a few basic questions and some strategies for becoming more reflective about your teaching. I hope you will take this as an invitation to reflect constantly on what is taught and learned in your classroom between now and the end of your career. These questions may seem less attractive than the answers promised by those glitzy textbooks and teaching materials. But in the end, I hope that they will invite you to engage in the same constant process of making connections that you help your students to discover in the days to come.

Explorations

1. **Name Your Own Exploration.** Have fun!

References

Judy, S. (1981). *Explorations in the Teaching of English.* New York: Harper & Row Publishers.

Purves, A.C. (1990). Can literature be rescued from reading? In E.J. Farrell & J.R. Squire (Eds.), *Transactions in Literature: A Fifty Year Perspective,* pp. 79-93.

Vygotsky, L.S. (1962). *Thought and Language.* Cambridge, MA: MIT Press.

Susan Hynds

Susan Hynds is Associate Professor and Director of the English Education program at Syracuse University. Before beginning her university career, she was a teacher of English, speech, and drama on the middle school and high school level in Nashville, Tennessee for nine years. Her work with teachers focuses on the areas of language across the curriculum, writing, and response to literature. She has written articles and book chapters on language teaching and has co-edited two books: *Perspective on Talk and Learning* (with Don Rubin) and *Developing Discourse Practices in Adolescence and Adulthood* (with Richard Beach.)

Index

Applebee, Arthur, 179
Artistic learning, 8
Assessing student attitudes and beliefs, 244-247
Atwell, Nancie, 101, 102
   on giving students choices, 120, 122
   on setting goals for students, 205
Audience, as distinct from outcome, 73-74
Author cards, 208
Author day, 206-207

Berthoff, Ann, 25, 193
   on meaning of research, 180
Biklen, Douglas, and facilitated communication, 87
Boyer, Ernest, 28
Brainstorming, 16
Britton, James, 179
   on artistic dimension of learning, 8
   on learning as a social activity, 12
   model of language functions, 29
Burns, Marilyn, 130, 132

Calkins, Lucy, on giving students, choices, 120
Choice, 117-143
   closing down and opening up, 126
   creating a climate of, 122-123
   as dimension of learning climate, 222
   and evaluation system, 250-251
   in finding solutions to math problems, 130
   modelling, 126-127, 127 (fig.)
   provided to students, 120-121, 121 (fig.)
   related to learning, 10
   related to structure, 123
Clustering, 62-63, 62 (fig.)
Collaboration, 147-148
   and grading process, 251
   related to learning, 10-11, 222
Collaborative goal-setting, 187
Collaborative grant writing, 188, 190-191 (fig.)
Collaborative learning, as distinct from cooperative learning, 168
Collaborative writing, 158-160
Commitment
   as dimension of learning climate, 222
   and evaluated activities, 251-252
   and language acts, 178
Communicative writing, 8
Competencies, as focus of teacher's evaluation of student, 242-244, 243 (fig.)
Competency examinations, 27-29, 123
Computer day, free, 164
Concept map, 62, 63
Connecting, 51-52
Connections, 15

Cooperative learning, as distinct from collaborative learning, 168
Crossley, Rosemary, on facilitated communication, 87
Culminating project, 65

Deficit view of learners, 49
Demonstrating, as distinct from sharing, 150
Developmental stages models, 49
Dialogue journal, 152
Dimensions of language and learning, 4, 7-12, 13 (fig.)
   applied to classroom experience, 15-16
Double-entry journal, 56, 57, 58 (fig.), 61

Editing written work, 111
Elbow, Peter
   on concept of freewriting, 11
   on writing purposes and techniques, 148
   on writing tentatively, 177-178
Emig, Janet, on presenting writing developmentally, 98
Evaluating groups of students, 242-244
Evaluating student growth, 234-241
Evaluating writing, 215
Evaluation, of student's work, 225-254
   formative, 227
   by peers, 228
   by student, 227-228
   summative, 227
Expectations, of teachers and students, 1-2, 19-20
Explorations, xvii
Exploratory language, 11
   and research papers, 178, 187
Extending, 51, 52

Fable stories, 114
Facilitated communication, 87, 88
Formative evaluation, 227
Foxfire Teacher Outreach Network, 186

Free choice writing topics, 101-102
Freewriting, 11
Frightening freedom, 140-141

Gardner, Howard, 50
   on human development, 48
Goal-setting, collaborative, 187
Grading, 229-230, 248
   and collaboration, 10-11
   group work, 161
Grant writing, collaborative, 188, 190-191 (fig.)
Graves, Donald, 91
   on children's desire to write, 71-72
   on giving students choices, 120, 123
   on young writers, 102

Hierarchical approaches to learning, 7, 8
Hierarchical thinking, 48
   and curriculum plan, 49
   effect on schools, 49
   faulty assumptions of, 50
Human purposes, of language, 24-25, 25 (fig.)
Humphreys, Cathy, 130, 132

Idiomatic expressions, identifying and using, 107
Independence, related to learning, 10-11
Informational reading, compared with literary reading, 73
Instructional scaffolding, 123, 140
Invented spelling, 99
Invested language activities, 25 (fig.), 26, 43

Journals
   dialogue, 152
   double-entry, 56, 57, 58 (fig.), 61
Journal writing, 35-41
   as independent or collaborative activity, 150-151
   viewed negatively by students, 117-120

"Knowing places," creation of, xv

Language
  and creation of knowledge, xv
  purposes for using, 30-33
Language acts, exploratory and permanent, 178-179
Language and learning
  applied to classroom experience, 15-16
  dimensions of, 4, 7-12, 13 (fig.)
Language event, 2-3
Language forms, 16-18, 18 (fig.), 19
  and school purposes, 26-27, 43
Language learning, 2-3
Language outcomes, 75 (fig.), 76
  for distant others, 76, 77, 82-84
  for intimate others, 76, 77, 80-82
  for self, 76, 77, 78-80
Language techniques, 16-17, 17 (fig.)
Learners, deficit view of, 49
Learning
  and change, xvii, 12
  collaborative, 10-11, 168
  related to independence, 10-11
  as transactive process, 12
Learning climate, xv, 2
  designing the, 4, 12
  related to language event, 16
  three dimensions of, 222
Learning stances, 7-8
  connecting, 51
  defined, 50
  as distinct from thinking level, 50
  and evaluation process, 249
  expanding students' awareness of, 66-67
  extending, 51
  recognizing students', 52-55, 66
  replicating, 51
  and teacher's intentions, 67
Learning strategies, 3-4
Learning techniques, related to independence and collaboration, 148-150, 149 (fig.)
Literary reading, compared with informational reading, 73

Logical learning, 8

Mathematics learning, enhanced by writing activities, 128-138
Mathematics notebook, 130
Mathematics Teacher, The (Erickson), 135
Mini research project, 180-184, 196
Moffett, James
  on human development, 49
  on language users, 9
Motivation, 24
Movement, between self and world, 9-10
Murray, Donald, on teacher's control of students, 122

NCTM Commission on Standards for School Mathematics approach, 129
Network of Empire State Teachers, 186
Newkirk, Tom, 50
  on human development, 49

Outcome, 71-94
  as distinct from audience, 73-74
  and evaluation process, 249-250
  and influence on writing, 9, 10, 73
  for listening, 74
  for reading, 72-73
  for talking, 74
Ownership of work, by students, 123

Peer evaluation, 228
Permanent language, 11, 178-179, 188
Piagetian concept of learning, 48, 49
Privacy, of students, 91, 167
Process grade, 192, 229
Program evaluation, 228-229
Project journal, 192
Protecting students' privacy, 167
Purposes for using language, 30-33
  and evaluation process, 248-249
Purposeful learning, 7
Purposeful writing, 7
Push in resource program, 201

Reading corners and student privacy, 91
Recognizing students' learning stances, 52-55, 66
Reflections, xvii
Replicating, 51-52
Replicative language, value of, 55
"REsearch," 180
Research, as a process, 180-184
Research papers, 174-178, 175 (fig.)
  and exploratory language, 178
  grading, 192
Resource teacher, 110
Response, as inspiration and guidance to students, 226, 230-234
Revising written work, 106, 110
Rogers, Carl, xvi
Rosenblatt, Louise
  on different kinds of reading, 73
  on transaction in learning, 12

Science, enhanced by language activities, 60-65
Scope and sequence charts, 2, 47
Self-evaluation, 227-228
Sense of community, xvi
Sharing, as distinct from demonstrating, 150
Sharing writing, 9
Staton, Jaha, and concept of dialogue journals, 152
Story map, 103
Story problems, as math exercises, 135-138, 138 (fig.)
Student, as expert, 91-93, 124
Students' purposes in using language, 41-43
Summative evaluation, 227

Tchudi, Stephen, on evaluation approaches, 227
Teacher
  as classroom expert, 123
  as dominant classroom talker, 74
  as intermediate audience, 74
  roles in accepting and responding to students' language, 84, 91
Teaching tale, 33-35

Theory, and teaching, xvii
Thinking level, 50
Topic sentences, 109-110
Transformation, through learning, 12

Vygotsky, L., 3, 251

Whole language movement, 3
Wigginton, Elliot, 186
Word processing children's stories, 113
Writing
  collaborative, 158
  as a process, 2
  as tool for learning math, 128-138
Writing poetry, 104-105
  as a collaborative activity, 155-158, 157 (fig.)
Writing science fiction stories, 64
Writing topics, free choice of, 101-102